CHAUCER'S PARDONER
AND GENDER THEORY

THE NEW MIDDLE AGES

BONNIE WHEELER
Series Editor

The New Middle Ages presents transdisciplinary studies of medieval cultures. It includes both scholarly monographs and essay collections.

PUBLISHED BY ST. MARTIN'S PRESS:

Women in the Medieval Islamic World: Power, Patronage, and Piety
  edited by Gavin R. G. Hambly

The Ethics of Nature in the Middle Ages: On Boccaccio's Poetaphysics
  by Gregory B. Stone

Presence and Presentation: Women in the Chinese Literati Tradition
  by Sherry J. Mou

The Lost Love Letters of Heloise and Abelard:
Perceptions of Dialogue in Twelfth-Century France
  by Constant J. Mews

Understanding Scholastic Thought with Foucault
  by Philipp W. Rosemann

For Her Good Estate: The Life of Elizabeth de Burgh
  by Frances Underhill

Constructions of Widowhood and Virginity in the Middle Ages
  edited by Cindy L. Carlson and Angela Jane Weisl

Motherhood and Mothering in Anglo-Saxon England
  by Mary Dockray-Miller

Listening to Heloise: The Voice of a Twelfth-Century Woman
  edited by Bonnie Wheeler

The Postcolonial Middle Ages
  edited by Jeffrey Jerome Cohen

Chaucer's Pardoner and Gender Theory: Bodies of Discourse
  by Robert S. Sturges

CHAUCER'S PARDONER AND GENDER THEORY

BODIES OF DISCOURSE

Robert S. Sturges

St. Martin's Press
New York

ISBN 0-312-21366-2

Library of Congress Cataloging-in-Publication Data
Sturges, Robert Stuart, 1953–
    Chaucer's Pardoner and gender theory : bodies of discourse /
Robert S. Sturges
        p.   cm.
    Includes bibliographical references (p.) and index.
    ISBN 0-312-21366-2
    1. Chaucer, Geoffrey, d. 1400. Pardoner's tale.   2. Chaucer,
Geoffrey, d. 1400. Canterbury tales. Prologue.   3. Homosexuality
and literature—England—History—To 1500.   4. Christian pilgrims
and pilgrimages in literature.   5. Gender identity in literature.
6. Storytelling in literature.   7. Body, Human, in literature.
8. Clergy in literature.   9. Sex in literature.   I. Title.
PR1868.P3S78   1999
821'.1—dc21   99-27777
                                                                          CIP

Book design by Letra Libre

First edition: March 2000
10   9   8   7   6   5   4   3   2   1

For Jim Davidson
leue grom

CONTENTS

SERIES EDITOR'S FOREWORD

The New Middle Ages contributes to lively transdisciplinary conversations in medieval cultural studies through its scholarly monographs and essay collections. The series provides focused research in a contemporary idiom about specific practices, expressions, and ideologies in the Middle Ages. Robert Sturges' *Chaucer's Pardoner and Gender Theory: Bodies of Discourse* is the fourteenth book in the series. Here Sturges investigates the fixities and fluidities of fourteenth-century discourses about gender by focusing on its most notably unsettled representative, Chaucer's Pardoner. This book provides richly sedimented readings of the discoherent and discontinuous rhetorics of gender and power mapped in the figure of the Pardoner. In this keenly insightful study, Sturges provokes us, among other things, to examine anew our usual suppositions about Chaucer's notions of patriarchy and politics.

Bonnie Wheeler
Southern Methodist University

ACKNOWLEDGMENTS

Several friends and colleagues have read portions of this book in draft form, and have made helpful suggestions; other friends, colleagues, and Internet acquaintances (known to me through the online discussion groups medgay-l, medfem-l, chaucernet, and medtext-l) have asked pertinent questions, offered bibliographical assistance, and kept me from pursuing a number of wild-goose chases. I wish to thank them all: Mark Allen, Donna Burnell, Anne Charles, Jeffrey Jerome Cohen, Sheila Delany, Laurie Finke, Hoyt Greeson, David Greetham, Norman Hinton, Laura Hodges, Brian S. Lee, Catherine Loomis, Peter Schock, R. Allen Shoaf, Kristine K. Sneeringer, Lorraine Kochanske Stock, and Bonnie Wheeler, as well as a sympathetic and observant anonymous reader for St. Martin's Press, a couple of whose comments I have incorporated into my preface. I also thank my graduate students in several seminars on medieval literature and gender, where I first tried out some of these ideas, and my production editor at St. Martin's, Alan Bradshaw.

This book probably could not have been written, and would certainly be very different, if it were not for the intellectual comradeship of two further friends and colleagues who have, over the course of conversations too numerous to count, through shared meals, drinks, conferences, and classes, taught me a considerable amount about gender and about the Middle Ages: Miriam Youngerman Miller and Jessica Munns. Most important, I thank this book's dedicatee, my companion Jim Davidson, for the years of emotional support without which it would not exist.

I thank the University of New Orleans, and John Cooke in particular, for institutional support in the form of a sabbatical leave and course reductions, which allowed this book to be written more quickly than would otherwise have been possible.

A substantially different version of chapter 4 has previously appeared under the title "The Pardoner, Veiled and Unveiled," in *Becoming Male in the Middle Ages* (ed. Jeffrey Jerome Cohen and Bonnie Wheeler [New York: Garland, 1997], pp. 261–277). Some of the ideas I presented as respondent to David Greetham in the *Exemplaria* session entitled "Theories of Editing and Editing Theory" at the Medieval Institute's International Congress on

Medieval Studies, at Western Michigan University in May 1998, have been reworked for the conclusion to this book. I presented an earlier version of the introduction at the University of Denver in March 1999, and I thank the Denver audience for their kind reception and useful comments.

ABBREVIATIONS

U nless otherwise noted, all Chaucer quotations are from *The Riverside Chaucer,* 3rd ed., ed. Larry D. Benson et al. (Boston: Houghton Mifflin, 1987). Quotations from *The Canterbury Tales* are identified in the text by fragment and line numbers. Other works of Chaucer are also cited by line numbers in the text; their titles are abbreviated as follows:

BD	*The Book of the Duchess*
CP	"Complaint to His Purse"
HF	*The House of Fame*
PF	*The Parliament of Fowls*
T&C	*Troilus and Criseyde*

I also use the following standard abbreviations:

EETS, e.s.	Early English Text Society, extra series
EETS, o.s.	Early English Text Society, original series
MED	*Middle English Dictionary*
OED	*Oxford English Dictionary*
PL	*Patrologiae cursus completus, series latina,* ed. J.-P. Migne.

PREFACE

THE PARDONER IN DISCOURSE:
THEORIES, HISTORIES, METHODS

> *Humanity does not pass through phases as a train passes through stations: being alive, it has the privilege of always moving yet never leaving anything behind. What-ever we have been, in some sort we still are.*[1]

> *Language is a product of the sedimentation of languages of former eras. It conveys their methods of social communication. It's neither universal, nor neutral, nor intangible. . . . [E]very era has its own specific needs, creates its own ideals, and imposes them as such. Some are more historically durable than others: sexual ideals are a good example here. These ideals have gradually imposed their norms on our language.*[2]

By beginning with the two quotations above, from C. S. Lewis and Luce Irigaray, writing respectively over sixty and less than ten years ago, I hardly wish to imply—rare thought—that Lewis and Irigaray were engaged in essentially similar projects. Nevertheless, I find their juxtaposition illuminating. Both do suggest that certain long-term continuities in discourses about the relations between the sexes (for Lewis was writing about love, Irigaray about sex) continue to influence our current languages and ways of thinking about them. Lewis' "moving yet never leaving anything behind" and Irigaray's "sedimentation of languages of former eras" both may be understood to mean that older, even medieval, discourses of what we have come to call sex, gender, and sexuality may remain consciously or unconsciously embedded in modern, even postmodern, discourses. I hope this book will make the same point specifically with regard to Chaucer's figure of the Pardoner in *The Canterbury Tales:* the clash of medieval discourses of gender (theological, juridical, grammatical, medical, literary, political) that produced such an ambiguous figure in the fourteenth century remain embedded (though, to be sure, historically transformed), in our (post)modern discourses. In each of the following chapters, therefore, I will be attempting both a historical argument, one that seeks to understand the Pardoner by means of the multiple discourses of gender available to Chaucer in fourteenth-century England, and a theoretical (and transhistorical) argument, one that assumes that such modes of thought, and especially the disjunctions among them, remain sedimented in our own ways of thinking about gender. I hope that this book will demonstrate that postmodern discourses can be used to excavate this sedimentation and that they are therefore equally illuminating, in their own way, of the Pardoner. In the remainder of this preface, I shall attempt to explain this book's underlying assumptions and methods, assumptions and methods that will be discussed only rarely in the chapters that follow, but that nevertheless make those chapters possible.

Bringing the traditional medievalist and the postmodern feminist together as I just did is obviously a strategic move on my part, one intended to justify my continual juxtaposition of history and theory throughout this book in a way that both the historically minded, who sometimes insist on the unique specificity and alterity of the Middle Ages, and the theoretically minded, who may also insist on historical discontinuity, might find objectionable. Implicit throughout this book is the belief that the postmodern is not, or not only, a historical period; as the editors of a recent collection entitled, tellingly, *Postmodernism Across the Ages* have it,

> Our anachronisms are not falsehoods, but the thinking of the unaccountable and yet necessary phrase-events upon which every act of historical recounting or epistemological accounting is based. This is a denial of a certain history, but it is also a rigorous thinking of temporality, a refusal to think of time as something that befalls phrases. History is no longer an envelope or medium within which things happen; our historical awareness is of the conventional modernist account of history as the effect of a certain unacknowledged arrangement of phrases. It is this awareness, which comes both after modernism and before it, that we pose "across the ages."[3]

Historical periodization is both unaccountable and necessary, and while I shall not be arguing that Chaucer "is" in some way postmodern, I do not hesitate to use postmodern thought to illuminate the Pardoner. Some theorists of gender to whom I will be referring themselves refer regularly to their reading of the premodern as a source of their own theories (Jacques Lacan, Julia Kristeva, Jonathan Dollimore[4]), others do not; but if Lewis and Irigaray are correct, all could, and I shall.

I hope my strategy here is more than mere self-justification, however. It also demonstrates the manner in which I negotiate what is perhaps the central historical and theoretical problem encountered when embarking on any enterprise within the category of "gender studies": the classic (or possibly just tiresome) question of where to position oneself in the ongoing debate on the degree to which gender, sexuality, and (sexed) bodies themselves are and are not to be understood as social or cultural constructions. Do terms like "homosexual" and "heterosexual," "masculine" and "feminine," or even "female" and "male" represent core identities that remain stable (regardless of how they are perceived) across cultures and historical periods, or do they represent linguistic elaborations without any essential core, dependent entirely upon culturally and historically differing discourses? It is an issue that continues to haunt gender studies—especially lesbian, gay, and queer studies, but women's studies and the emergent field of critical studies in masculinity as well—despite various attempts to lay it to rest. (That this issue is alive and well among medievalists is attested to by an interesting debate about it that took place on the electronic discussion list medgay-l in June 1999.)

As recently as 1990 the historian of medieval sexuality John Boswell could write of the "constructionist/essentialist debate" that "one of the many ironies about the controversy is that no one deliberately involved in it identifies himself as an 'essentialist,' although constructionists (of whom, in contrast, there are many) sometimes so label other writers. Even when applied by its opponents the label seems to fit extremely few contemporary scholars."[5] Boswell himself has come in for considerable criticism over the years for claiming to have found evidence of a "gay subculture" in medieval Europe, an apparently essentialist claim, though he himself pointed out that "even if societies create or formulate 'sexualities,' it might happen that different societies would construct similar ones, as they often construct similar political or class structures."[6] And of course, anti-essentialism has not prevented scholars from writing women's or queer history, including literary history—an obvious point, but one that does imply a recognition of some basic commonality with the past: as Irigaray points out, "sexual ideals" in particular have been "historically durable." People with similar genitals have desired each other in many times and places, and patriarchy transcends cultural particulars. (As Samuel R. Delany, perhaps our most brilliant novelist, points out: "as long as power, whether it goes with or against the law, is named male, the law itself will *be* male."[7])

If no one was willing to label himself or herself an essentialist in the early nineties, many were interested in negotiating a position between essentialism and constructionism. The authors of two of the most influential works of Queer Theory, Eve Kosofsky Sedgwick and Jonathan Dollimore, both did so. In Sedgwick's famous discussion (in 1990) of the "minoritizing" (roughly essentialist) and "universalizing" (roughly constructionist) views and their overlaps, despite her commitment to the constructionist position, she acknowledged that "[t]o question the natural self-evidence of this opposition between gay and straight as distinct kinds of persons is not . . . to dismantle it. Perhaps no one should wish it to do so; substantial groups of women and men under this representational regime have found that the nominative category 'homosexual,' or its more recent near-synonyms, does have a real power to organize and describe their experience of their own sexuality and identity." This in spite of the "enormous accompanying costs"[8] involving the oppressive hierarchization that invariably accompanies this sort of categorization, a terminology suggesting that Sedgwick places herself more in the "universalizing" or constructionist camp, despite the political sympathies for the essentialist position enunciated in the previous passage.

The same might be said of Dollimore writing in 1991. Like Sedgwick, he finds that "the essentialist quest in the name of an authentic self has proved wanting, especially within dominant cultures, and many of its adherents have lost their faith when confronted with the post/modern repudiation of such a self."[9] But at the same time, he follows Gayatri Spivak in recognizing the necessity of at least a strategic essentialism pursued for political ends, and furthermore follows Diana J. Fuss' revaluation of essentialism in *Essentially Speaking* as well: "In a recent study Diana Fuss suggests that essentialism and the theories of identity deriving from it must be neither sanctified nor vilified but simultaneously assumed and questioned. . . . [T]he essentialist/anti-essentialist opposition is rather less stable than is often supposed in theoretical discourse."[10]

Theorists of sex and gender have generally been even less thorough going in their rejection of essentialism than theorists of sexuality. The very notion of *écriture féminine,* so influential in the seventies (and today[11]) would seem to rely on a biologically essential female (and hence also a male) identity, as would Irigaray's more recent theorizing of difference.[12] And despite widespread criticism of such essentialism,[13] it has also had important defenders, notably Fuss, who goes so far as to identify constructionism as itself a form of essentialism, grounding her understanding of this relationship in John Locke's category of nominal essences: "an essentialist assumes that innate or given essences sort objects naturally into species or kinds, whereas a constructionist assumes that it is language, the names arbitrarily affixed to objects, which establishes their existence in the mind."[14] As Dollimore notes, Fuss' influential study destabilizes the apparent opposition between essentialist and constructionist for gender studies in general. Indeed, Fuss implicitly questions whether signification itself would be possible without essentialism: "the constructionist strategy of specifying more precisely these sub-categories of 'woman' does not necessarily preclude essentialism. 'French bourgeois woman' or 'Anglo-American lesbian,' while crucially emphasizing in their very specificity that 'woman' is by no means a monolithic category, nevertheless reinscribe an essentialist logic at the very level of historicism."[15] If "woman" has any referent at all, some degree of essentialism must be admitted.

Recently, even lesbian/gay/queer studies have seen a remarkable return of essentialism, not only in the work of scientific researchers,[16] but in that of historians as well. Rictor Norton is representative: "In the social constructionist view, knowledge is constructed, deconstructed and reconstructed through ideological discourse. In my essentialist view, knowledge is discovered, repressed, suppressed, and recovered through history and experience. Social constructionism emphasizes revolutionary development (the dialectic); I see evolutionary development, cultural growth and permutation, and sometimes mere change in fashion."[17] In literary history, too, it has now become possible, for instance, for Gregory Woods to declare flatly of the Pardoner that "he is famously described as 'a geldyng or a mare' (I, 691), which most commentators take to mean, after all the niceties of definition have been worried over for a sufficient period, that he is homosexual."[18] In short, despite all the attempts to deconstruct and destabilize it, the opposition between essentialist and anti-essentialist positions remains stubbornly at the center of gender studies. Nevertheless, I wish to make another attempt to deconstruct it, by means of the concept of sedimentation outlined above.

To insist that the discourses of gender available to Chaucer may remain sedimented in our own ways of thinking about gender is not necessarily to take an essentialist position. I do not suggest that these discourses represent some essential truth of gender. Rather, what I hope will be demonstrated here has much in common with Judith Butler's rigorously anti-essentialist theory of gender performativity and reiteration.

> Construction not only takes place *in* time, but is itself a temporal process which operates through the reiteration of norms; sex is both produced and destabilized in the course of this reiteration. As a sedimented effect of a reiterative or ritual practice, sex acquires its naturalized effect, and, yet, it is also by virtue of this reiteration that gaps and fissures are opened up as the constitutive instabilities in such constructions, as that which escapes or exceeds the norm, as that which cannot be wholly defined or fixed by the repetitive labor of that norm.[19]

I will be investigating both tendencies with regard to the Pardoner. On the one hand, he is produced by a variety of medieval discourses whose reiteration in time tends to fix or define him in terms of sex, gender, and sexuality; those discourses reemerge in modern critical approaches to Chaucer. On the other hand, the discourses that produce him are not univocal, despite the efforts of medieval writers and thinkers to police the boundaries of gender, and it is their very incoherence that most significantly remains sedimented in patriarchal discourse, a sedimentation that makes possible the postmodern deconstruction of the very boundaries these discourses attempt to fix.[20] I will be arguing this point most directly in part I of this book, but it will remain an unspoken, but enabling, assumption throughout part II as well.

The essentialist/constructionist problem, then, might be more fruitfully recast in historical terms. We might ask not only what specific constructions of sex, gender, and erotic practice were available in different periods and to different cultures, but also what historical effects such constructions may have had on later ones. Asking what are the paths of transmission by which an earlier medieval construction might influence a later one, and to what extent a medieval construction might still be partially embedded in our own, may help us to understand the commonalities among such constructions without resorting to a transhistorical (or ahistorical) concept of essential gender identity. As Dollimore has stated, "[o]nly critical theory and history conjoined can begin to reveal the tenacious yet mobile forms of discrimination, sexual and otherwise, which organize culture."[21] This book explores both the tenacity and the mobility of various gender discriminations as they appear in medieval and modern discourses.

Social—or linguistic—construction thus need not imply a complete lack of historical continuity, as is sometimes claimed (and more often merely assumed). But neither does the concept of sedimentation imply a completely unbroken continuity. It does not claim even a linguistic transhistorical or transcultural essence (as Fuss might). But it does place certain modern constructions of sex, gender, and sexuality into a proper historical perspective. And such sedimentations need not remain undisturbed; any language conceived historically contains the seeds of its own deconstruction, as Glenn Burger has suggested with regard to the Pardoner.[22] Despite Chaucer's anxieties about improper language and improper sex, the same language that expresses these anxieties also makes visible the very possibilities it deplores, and opens its condemnations to deconstruction; Chaucer's own discourse allows us to deviate from his intentions. A theoretical analysis that is also and simultaneously historical thus reveals not a transhistorical or essential sex, gender, or erotic practice, nor merely discontinuous cultural constructions, but a gradual accumulation of discursive constructions of all categories that cannot be accommodated in "proper" language—an accumulation or sedimentation that only in recent years has begun to be excavated with the use of new theoretical languages.

The theoretical positions outlined above enable my demonstration, in part II, of the utility of recent gender theory to a rigorous rethinking of Chaucerian identity and textuality. If medieval constructions of gender are sedimented in modern ones, current theoretical critiques of these modern gender constructions may legitimately help us to deconstruct Chaucer's representation of the Pardoner's sex, gender, and sexuality without risking mere anachronism. Recent antihomophobic Chaucerians like Burger, Steven F. Kruger, and Carolyn Dinshaw have refused to accept any simple definition of the Pardoner's sexuality or gender identity, and have effectively read his ambiguity in a more productive and less anxious way than earlier critics: in a formula to which I shall be returning, Burger writes that the Pardoner is "a nexus of intermingling discourses about the subject and its meaning that cannot settle into a reassuring ordered hierarchy but must work in conjunction, even in competition, with one another."[23] For such critics, this competition itself reveals the constructed nature of all gender identities, and I place myself in their company.

All of the above is by way of saying that both elements of my title, "Chaucer's Pardoner" and "Gender Theory," are equally important to me. This book seeks to examine how theories of gender—crucially, both medieval and postmodern ones—can illuminate the figure of the Pardoner, but it also represents an investigation of the historical continuities and discontinuities between the two. The plural "Bodies of Discourse" in my subtitle is important to me, too: it is the very plurality of the discourses that produce Chaucer's representation of the Pardoner's body, gender, and erotic practices that interests me here.

This book is not primarily a work of "Queer Theory," though many of the most useful recent discussions of the Pardoner have drawn on the work of various Queer Theorists. In fact, for that very reason I have chosen not to focus exclusively or even primarily on representations of what we call sexuality, but instead to discuss them as one aspect of a larger variety of gender issues. I prefer to think of this book as a contribution to the emerging field of Gender Studies. Fuss has suggested that the discourse of feminism "presumes upon the unity of its object of inquiry (women) *even* when it is at pains to demonstrate the differences within this admittedly generalizing and imprecise category."[24] What is needed at this juncture, I am convinced, is a post-postmodern feminism that takes the imprecisions in all the categories of sex, gender, and erotic practice, their overlaps, incoherencies, and contradictions, as its object. Such a feminism is not to be found in Women's Studies, Men's Studies, or Queer Theory, but in the relations among them that I call Gender Studies or Gender Theory.

Therefore, the following post-postmodern discussions of the Pardoner do not, it should also be emphasized, "add up" to a single, coherent view of him, nor do they constitute a "reading." Neither do the more historical discussions. Instead, they provide multiple, non-coherent, or, to adopt Dollimore's term, "discoherent" perspectives.[25] Luce Irigaray and Monique Wittig, for only one example, entertain what seem to me mutually exclusive views of sexual dimorphism, and Butler and Fuss critique them both; nonetheless, I deploy all four at various points in my arguments.

Methodologically, postmodern psychoanalysis will play a large role in this book, especially throughout part II, in part because the willingness to turn to the premodern as a source of modern and postmodern thought mentioned above has been most explicit in the work of psychoanalytic theorists. As R. Howard Bloch has argued,

> The question is not whether the Chaucerian moment is the same as the Freudian moment, since any historian must recognize that no two moments are ever really the same; rather, the question is how Chaucer, as later Shakespeare, contributed to the development of a psychology of depth that will culminate in the West in the Freudian model of personality which still dominates many of our assumptions about the world; and which, properly exploited, also contains the possibility of certain critical interpretive moves—suspicious, all-embracing, deterministic ones—that are the essence of a certain subversive modernism.[26]

Julia Kristeva's critical moves illustrate this process especially well: as a medievalist, she may well, consciously or unconsciously, derive the constellation of subversive effects discussed in chapter 5 in part from medieval sources. This is the "sedimentation" Irigaray refers to in *Je, tu, nous.* Thus even if one does not accept the validity of psychoanalysis for the understanding of psychic realities, it has shown itself a valuable tool in analyzing cultural productions such as literature—perhaps because it is derived from cultural productions rather than from life. I would also argue that many modes of postmodern thought beyond psychoanalysis might also find their roots in the premodern.

But the philosophical underpinnings of postmodern feminism are even more important to me than psychoanalysis, and in the introduction I attempt to ground all my subsequent findings in material reality—the history and economic structures of fourteenth-century England—in hopes of avoiding the psychoanalytical "assumption that the subject is raceless and classless."[27] This capacious, and even contradictory, method, and the book's resulting baggy structure, are justified by the discoherent, contradictory elaboration of various gender problems to be found in medieval discourses—and in Chaucer's own language; it is the contradictions themselves that remain sedimented in modern discourses on gender, and that continue to be played out in such theoretical disagreements. It is these disjunctions that I find most useful, and I stress multiplicity and heterogeneity, rather than synthesis, throughout, as a challenge to the whole history of interpretation of the Pardoner and by implication of the Middle Ages more generally.

Returning to Woods' declaration that the Pardoner "is homosexual" underneath the accumulation of critical "niceties of definition": it is precisely the niceties, not only of sexuality, but of sex and gender as well, in all their worrisome ambiguity, that I will be examining in the following chapters. Part I provides contexts, medieval and (post)modern, for reading the Pardoner's body, gender, and erotic practices; Part II uses those contexts in a discontinuous series of readings, each of which takes off from a specific textual observation (the Pardoner's veils, his voice, his obsession with dismemberment) and follows it through a chain of associations in an attempt to chart the cultural Imaginary that produces it. I am aware that my associative method may seem to strain the boundaries of evidence and that some of these readings may appear highly speculative. That is my intention; the works of scholarship and criticism that I have found most inspiring have usually been works of bold speculation, and I place myself in their company too, despite the intellectual risks of doing so.

I take comfort in several contributions to a 1996 *PMLA* roundtable on "the status of evidence." In it, Nancy J. Vickers asserts that "[t]here is a place for argument in the marketplace of ideas that is not necessarily proof but that will stimulate a next stage of argument,"[28] and that is the kind I attempt here. Even more interestingly, Antoine Compagnon raises the issue of "how the unsaid has become evidence—a crucial transformation. When evidence par excellence is the unsaid . . . what are the criteria of truth, of demonstration?" To which Martha Banta responds with the notion of "traces": "I don't use words like *truth, knowledge, law*. It's just glimmers, traces. . . . Of course, in feminist criticism there is what is said between the lines, fascinating traces that are fading like graffiti on the wall, or the silences of all the things that were not said."[29] It is the unsaid, these glimmers, traces, and even silences concerning sex, gender, and sexuality, that provide the "niceties of definition," and about which I shall be speculating, with regard to the Pardoner.

INTRODUCTION

THE PARDONER, THE PREACHER, AND (GENDER) POLITICS

Nay, lat hym telle us of no ribaudye! (VI, 324)

In the following chapters, I shall be analyzing Chaucer's Pardoner as a potentially subversive figure in terms of gender; one who, in his unanchored oscillation among various possible sexes, genders, and erotic practices, could pose a threat to patriarchal authority. But he will also appear as Chaucer's straw man, a figure who introduces this subversive potential only so that it can be disciplined by representatives of medieval authority, especially the Host and the Knight. In addition, the Pardoner will appear as a patriarchal figure himself, one who rejects the feminine and is anxious to assume the signs of a phallic and authoritative masculinity. But first, in this introduction, I would like both to ground these fluctuations in material reality and in poetic language, and to forecast some of the specific arguments I shall subsequently pursue in more detail. How might these disjunctive, discontinuous versions of the Pardoner function in terms of fourteenth-century politics? In what ways might gender be a factor in the political life of late medieval England? How might the economy of court patronage affect and be affected by the politics of gender? And how might all of these questions be related to Chaucer's own status as court poet?

In chapter 5, I shall specifically examine the Pardoner's use of the nonscriptible, presymbolic, "heterogeneous" elements of language as one of the ways in which he exercises the patriarchal authority of the Church; I shall simultaneously argue that these elements are also troubling to this very authority in their alignment with the feminine—and also in their alignment with rebellious peasant speech. It is worth recalling at this point that the insurgents of 1381 directed their revolt not against the king, Richard II, with whom they often identified themselves, but rather against his advisors,

primarily his hated regent, the Duke of Lancaster. And the Duke of Lancaster is better known to Chaucerians as John of Gaunt, Chaucer's patron
throughout much of his poetic career. It is not surprising, then, that
Chaucer's most direct reference to the peasant insurgents is an unflattering
one: the famous passage from *The Nun's Priest's Tale* that compares the peasants' sound-world to that of barnyard animals: "They yolleden as feendes
doon in helle; / The dokes cryden as men wolde hem quelle; / The
gees for feere flowen over the trees; / Out of the hyve cam the swarm of bees. / So
hydous was the noyse—a, benedicitee!—/ Certes, he Jakke Straw and his
meynee / Ne made nevere shoutes half so shrille / Whan that they wolden
any Flemyng kille, / As thilke day was maad upon the fox" (VII, 3389–97).
John of Gaunt's patronage supplies a clear-cut economic motive for
Chaucer's hostile (though comic) portrayal of the peasants.

The Pardoner is, in some ways, another matter: the kind of threat he
poses is not one of direct rebellion, but rather of the potential for the disruption of patriarchal hierarchies more generally, a potential that must be
disciplined. Nevertheless, the Pardoner, like the peasants, is also aligned with
nonscriptible speech: in *The General Prologue,* his sound-world, too, is animalistic: "[a] voys he hadde as smal as hath a goot" (I, 688). And he is, again
like the rebellious peasants, potentially disruptive of the good order of the
Canterbury pilgrimage; in his *Introduction,* the "gentils" of the company fear
his potential for "ribaudye" when the Host invites him to tell a tale:

> " . . . Thou beel amy, thou Pardoner," he sayde,
> "Telle us som myrthe or japes right anon."
>   "It shal be doon," quod he, "by Seint Ronyon!
> But first," quod he, "heere at this alestake
> I wol bothe drynke and eten of a cake."
>   But right anon thise gentils gonne to crye,
> "Nay, lat hym telle us of no ribaudye!
> Telle us som moral thyng, that we may leere
> Som wit, and thanne wol we gladly heere." (VI, 318–26)

As usual, the Pardoner is an ambiguous figure in this passage: the gentlefolk among the pilgrims perceive him as equally capable of "ribaudye" and
of "som moral thyng," though they suspect he is more prone to the former. Ribaldry is an accusation also leveled at the peasant insurgents of
1381 in their own relations with gentlefolk: according to Thomas Walsingham, for instance, they are "rustici, ribaldi perditissimi, ganeones dæmoniaci" [peasants, doomed ribalds and whores of the devil].[1] Ribalds, and
also whores: the connection of the Pardoner to the peasants points the way
toward gender disruption.

This link, however, may seem somewhat tenuous: the Pardoner, after all, is not a peasant, and even seems anxious, not to destroy, but to participate in that very patriarchal power structure that the "gentils" fear he will disrupt. Nevertheless, I believe there is a connection to be drawn.

Other critics have recently argued for such links between some of the other pilgrims and the Peasants' Revolt, in addition to the Nun's Priest's direct mention of it. In *The Knight's Tale,* the cruel god Saturn claims that one of his effects on human life is "[t]he murmure and the cherles rebellyng" (I, 2459), and critics have sometimes associated the remainder of Fragment I with the Revolt. Alfred David refers to *The Miller's Tale* as "a literary Peasants' Rebellion."[2] Steven Justice points out geographical and other similarities between the Revolt (specifically Richard II's failure to grant a requested audience to the peasants at Greenwich) and Chaucer's description of the argument among the Miller, the Reeve, and the Host in *The Reeve's Prologue* (I, 3855–3920): "What are we to do with these lines? The situation—Greenwich; an angry peasant; a king (an innkeeper speaking as lordly as one); a failed intervention; violence in consequence—almost invites recollection of that crucial moment from which the violence in London flowed."[3] For Justice, however, these potential memories of the Revolt are contained or "warded off" in Chaucer's substitution of individual conflict for political action.[4] Similarly, Lee Patterson reads Fragment I as a whole in terms of successive rebellions that can be understood with reference to the Revolt, and concludes that "the Cook's rebelliousness, and rebelliousness per se, stand for all that must be annulled if the *Canterbury Tales* is to be brought to its appointed and orthodox conclusion."[5] Paul Strohm, on the other hand, finds a more positive value in the Miller's rebellion against the Host's authority: "[r]estated in terms of style," it dialectically allows "the incorporation of the challenger into the resultant new order" rather than functioning merely as the containment of rebellion.[6]

Perhaps even more interesting for our purposes, Susan Crane draws a connection between the Revolt and the Wife of Bath in terms of gender: "the analogies between the *Wife of Bath's Prologue* and the rising of 1381 are so striking as to deserve commentary. Alison shares with the rebels inferior status, exclusion from literate circles, a sense of undervaluation by the powerful, and a consequent hostility to writing as the instrument of these interrelated oppressions."[7] The Pardoner, too, is more involved with the material, acoustic qualities of spoken language than with writing, as we shall see in chapter 5. Although he does brandish written documents, they are secondary to his oral self-presentation, and it is as material objects rather than as writing per se that he claims to use them in his *Prologue:*

> First I pronounce whennes that I come,
> And thanne my bulles shewe I, alle and some.
> Oure lige lordes seel on my patente,
> That shewe I first, my body to warente,
> That no man be so boold, ne preest ne clerk,
> Me to destourbe of Cristes hooly werk.
> And after that thanne telle I forth my tales;
> Bulles of popes and of cardynales,
> Of patriarkes and bishopes I shewe,
> And in Latyn I speke a wordes fewe,
> To saffron with my predicacioun,
> And for to stire hem to devocioun. (VI, 335–46)

These documents are quickly assimilated to the power of the Pardoner's oral language: the "bulles" are merely another way in which he can "telle forth" his "tales," the "seel" and "patente" guaranteeing his material "body." They are merely props in an oral performance, sandwiched between his opening pronouncement and his "saffron" words of Latin, which, again, are valued for their nonscriptible acoustic properties rather than for their symbolic meaning. Nevertheless, this writing and the oral language that contains it also represent the Pardoner's attempts at exerting the patriarchal authority of the Church; rather than disrupting it, he tries to become a part of it. Unlike Alison, the Pardoner would never burn a book—though he would happily misuse it.

While he tries repeatedly to assume a position within the pilgrimage's powerful circles, however, we witness the process by which he is ultimately undervalued by, and excluded from, those circles, like the rebellious Wife in Crane's analysis. The process begins during his *Prologue,* when those "gentils" assume he will tell a tale of "ribaudye," associating him with the ribaldry and whorishness that Walsingham attributes to the rebels. It concludes in his humiliation by the Host and in the Knight's reestablishment of order.

As for his social status outside the pilgrimage, while it is true that the Pardoner is not a peasant, neither are the other pilgrims who have been associated with the Revolt: the Miller and the Wife are both, in modern terms, of the middle class rather than the peasantry. And, as Strohm has pointed out, "participants in the Peasants' Revolt included many yeomen, artisans, and craftsmen."[8] In fact, one of the leaders of the Revolt, John Ball, was, like the Pardoner, a preacher.

Accounts of John Ball's sermons and the famous letters attributed to him provide some interesting parallels with the words of the Pardoner. According to Walsingham, Ball, like the Pardoner, was a deceiver of the common people, a preacher whose linguistic sophistication seduced them: "Nec defuerunt ei de communibus auditores, quos semper studuit per detractiones prælatorum, et placentia verba, allicere ad sermonem" [Nor did he lack hearers among the common people, whom he always strove to entice to his sermons by pleasing words, and slander of the prelates].[9]

For Walsingham (and the other chroniclers of the Revolt), Ball's sermons had a political and heretical purpose, promoting Wycliffite doctrines and social egalitarianism.[10] The first letter attributed to Ball, however, may remind us instead of the Pardoner's own sermon: "Nowe regneþ pride in pris, and covetys is hold wys, and leccherye wiþouten shame and glotonye wiþ outen blame. Envye regniþ wiþ tresone, and slouthe is take in grete sesone. God do bote, for nowe is tyme. Amen."[11] These sentences, partaking as they do of the familiar discourse of the Seven Deadly Sins, could almost be understood as the moral of *The Pardoner's Tale*. Lechery, gluttony, and sloth are the sins of the three rioters in its opening scene; the rioters demonstrate unseemly pride in dealing with the Old Man; and covetousness, envy, and treachery prove to be their downfall in the fight over the gold. In the context of the Revolt, the sentiments attributed to Ball may be taken as a criticism of those in power. In *The Pardoner's Tale,* their application is more general, but, still, the Pardoner's exemplum belongs to the same discursive tradition as Ball's letters.

The Pardoner also has in common with John Ball the attempted usurpation of power properly belonging to others. It is worth recalling here that the chroniclers of the Peasants' Revolt agree that Ball, while preaching egalitarianism, hypocritically desired a position of power for himself. According to Walsingham, Ball's sermons inflamed the commons to acclaim him archbishop:

> Cum hæc et plura alia deliramenta prædicasset, commune vulgus eum tanto favore prosequitur, ut acclamerent eum Archiepiscopum futurum, et regni Cancellarium; solum eum dignum Archipræsulatus honore; Archiepiscopum, qui tunc superstes erat, communium et regni proditorem fuisse, et idcirco decapitandum, ubicunque posset in Anglia comprehendi.

> [And when he had preached these and many other ravings, he was in such high favour with the common people that they cried out that he should be archbishop and Chancellor of the kingdom, and that he alone was worthy of the office, for the present archbishop was a traitor to the realm and the commons, and should be beheaded wherever he could be found.][12]

According to the *Anonimalle Chronicle,* Ball was not merely acclaimed by the commons, but actually laid claim to this position for himself:

> En quel temps les communes avoient a lour conseil une chaplein de male part, sire Johan Balle par noune, le quel sire Johan les conseilla de defair

toutz les seignurs et lercevesques et evesques, abbes et priours et plusours moignes et chanouns, issint que nulle evesque serroit en Engleterre forsque une ercevesque, le quel il serroit mesmes. . . .

[At this time the commons had as their counsellor a chaplain of evil disposition named Sir John Balle, who advised them to get rid of all the lords, archbishops, bishops, abbots and priors as well as most of the monks and canons so that there should be no bishop in England except for one archbishop, namely himself. . . .][13]

Despite the egalitarian impulse of the Revolt's leaders as exemplified in Ball's sermons,[14] chroniclers contemporary with Chaucer thus perceived Ball himself as a usurper of power, one who desired, not equality with the peasants, but to take the place of the archbishop (and the archbishop's death at the hands of the insurgents is the scene given the most emotional weight by several of these chroniclers).

The Pardoner, in a similar fashion, tries to promote himself, and to usurp the Host's position of authority, at the conclusion of his *Tale:* "It is an honour to everich that is heer / That ye mowe have a suffisant pardoneer / T'assoille yow in contree as ye ryde. . . . / I rede that oure Hoost heere shal bigynne, / For he is moost envoluped in synne. / Com forth, sire Hoost, and offre first anon, / And thou shalt kisse the relikes everychon, / Ye, for a grote! Unbokele anon thy purs" (VI, 931–33, 941–45). The Pardoner here attempts to assert his own (specifically religious) authority against the ordained leader who was chosen by the community at the beginning of the pilgrimage ("And we wol reuled been at his devys / In heigh and lough; and thus by oon assent / We been acorded to his juggement" [I, 816–18]). As John Ball wished to do on a larger, national scale (according to the chroniclers), the Pardoner wishes, in the microcosm of the pilgrimage, to usurp patriarchal authority for himself.

Ball and the Pardoner also come to similar bad ends. The Pardoner, as we shall see in chapter 4, is verbally dismembered by the offended Host, who, at the end of *The Pardoner's Tale,* exposes the Pardoner's ambiguous relation to phallic power, either threatening him with castration or exposing his apparent status as eunuch (or both): "I wolde I hadde thy coillons in myn hond / In stide of relikes or of seintuarie. / Lat kutte hem of, I wol thee helpe hem carie; / They shul be shryned in an hogges toord!" (VI, 952–55). In chapter 6 we shall examine further examples of the Pardoner's obsession with dismemberment, which is John Ball's fate as well: the chronicles report that, in Walsingham's words,

Hoc die præterea, Johannem Balle, presbyterum, captum a viris Coventrensibus, et pridie ductum ad Sanctum Albanum et Regis præsentiam, cujus

majestatem convictus est læsisse enormiter, auditum et confessum turpissima
scelera, tractioni, suspendio, decollationi, exentrationi, et quarterizationi, ut
usu vulgari loquar, idem Robertus adjudicavit. . . .

[Moreover, on that day {Saturday 13 July} the same Robert {Tresilian} sen-
tenced John Balle, priest, after hearing of his scandalous and confessed
crimes, to drawing, hanging, beheading, disemboweling, and—to use the
common words—quartering: he had been taken by the men of Coventry
and on the previous day brought to St. Albans and into the presence of the
king whose majesty he had insulted so gravely.]¹⁵

Dismemberment in the presence of an ordained leader he has insulted:
once again the careers of these two preachers, John Ball and the Pardoner,
follow a similar trajectory.

These parallels are at least as striking as those between the Miller or the
Wife and the insurgents as analyzed by Justice and by Crane: in both cases
(of Ball and the Pardoner), we have a preacher who is associated with the
community's lower orders (and with orality); who is linguistically sophisticated; who is a hypocrite; who uses his pleasing words to deceive an audience of peasants; who desires power for himself; who tries to usurp that
power from the community's ordained authority; and who is punished by
that leader with dismemberment. From this perspective, the Pardoner may
be regarded, not as an allegory of the Revolt or even as a fictionalized John
Ball, but perhaps as a hostile parody of Ball, and thereby of the Revolt
more generally. If, as Justice suggests, the Miller's encounter with the
Reeve and the Host "invites recollection" of the Peasants' Revolt, a similar recollection of John Ball is invited by the Pardoner's entire performance, including his encounter with the Host—and that with the Knight.

It is the Knight who restores order in *The Canterbury Tales* after the Pardoner's attempted insurrection, and if we broaden the parallels beyond
John Ball to include other aspects of the Peasants' Revolt, we may discover
a comparable movement from disorder to order in the chroniclers' accounts of it. The insurgents' behavior is regularly decried in the chronicles
as madness, and this insanity takes the form of a reversal of the "natural"
order. It is, in particular, characterized by an overemphasis on the body, indeed on the very sins of pride, gluttony, and lechery apparently imputed to
the ruling classes in the letters attributed to John Ball:

[S]ol altius elevatus incaluisset, et ipsi pro votis ubique vina diversa et pretiosis-
sima pocula præegustassent, et facti fuissent non tam ebrii quam dementes. . . .
    Et cum hæc omnia facerent, et, ut diximus, plerique soli in cameras con-
cessissent, et sedendo, jacendo, jocando, super lectum Regis insolescerent; et
insuper, matrem Regis ad oscula invitarent quidam; non tamen—quod

mirum dictu est,—audebant plures milites et armigeri unum de tam incon-
venientibus actibus convenire, non ad impediendum manus injicere, nec
verbis secretissimis mussitare. Intrabant et exibant ut domini, qui quondam
fuerant vilissimæ conditionis servi; et præferebant se militibus non tam mil-
itum, sed rusticorum, subulci.

[{T}he sun had climbed higher and grown warm and the rebels had tasted
various wines and expensive drinks at will and so had become less drunk
than mad. . . .
    After the rebels had done all these things and had gained access singly
and in groups to the rooms in the Tower, they arrogantly lay and sat on the
king's bed while joking; and several asked the king's mother to kiss them.
But (marvelous to relate), the many knights and squires present dared not
resist any of these unseemly deeds, nor raise their hands in opposition nor
keep the rebels quiet by means of secret words. The rebels, who had formerly belonged to the most lowly condition of serf, went in and out like
lords; and swineherds set themselves above soldiers although not knights but
rustics.][16]

Walsingham quickly assimilates the bodily sins of drunkenness and lechery
to the incomprehensible social madness whereby peasants usurp the place
of knights, and the knights fail to respond appropriately. Here we are undoubtedly, though perhaps unconsciously, in the presence of the metaphor
of the body politic. The disordered, drunken (peasant) body is directly
analogous to disorders in the social body by which the lower members
rebel against the sovereignty of the head, for instance in the accounts of
this metaphor given by John of Salisbury, Marie de France, and Christine
de Pizan.[17] (And it is worth noting how often the chroniclers dwell on the
beheading of the peasants' victims:[18] the insurgents literally enact the political metaphor of rebellion of body against head.)
    As we shall see in chapter 4, the Pardoner, too, privileges, in his concern
with bodily fragmentation, not the head, but the (in his case possibly absent) sex organs. And the bodily sins here imputed to the peasants, including sexual sins, are also those of which the Pardoner accuses himself. His
desire for drink is apparently what first arouses the suspicion of the pilgrimage's gentlefolk, and the accusation of "ribaudye." Shortly after (in his
Prologue), the Pardoner associates this desire with lechery as well: "Nay, I
wol drynke licour of the vyne / And have a joly wenche in every toun"
(VI, 452–53). As in Walsingham's account of the peasants' behavior, what
begins with drink ends with a socially disruptive invitation to a kiss: if the
insurgents demand kisses from the king's mother, the Pardoner demands a
kiss—of his relics—from the Host, a kiss that the Host, with his references
to fouled breeches and "coillons," interprets in its most carnal sense. Both

kisses thus literally represent the "unnatural" dominion of the lower body over the head, and figuratively represent an equally unnatural social or political disorder, in terms of the body politic.

The chivalric class responds to this conflict more positively in *The Canterbury Tales* than in the chronicles, however. Unlike the knights of Walsingham's chronicle, made passive by the peasants' usurpation of power, Chaucer's Knight, at the conclusion of Fragment VI, steps in to repair the relations between the Pardoner's attempted usurpation and the Host's authority with another kind of kiss:

> But right anon the worthy Knyght bigan,
> Whan that he saugh that al the peple lough,
> "Namoore of this, for it is right ynough!
> Sire Pardoner, be glad and myrie of cheere;
> And ye, sire Hoost, that been to me so deere,
> I prey yow that ye kisse the Pardoner.
> And Pardoner, I prey thee, drawe thee neer,
> And, as we diden, lat us laughe and pleye."
> Anon they kiste, and ryden forth hir weye. (VI, 960–68)

In restoring good order to this community, the Knight recalls the eventual suppression of the Peasants' Revolt by Richard II's knights and justices rather than the passivity exhibited by the knights during the revolt itself. Froissart describes Richard II's raising of "cinq cents lances et autant d'archers" [five hundred spears and as many archers] to bring "le royaume en son droit point" [bring again his realm in good order].[19] Walsingham exaggerates the size of the king's army to "quadraginta millia equitum, decentissime armatorum" [40,000 properly armed horsemen], and describes the slaughter of five hundred peasants.[20] The justices' punishment of the insurgents was also severe, and in some cases, according to Walsingham, mirrored John Ball's dismemberment:

> Usi sunt tamen prius judices, qui sederunt in Estsexia, Kancia, et Londoniis, propter multitudinem perimendorum, decollationibus rusticorum, donec visum fuisset pœnam capitalem non correspondere tantis tamque facinoribus manifestis; quia quodammado erat nimis secreta punitio tam evidenti delicto. Ob quam causam, expost, juxta regni consuetudines, decreverunt omnes repertos sceleratiores, ut diximus, protractione, suspensione, punire: et in Estsexia res utique taliter se habebant.

> [Previously, the judges who sat in Essex, Kent and London had beheaded many rustics because of the multitude of people to be executed—until it seemed that this type of capital punishment no longer corresponded to the

crimes committed. Such a penalty was too mild a punishment for the cases
in question. Wherefore it was later decreed, according to the customs of the
realm, that all those discovered to be criminals should, as we have said, be
punished by drawing and hanging; and this was the method employed in
Essex.][21]

If, as Strohm has it, the Miller's social reintegration is relatively painless
compared to that of the real peasant rebels, the same might be said of the
Pardoner, though whether he is, like the Miller, successfully reintegrated
into the pilgrimage community is open to question. As in the discourses
surrounding the suppression of the Peasants' Revolt, the motivation of
Chaucer's Knight is the restoration of order ("as we diden, lat us laughe
and pleye") and "*pacis regni*," "the peace of the Realm."[22] In *The Canterbury Tales,* however, this peace is signified in uncomfortably gendered—and
erotic—terms. The Kiss of Peace proposed—with good intentions but no
sense on the Knight's part of the typically Chaucerian irony perceptible to
readers—follows the Pardoner's proposal that the Host kiss his relics and
the Host's angry response invoking an imagined kiss of the Pardoner's
breeches. The Host appears to be responding to the unwelcome erotic possibilities implied in the Pardoner's invitation to unbuckle his purse and kiss
his relics: chapter 4 will examine the fetishized, quasi-phallic meaning of
the Pardoner's relics (which have also been discussed by Carolyn Dinshaw[23]). And the use of the purse as a double entendre for male sex organs
is established by the Wife of Bath ("Yblessed be God that I have wedded
fyve! / Of whiche I have pyked out the beste, / Bothe of here nether purs
and of here cheste" [III, 44–44b]). The double reference to purse and relics
requires a sodomitical reading, and that is how the Host understands it,
hence his furious refusal.

In this context, the image of two men kissing, as proposed by the
Knight, ironically raises exactly the sodomitical possibilities that the Host
angrily disavowed: the previous passage makes a mockery of the sacred kiss
that follows by changing its register of meaning from spirituality to eroticism.[24] The Host's phallic power—we may recall that he considers himself
"perilous wyth knyf in honde" (VII, 1919)—is threatened by the Pardoner,
and the Host responds by using his verbal knife to castrate him. Compare
the Pardoner's threat to the Host with that posed by the Host's wife Good-
elief: she, too, rebels against her husband's authority specifically by threatening his masculinity, as in this passage from *The Monk's Prologue:* "Whan
she comth hoom she rampeth in my face, / And crieth, 'False coward, wrek
thy wyf! / By corpus bones, I wol have thy knyf, / And thou shalt have my
distaf and go spynne!'" (VII, 1904–1907). The Host perceives a similar
threat in the Pardoner's invitation to a kiss; and if he cannot control his

masculinized wife, he demonstrates that he can put the Pardoner, at least, into a powerless, feminized position. This feminization of the Pardoner is confirmed in the Knight's invitation to the Kiss of Peace: he is merely to "draw near" at the Knight's command and passively receive the kiss from the Host, who is to take the active role in bestowing it. The Knight's proposal both unintentionally confirms the erotic overtones of the Pardoner-Host encounter, and turns the Pardoner into the passive partner in it. Ironically, the Knight does restore a kind of order after all, but it is the order of the patriarchal gender hierarchy, not the spiritual order he apparently intends. And it is an order that the Pardoner, in his furious silence, refuses to accept.

The eroticized language of the Pardoner's encounter with the Host suggests that the Pardoner's entire rebellion, as well as its suppression in a kiss, is to be understood in terms of gender and the erotic. If the rebellions of Fragment I recall the Revolt only to defuse that recollection by making them personal and literary or stylistic rather than political, as Justice and Patterson argue, the Pardoner's transgression, by contrast, is perhaps rendered more rather than less potent in being generalized to include gender politics. The effect of the interaction among Pardoner, Host, and Knight seems to be the Pardoner's exclusion rather than his reintegration: he is silenced and does not reappear in *The Canterbury Tales* after this moment. But the introduction of gender issues into his moment of transgression allows him to remain troubling in his very absence. Order may be restored to the pilgrimage, but hardly peace: the Host's verbal castration and exposure of the Pardoner cannot be resolved or undone, and the Pardoner cannot be reinscribed within the patriarchal community.

The concern with gender issues—the feminine and the sodomitical—is not absent from contemporary accounts of the Peasants' Revolt, either. Any discussion of the rebellion of the lower orders of a hierarchy against the higher is inevitably, if unconsciously, a gendered act, especially when the rebellion is, like the Peasants' Revolt in Walsingham's account, imagined as a revolt of the lower body against the head. Caroline Walker Bynum succinctly makes the essential point that in the Middle Ages woman commonly "symbolized the physical, lustful, material, appetitive part of human nature, whereas man symbolized the spiritual or mental." But anatomical men, too, or those culturally constructed as male, can discursively play this feminine role; to quote one further feminist medievalist perspective, the critical task is to promote "an understanding not simply of sexual difference—'man' versus 'woman'—but rather of the various ways in which sexed identities take shape, in all their complexities and contradictions, according to historically specific configurations of power and power relations."[25] The male peasant rebels, and in some respects the Pardoner too, can thus occupy the "feminine" position, and I would argue that within the discursive framework under discussion, they often do.

Biological women, however, did play key roles in power relations among the classes at certain moments in the Revolt, as recounted in the chronicles. Susan Crane cites the actions of an old woman who expressed the anticlerical sentiment of the rebels in Cambridge when they burned the scholars' books: "[e]t vetula quedam nomine Margareta Starre cineres collectos in ventum sparsit clamando abcedat clericorum pericia abcedat" [a certain old woman named Margaret Starre scattered the heap of ashes to the wind, crying, 'Away with the knowledge of clerks, away with it'].[26] Crane argues that this action is treated not just as one rebellious moment among many, but as an epitome of the insurgents' disorderly conduct and as the ultimate justification for their punishment.[27]

The *Anonimalle Chronicle* also reports that it was a woman who prevented the archbishop of Canterbury's escape from the insurgents:

> . . . et en celle temps, en la matyne conseilla lercevesque de Kaunterbury et les autres qe furont adonqes en la Toure de aler a la petit port devers la eaw et prendre une bataille et salver lour mesmes. Et lercevesqe fist en celle maner, mes il fuist escrie par une malveys femme et retourna a la Toure a sa confusione de mesme.

> [And at this time of the morning {the king} advised the archbishop of Canterbury and the others who were in the Tower, to go down to the little water-gate, and take a boat and save themselves. And the archbishop proceeded to do this; but a wicked woman raised a cry against him, and he had to turn back to the Tower, to his own confusion.][28]

The beheading of the archbishop—one of the defining moments of the Revolt—follows in short order.

Such examples imply that the paradigm of woman as unruly body, opposed to things of the mind or spirit (as in the medieval Orpheus tradition explored in chapter 6), is unconsciously at work here in tandem with the metaphor of the body politic. As Crane points out, "the topos of woman's incoherence, which R. Howard Bloch has recently termed 'woman as riot,' again resonates with literary representations of the rebels as self-contradictory, irrational, and noisy—which is to say effectively voiceless."[29] A further sign of the seriousness of the Revolt's disorder is the passive, and hence discursively feminized, behavior of the knights cited by Walsingham earlier. Indeed, Henry Knighton describes the behavior of the king's knights during the revolt specifically as womanish: "Milites uero qui ituri erant cordis strenuitatem quasi tabescentes uecorditer amiserunt, et mentis audaciam quod dolendum

est sub calle dederunt, nec egredi quasi timore femineo percussi ullatenus audebant, set se in Turri continebant" [The knights who were to accompany
him foolishly allowed their ardor to cool, lamentably hiding the boldness of
their spirit, and as though struck by some womanish fear, not daring to go
out, stayed in the Tower].[30]

Given the sodomitical implications of the Pardoner's exchange with the
Host, we may also recall at this point that both rebellion and sodomy were
commonly associated with heresy in Chaucer's period; in the words of one
recent historian, after the thirteenth century, "[h]omosexuality became an
inevitable concomitant of accusations of heresy and witchcraft."[31] The
Peasants' Revolt is specifically, and regularly, associated with Lollardy in the
contemporary chronicles, John Ball having supposedly taught "perversa
dogmata perfidi Johannis Wyclif" [the perverse doctrines of the perfidious
John Wycliffe].[32] If we take the Pardoner's connection with Ball one step
further, we may find Chaucer substituting sodomy for heresy in a move
that would have been familiar to a late medieval audience.

It should not be too far-fetched, then, to suggest that the Pardoner's in-
sufficient manliness be regarded as another link with the Peasants' Revolt:
he epitomizes the body out of control, which is to say the sodomitical
body or the body feminized, and for that very reason, dangerous. When, in
Froissart's chronicle, the peasants make their demands known, they employ
a discourse of loss or lack that may remind us of the Pardoner:

Adonc dit le roi: "Seigneurs, que voulez-vous dire? Dites-le-moi; je suis ci
venu pour parler à vous." Ils lui dirent de une voix . . . : "Nous voulons que
tu viennes sur terre, et nous te montrerons et dirons . . . ce qu'il nous faut."

[And the king demanded of them what they would, and said how he was
come thither to speak with them, and they said all with one voice: "We
would that ye should come aland, and then we shall shew you what we
lack".]

Other chronicles also make it clear that the insurgents saw their own status as a condition of loss, of the unjust deprivation of an original equality
with the aristocracy.[33] The Pardoner, too, is attempting to make good what
he apparently lacks, to find an acceptable substitute—money, authority—
for that which he is apparently missing, whether testicles or manliness in
general. The Pardoner's attempted usurpation thus makes explicit the gendered nature of political insurrection that remains implicit in the chronicles. His attempt to place the Host in a passive, powerless, quasi-erotic
position with regard to himself must, then, almost inevitably be punished
in terms of gender, by the verbal castration that puts him back into his
proper place: the political solution to conflict within this little community

of the pilgrimage must also be a gendered solution, the necessary silencing of the feminine or potentially feminine when it aspires to masculine power. The reaction of Host and Knight, like the brutal response to the Revolt, is a form of revenge for the threat of passivity and feminization raised by the Pardoner, as by the rebels. It reclaims a specifically masculine authority that has been threatened and does so by means of a literal or figurative dismemberment and castration, the definitive un-manning of gendered political insurgency.

I do not necessarily wish to argue that the encounter of Host, Knight, and Pardoner is a deliberate rewriting, in gendered terms, of contemporary perceptions of the Peasants' Revolt, though the parallels are interesting. I do wish to argue that contemporary representations of the Revolt and the Pardoner's failed attempt to usurp the Host's position should be seen within the same discursive framework: both are concerned with disorder in the body politic, and both, though more explicitly in the case of the Pardoner, connect that disorder to the presence of the feminine (lower body versus head, undisciplined sound versus scriptible language), which not only characterizes the insurgents themselves (peasants or Pardoner), but also threatens the dominant authority (archbishop, knights, Host) with feminization. In both cases the feminine threatens to usurp masculine power by feminizing those who hold it, and in both cases this threat is averted by reestablishing the preexisting political and gender hierarchies.

If John of Gaunt was threatened by the Peasants' Revolt, then, Chaucer here provides him with a displaced, literary rebellion whose suppression is both politically satisfactory and provides the extra benefit of feminizing insurgency. We may find here the economic motive underlying the text's need to silence the Pardoner. If this figure appears initially as a means of exploring gender ambiguities, the very fact that such ambiguities call into question what are at bottom political hierarchies ensures that the Duke of Lancaster's patronage will require their ultimate suppression. But why should this suppression take place in terms of gender at all?

One reason may have to do with the contemporary circulation of rumors of sodomy at Richard II's court. While Richard tried to clear his ancestor Edward II's name of such accusations, he himself suffered from similar allegations leveled by, for instance, Walsingham, who depicted Richard's political patronage of Robert de Vere as an example both of effeminacy and of sodomitical desire: "tantum afficiebatur eidem, tantum coluit et amavit eundem, non sine nota, prout fertur, familiaritatis obscoenae" [he was so much attached to him, he associated with him and loved him so much, not without indication of indecent familiarity].[34] The representation of an "official" suppression of rebellion specifically as it might be linked to unorthodox sexuality, then, might have been especially welcome to Chaucer's patrons.

The discourses of gender, however, are rarely self-consistent or monophonic. Whatever orthodoxy Chaucer's relations with his patron required may, like all such orthodoxies, have also tended to deconstruct itself when it was cast into the form of poetic language. The concatenation of patronage, poetry, and gender politics can be further illuminated by a brief examination of one of Chaucer's best-known shorter poems, the "Complaint to His Purse," which demonstrates that the relations between patron and poet are always already gendered, and gendered in ways that escape the poet's and the patron's control. This poem was written, or at least completed, under the reign of Henry IV, but it may nevertheless demonstrate the ways in which all of Chaucer's attempts to discipline and suppress unorthodox erotic practices in a political context may, despite his best efforts, escape his control. The very attempt to reproduce patriarchal discourse opens up the possibility of deconstructing that discourse, both in the "Complaint" and in the figure of the Pardoner.

This poem is constructed in terms of analogous hierarchies registered in various kinds of figurative language. It begins by stating an equivalence between the linguistic registers of money and love: "To yow, my purse, and to noon other wight / Complayne I, for ye be my lady dere" (CP, 1–2). Typically a form for love poems, the complaint is here used to discuss the poet's financial situation: money stands in for love, and the purse occupies the position generically occupied by the beloved lady. But the positions can also be reversed: the literal addressee of the poem at this point is the purse, and the lady thus occupies the purse's position only figuratively. The equation works both ways: lady equals purse, purse equals lady. The desire for money is analogous to heterosexual desire. But if the purse here plays the same figuratively erotic role we have observed elsewhere, gender confusion has already set in: the purse, in *The Canterbury Tales* regularly representative of the male genitals, here stands in for the female beloved.

The first two stanzas of the poem explore the sometimes comical conjunctions and disjunctions that result from the equation of purse and lady, and, at the end of the second stanza, add a third register of figurative language, the religious: the purse is also "Quene of comfort" (CP, 13), an epithet sometimes applied to the Virgin Mary. This religious register dominates the third stanza, in which the purse becomes the poet's "saveour" (though only "doun in this world here" [CP, 16]), a divinity to whom the poet can pray for assistance: "Out of this toune helpe me thurgh your myght" (CP, 17). The earlier figurative registers are not forgotten in this stanza, but also remain in play: the purse itself reappears in line 15 ("Now purse that ben to me my lyves lyght"), and it is addressed not only as a purse and as a god but also again as a courtly lady (to whom a poet might also pray) at the end of the stanza: "But yet I pray unto your cur-tesye / Beth hevy agen, or elles moot I dye" (CP, 20–21). The equation now works in three registers: lady equals purse equals God.

The categories being humorously invoked here are familiar to any stu-dent of the Great Chain of Being, or of medieval hierarchical and analog-ical thought: the hierarchy in which the lady dominates the lover is regularly conflated, in medieval love poetry, with the religious hierarchy in which the worshipper is subjected to God. To that extent the lady is placed discursively in an apparent position of masculine power also suggested by the purse's connotation of masculinity (though, as the lady's power de-pends entirely on male erotic desire, it is more apparent than real). To this constellation Chaucer adds an economic hierarchy in which the purse dominates the poor poet:

Like the courtly lady in the register of love poetry, the monarch in the register of politics normally occupies the position at the top of the hierar-chy analogous to God's position in the religious hierarchy, and Chaucer's poem completes this series of interchangeable hierarchies in the envoy: "O conquerour of Brutes Albyon, / Which that by lyne and free eleccion / Been verray kyng, this song to yow I sende, / And ye, that mowen alle oure harmes amende, / Have mynde upon my supplicacion" (CP, 22–26). The addressee is now the new king, Henry IV, who is smoothly moved into the structural position formerly occupied by God, by the lady, and especially by the purse: he is now the addressee of the poem, as the purse was ini-tially, and, like the purse (and God, and the lady), he is to respond to his subject's "supplicacion." The king is most specifically analogous to the purse; the point, after all, is that, like the purse, he is to provide money for the poet: king equals purse. More flatteringly, the king in his political rela-tionship with his subject is analogous to God in his religious relationship with the worshipper ("ye, that mowen alle oure harmes amende"): king equals purse equals God.

And this seems to be the point of the poem: to flatter the king by plac-ing him at the top of a political hierarchy, thereby making him godlike in his power, and thus also, comically, to turn him figuratively (and in terms of the poem's construction, structurally) into a purse, a source of money to the poet.

What Chaucer's envoy silences, of course, is the remaining term of the equation: in the envoy, the lady has disappeared from the language of the poem, and with her the erotic register of meaning with which it began. In terms of structure, however, the various registers of meaning have been, up to this point, interchangeable, and so the nagging memory of that erotic register must remain: if the king in relation to his subject is also God in his relation to his worshipper and the purse in relation to the poet, he must also be the lady in relation to the lover—a lady who retains power as long as she has what the poet wants. From the structural perspective, then, the heterosexual desire of the "Complaint"'s opening evolves into a sodomitical, male-male desire by its conclusion (a desire also reinforced by the purse's male-genital characteristics). By the same token, the formerly heterosexual desire for money has been re-cast as a form of male-male eroticism. And the purse has taken up again its function as a signifier of male sexuality and sodomitical desire that we observed in the Pardoner's interaction with the Host. The patron-poet relationship can be deconstructed as a relation that is, in a fairly complex fashion, both gendered and eroticized: like any discourse of desire or lack, the economic discourse has its gendered aspect.

I do not wish to argue that this is Chaucer's intention. But the discourse of gender—and perhaps poetic discourse itself—is so slippery and ambiguous that it seems inevitably to deconstruct itself, to allow prohibited meanings to manifest themselves in the very language that attempts to silence them. If sodomy and revolt are both like heresy in their rebellion against God's order, which includes the authority of the king, Chaucer must condemn them in the person of the Pardoner; and yet, sodomy itself escapes such discursive orthodoxies. Chaucer must introduce the possibility of sodomy into the Pardoner's interaction with the Host in order to discipline it; it cannot be uttered directly, but neither can it remain merely unspoken. As in the "Complaint," this sodomitical possibility is introduced by way of money, and specifically by way of a reference to a purse belonging to the community's leader. The Pardoner has often, rightly, been cited as a figure of the poet[35]; nevertheless, it may come as a surprise to find the poet placing himself, in the "Complaint," in the same position in which he placed the Pardoner: requesting that a person of authority open his purse in terms that hint—to the Host, at any rate—at sodomy. The Pardoner's request, and the Host's response to it, demonstrate how easily a speaker can lose control of his own discourse, and the "Complaint to His Purse" implicates Chaucer himself in this loss of control: in both cases the discourse of patronage—perhaps inevitably, as it involves two men in an unequal relation of power, that is, in a relation in which one of them is necessarily feminized—can be deconstructed as the discourse of same-sex desire.

If the "Complaint to His Purse" unconsciously works against its own heterosexual presumptions, might the same be said of *The Canterbury Tales?* In the concluding chapter of this book I shall return to this question and argue that perhaps it does; that, as in the "Complaint," the form of the text may actually embody the very confusions in gender categories that are so troubling to the text's content and that it continually tries to suppress.

PART I

CONTEXTS: THE PARDONER'S
GENDERS, SEXES, EROTIC PRACTICES

CHAPTER 1

THE PARDONER'S GENDERS:
LINGUISTIC AND OTHER

A voys he hadde as smal as hath a goot (I, 688)

In the first three chapters of this book, I will be examining a number of the discursive contexts in which Chaucer's Pardoner is situated, with specific reference to three related components of gender identity: the sexed body, socially constructed gender presentation, and erotic practice. While at least some late- twentieth-century readers distinguish among these three components, medieval sources sometimes do not, often assuming instead that what we call anatomical sex, gendered behaviors, and erotic object choice ideally function as one, expressing a univocal gender identity. Nevertheless, because this book as a whole will be questioning such univocity, it seems useful to distinguish among the three components at the outset, in order to clarify how they do and do not function, together and in themselves, in the Pardoner's case. And because what I intend to examine in this book is less often Chaucer's intentions than the cultural Imaginary that conditioned the production of his texts, I will also be calling upon recent gender theorists to shed light on various conjunctions and disjunctions among the three components, relations that reveal anxieties about gender that span the centuries since Chaucer wrote. Once again, I attempt both a historical and a transhistorical understanding of the problematics of gender as they are revealed through the Pardoner, in the hope that each can illuminate the other.

Of these three categories, it is gender, dependent neither upon specific types of body nor specific sex acts, that poses the greatest difficulties of definition. Gender may be conceived as a set of social performances or presentations referring variously to bodies and acts, specifically, as R. W. Connell has it, "in relation to a reproductive arena, defined by the bodily structures and processes of human reproduction. This arena includes sexual arousal and intercourse, childbirth and infant care, bodily sex difference and similarity."[1] Social ideals usually do demand that these processes be "ordered": sex acts and body types "should" conform to a masculine or feminine gender ideal (the Pardoner seems unconcerned with child rearing except insofar as he appears boyish rather than manly, a point to which I shall return below).

Judith Lorber offers another useful perspective on "gender as a social institution," suggesting that it "is built into the major social organizations of society, such as the economy, ideology, the family, and politics, and is also an entity in and of itself."[2] From this perspective, even the crossing of gender boundaries tends to reinforce rather than to challenge the ideology of gender: "Paradoxically, then, bending gender rules and passing between genders does not erode but rather preserves gender boundaries. In societies with only two genders, the gender dichotomy is not disturbed by transvestites, because others feel that a transvestite is only transitorily ambiguous—is 'really a man or woman underneath.'"[3]

Donna J. Haraway (following, like many theorists of gender, Gayle Rubin) insists that gender is necessarily a political concept: "Gender is a concept developed to contest the naturalization of sexual difference in multiple arenas of struggle. Feminist theory and practice around gender seek to explain and change historical systems of sexual difference, whereby 'men' and 'women' are socially constituted and positioned in relations of hierarchy and antagonism."[4] For Haraway, the politics of gender is an aspect of the larger postmodern and neo-Marxist project of critiquing the "natural" subject:

> The refusal to become or to remain a "gendered" man or a woman, then, is an eminently political insistence on emerging from the nightmare of the all-too-real, imaginary narrative of sex and race. Finally and ironically, the political and explanatory power of the "social" category of gender depends upon historicizing the categories of sex, flesh, body, biology, race, and nature in such a way that the binary, universalizing opposition that spawned the concept of the sex/gender system at a particular time and place in feminist theory implodes into articulated, differentiated, accountable, located, and consequential theories of embodiment, where nature is no longer imagined and enacted as resource to culture or sex to gender.[5]

My project here is an aspect of the one Haraway outlines: to take advantage of the Pardoner's apparently *un*natural gender transgressions in order to locate the specific historical discourses that constitute these apparently natural categories for the fourteenth century, and that remain sedimented at the end of the twentieth. The Pardoner cannot be "or-

dered" in the ways Connell and Lorber describe as normative; the ambiguities surrounding the categories of body type and erotic practice
with regard to the Pardoner ensure that his gender identity, too, will be
disordered and disjunctive. Donald R. Howard thus claims, on the one
hand, that "[n]owhere . . . is there any suggestion that his mannerisms
are effeminate—if anything, his bravura could be reckoned masculine";
but on the other, that "[t]he Pardoner . . . is *feminoid* in a starkly physical way—his voice, his hair, his beard are involved."[6] The Pardoner does
not exactly cross genders in the way Lorber describes; rather, and more
disturbingly, he engages in contradictory gender presentations or performances simultaneously, making it impossible to fix him as primarily
masculine or feminine. The Pardoner seems "queer" in reference to his
gender as well as in reference to his erotic practices; what Carolyn Dinshaw says of "heterosexuality" could be said equally well of "gender":
"[t]he queer empties out the natural, the essential, empties out the conventional foundations of representation and identity, shakes with his
touch the heterocultural edifice."[7]

It is impossible to discuss gender without referring to bodies and acts.
But while most Chaucerians have focused on the latter two issues in their
discussions of the Pardoner, it may nevertheless still be useful to try and
consider gender, at least briefly, as a social practice not quite identical with
bodies and acts, fraught with difficulties though such an attempt must be.
The difficulties themselves are actually instructive; as Connell puts it, gender itself is "historically changing and politically fraught" because "the
right to account for gender is claimed by conflicting discourses and systems of knowledge."[8] This is as true of Chaucer's period as of our own.

Monica McAlpine points out that the categories of anatomical sex,
erotic practice, and gender as social practice are even more confused in
medieval texts than they are for us. On the one hand, "Chaucer reflects one
ancient and widespread misunderstanding about male homosexuality, that
it involves in some a sense a man's becoming a woman"; but on the other
hand, "[j]ust as not all effeminate males were suspected of homosexuality,
so not all homosexual males were perceived as effeminate."[9] McAlpine's
essay, published in 1980, uses the modern term "homosexuality" to denote
male-male erotic practice, and assumes a transhistorical homosexual identity in a way few scholars would now find appropriate, but her larger point
is well taken: sex acts ("homosexuality"), anatomical sex ("male," "man,"
"woman"), and gender performance ("effeminacy") are conflated in some
medieval texts, though not in others.

As she remarks, the *Roman de la rose* at one point does conflate all three
categories: "Cous tes manches, tes cheveus pigne, / Mais ne te farde ne ne
guigne, / Ce n'apartient s'a dames non, / Ou a ceus de mavés renon, / Qui

amors par male aventure / Ont trovée contre nature" [Sew your sleeves and comb your hair, but do not rouge or paint your face, for such a custom belongs only to ladies or to men of bad repute, who have had the misfortune to find a love contrary to Nature].[10] Men who practice sodomitical sex acts ("men of bad repute," etc.) are assimilated to the other anatomical sex ("ladies"), and both are associated with a particular social practice or gender performance (the use of cosmetics).

It is worth recalling, however, that the fragmentary Middle English translation of this text, the *Romaunt of the Rose,* removes the association of effeminacy with "love contrary to Nature": "And kembe thyn heed right jolily. / Fard not thi visage in no wise, / For that of love is not th'emprise; / For love doth haten, as I fynde, / A beaute that cometh not of kynde."[11] A condemnation of effeminacy and its concomitant "unnatural" love in one text has become merely a condemnation of cosmetics, for both sexes, in another. Although this fragment of the *Romaunt* is not a genuine work of Chaucer's, it is contemporary with him and demonstrates that what appeared to be both effeminate and a sign of sodomitical desire in Guillaume de Lorris' period and culture might not have been either in Chaucer's. Gender, like sodomy in Foucault's famous phrase, is an "utterly confused category"[12] both now and in the Middle Ages, and I would argue that the Pardoner can be read as a figure for this confusion, just as he is for confusions about bodies and acts.

What, then, are the medieval discourses that try, in Connell's words, to claim "the right to account for gender," or to ensure that gender performances and erotic practices march in step with anatomical sex? Some—medical, theological, and legal, for instance—are discussed more fully in the following chapters, but here it seems useful to attend to two discourses specific to gender as a cultural construction. One is the linguistic or grammatical discourse surrounding gender; the other is a mythology of gender available to Chaucer and of particular relevance to the Pardoner. What they have in common is the anxiety, which is still with us, caused by that display of feminine characteristics by an ostensibly masculine person that we call "effeminacy."

Alan of Lille, among others, draws the connection between the gender of words and the gender of persons quite explicitly, and it seems worthwhile to explore these relations with regard to Chaucer as well. Alan unambiguously condemns gender transgressions, especially the "inappropriate" display of feminine gender attributes by men, for instance in his *Anticlaudianus,* in which Venus bemoans Achilles' cross-dressing: "Nunc mea tela iacent, quibus olim uictus Achilles / Cessit, degeneri mentitus ueste puellam; / Inque colum clauam uertens, in pensa sagittas, / In fusum pharetras, Alcides

degener armis / Totus femineos male degenerauit in actus" [Now my arms
lie idle, my arms through which Achilles, counterfeiting a girl in his degenerate clothes, was once overcome and yielded. The descendant of Al-
ceus, degenerate in arms, exchanges his staff for a distaff, his arrows for a
day's supply of wool, his quivers for a spindle and basely unsexed himself
completely in womanish action].[13] Alan's translator (perhaps displaying the
modern anxiety that continues to surround effeminacy) points out that the
details here are wrong, and that Alan's claim that Achilles "unsexed himself
completely" is "ludicrous."[14] In other words, Alan goes out of his way to
condemn this feminine gender performance by a man in terms stronger
than are warranted by the story itself. The same condemnation, but this time
in terms of grammatical gender, also occurs in Alan's twelfth-century allegory condemning sodomy, *The Complaint of Nature.*

We know that Chaucer was familiar with Alan's *Complaint* because he
refers to it directly in the *Parliament of Fowls:* "And right as Aleyn, in the
Pleynt of Kynde, / Devyseth Nature of aray and face, / In swich aray men
myghte hire there fynde" (*PF,* 316–18). Alan's allegorical figure of Nature
thus reappears, appropriately, in Chaucer's allegorical Valentine's Day celebration of male-female pairing, and as we might expect—given the nature
of Nature—she is, the poet tells us, unchanged from Alan's depiction of
her: natural characteristics are, or should be, universal and eternal. *The Parliament of Fowls* is usually dated to the early 1380s, while most of *The Canterbury Tales,* including all of the portions referring to the Pardoner, are
usually assigned to the late 1380s or 1390s[15]: Chaucer must therefore have
known Alan's *Complaint* ("the Pleynt of Kynde," as Chaucer calls it) well
before his creation of the Pardoner. We might therefore expect him also to
refer to this influential work on grammatical and human gender (and
erotic) deviance when describing his own ambiguously deviant character,
but no direct references to Alan are to be found in the description of the
Pardoner. The reason may have to do with the problem of translating Alan's
grammatical metaphors from Latin into a language whose grammar is significantly different.

Alan issues his condemnation of sodomy in figurative language, drawing on and elaborating a popular medieval metaphor in which Latin grammar represents erotic behavior.[16] Thus sodomy is seen as a linguistic
perversion above all; the improper verbal structure resulting, for example,
from the incorrect coupling of grammatical genders is condemned, in the
confusion of erotic practice with gender display that we observed above,
for its gender ambiguity, for being neither one thing nor the other, neither
masculine nor feminine—or, even worse, both things at once, which is to
say effeminate; which for Alan is to say, sodomical.

Two examples should suffice. In the opening poem, Alan says:

Actiui generis sexus se turpiter horret
Sic in passiuum degenerare genus.
Femina uir factus sexus denigrat honorem,
Ars magice Veneris hermafroditat eum.
Predicat et subicit, fit duplex terminus idem.
Gramatice leges ampliat ille nimis.
Se negat esse uirum Nature, factus in arte
Barbarus.

[The active sex shudders in disgrace as it sees itself degenerate into the passive sex. A man turned woman blackens the fair name of his sex. The witchcraft of Venus turns him into a hermaphrodite. He is subject and predicate: one and the same term is given a double application. Man here extends too far the laws of grammar. Becoming a barbarian in grammar, he disclaims the manhood given him by nature.][17]

According to Jan Ziolkowski, Alan is here condemning sodomy as a linguistic error, in which men assume both masculine and feminine roles by assuming the grammatical endings of both the masculine and feminine declensions.[18] The personified figure of Nature herself later clarifies this point, declaring:

Eorum siquidem hominum, qui Veneris profitentur gramaticam, alii solummodo masculinum, alii femininum, alii commune siue genus promiscuum, familiariter amplexantur. Quidam uero, quasi etherocliti genere, per hyemem in feminino, per estatem in masculino genere, irregulariter declinantur.

[Of those men who subscribe to Venus' procedures in grammar, some closely embrace those of masculine gender only, others, those of feminine gender, others, those of common, or epicene gender. Some indeed, as though belonging to the heteroclite class, show variations in deviation by reclining with those of female gender in Winter, and those of masculine gender in Summer.][19]

Leaving aside the specific question of sodomy for the moment, and turning to the more general issue of gender transgression, we may note with Ziolkowski that Nature's speech "exhausts the [Latin] vocabulary of noun classification"—masculine, feminine, and neuter—and that the metaphor of grammatical error makes sense only if grammatical gender is equated with the sexual gender of persons.[20]

For Monique Wittig as for Alan of Lille, gender is also a linguistic, even grammatical, construct, and she has pointed out in another context that while "English does not apply the mark of gender to inanimate objects," English and French both "as far as the categories of the persons are concerned . . . are bearers of gender to the same extent. Both indeed give way to a primitive ontological concept that enforces in language a division of beings into sexes."[21] But while Latin and its Romance derivatives such as French do so grammatically, English, including Chaucerian English, can do so only semantically.

Wittig's observations are true because Middle English grammar, in Chaucer's late-fourteenth-century London dialect, had eliminated grammatical gender. (This is perhaps the most literal example of how medieval discourse remains embedded in modern and postmodern ones.) Chaucer therefore could not reproduce this verbal metaphor in the form Alan of Lille gives it—unlike, say, Chaucer's visual description of Nature, drawn from Alan, which follows the passage from the *Parliament of Fowls* cited earlier. The classification of nouns as masculine, feminine, and neuter is simply not available in modern English, of which Chaucer's dialect is the late medieval forerunner. Chaucer must therefore rely on semantic ambiguity rather than grammatical impropriety to achieve a similar effect.

In the line "I trowe he were a geldyng or a mare" (I, 691), I believe we can see this process of translation from Latin grammar into English semantics at work. Notice that three terms in this sentence refer to the Pardoner: the pronoun "he," and the nouns "geldyng" and "mare." In other words, the masculine pronoun "he" is immediately rendered ambiguous by nouns suggesting, in their primary denotations, both a neutral or neuter asexuality ("geldyng") and a feminine sexual receptivity ("mare"). The three possibilities of Latin grammatical gender (masculine, neuter, and feminine) are here brought together as an undecidable set of lexical alternatives for the Pardoner's gender (with the resultant multiple possibilities for his erotic practices). Chaucer's narrator refuses—or is unable—to speak of the Pardoner's gender univocally, summoning instead an equivocal formula implying that the Pardoner cannot be so easily pinned down. As Dinshaw remarks, "[t]he Pardoner is uncertainly sexed and uncertainly gendered, a man who's not a man (the way others claim to be men), womanish but not a woman."[22]

For Luce Irigaray, it is precisely "the feminine" that cannot be defined in patriarchal language: "The question 'what is . . . ?' is the question—the metaphysical question—to which the feminine does not allow itself to submit."[23] This resistance to definition is, for Irigaray, linked as well to a multiplicity that is both sexual and linguistic or textual (in the sense of both verbal and social texts), similar to that which we find in the Pardoner: "So woman does not have a sex organ? She has at least two of them, but they are not identifiable as ones. Indeed, she has many more. Her sexuality, always at least double, goes even further: it is *plural*. Is this the way culture is seeking to characterize itself now? Is this the way texts write themselves/are written now? Without quite knowing what censorship they are evading?"[24] The plurality of feminine sex/gender/sexuality as imagined by Irigaray (and she collapses these categories as thoroughly as any medieval thinker), and her fluid passage back and forth between the question of bodies and the question of texts, may remind us disturbingly of the multiple and undecidable linguistic genders of the Pardoner as well as of the active/passive confusion deplored by Alan: this supposedly masculine character could, in his very undecidability, just as easily be constructed as feminine.[25]

If the grammatical and semantic construction of gender renders the Pardoner's gender status ambiguous, his resulting social performance of gender may be construed, *pace* Howard, as "effeminate," the term for a presumptive male who does not display solely the normative signs of masculinity in appearance and behavior, but appears to include the feminine in some fashion as well. The physical (bodily and behavioral) details of the Pardoner's description in the *General Prologue* connote femininity: his beardlessness and "smal" voice as well as his long, carefully arranged hair, on the one hand, and on the other the receptive sexuality that seems to be the point of his duet with the Summoner, would signal the feminine if they appeared in a female character; in one who is presumed to be male, these characteristics imply not exactly the feminine, but the effeminate. The very emphasis placed on the Pardoner's body, his very physicality itself, like his gender undecidability, may be taken as a sign of a closer connection to the feminine than would ideally be the case in a society in which, as Caroline Walker Bynum suggests, woman commonly represented the material, man the spiritual.[26]

Perhaps more precisely than "feminine" or even "effeminate," the term "not-masculine" may serve to indicate the Pardoner's problematic gender status. "Not-masculine" may imply more, or other, than the previous terms; it may, for instance, refer to boys as well as to women or girls. Although he is an adult, the Pardoner's high-pitched voice and beardlessness might be read as a reference to prepubertal youth as well as to the feminine, though critics have been uninterested in doing so.[27] His apparently receptive erotic practice with regard to the Summoner's "stif burdoun" would be understandable in this light: if, as in so many homoerotic ancient and medieval poems, puberty, signaled by the deepening of the voice and the growth of a beard, is regarded as the cutoff point for male same-sex eroticism, the Pardoner's boyish characteristics would make him a more likely candidate than most adult men for the role of catamite. (This may be the one way in which the Pardoner can be related to Connell's gender category of child rearing: the ancient erotic relationship of an

older man to a boy has commonly been regarded, in part, as an educa
tional one.)

Once again, however, I will leave the question of sodomy for another
chapter. Instead, I would like to focus here on the ambiguity of gender itself, and consider some further possible implications of the Pardoner's
voice, hair, and smooth face, and their relation to a particular myth that still
constituted one aspect of the discourse of gender in Chaucer's period. The
Pardoner's voice, and the way it relates him to tragedy, is our way into this
myth.

The Pardoner's portrait in the *General Prologue* heavily emphasizes the
voice, as we might expect in the portrait of one who makes his living from
preaching. It is, however, not his preaching but his *singing* voice that is the
primary focus of attention, both at the beginning of the portrait ("Ful
loude he soong 'Com hider, love, to me!'" [I, 672]) and at the end ("Therefore he song the murierly and loude" [I, 714]). And in the middle of the
portrait there appears the reference to his goatlike voice: "A voys he hadde
as smal as hath a goot" (I, 688). He sings, and he sounds like a goat.

"Goat-song," of course, is an etymology for "tragedy" well known
throughout the Middle Ages and into Chaucer's period. It appears early
on, in fourth-century texts by Evanthius and Donatus that remained influential. In his essay *On Drama,* Evanthius etymologizes "tragedy" thus:
"uel ἀπὸ τοῦ τράγου καὶ τῆς ὠδῆς, hoc est ab hirco hoste uinearum et a
cantilena" [This is from apo tou tragou kai tes oides—that is, from 'goat,'
an enemy of vineyards, and from 'song'].[28] The etymology offered by Donatus is more elaborate, but makes the same point:

haec autem carmina in pratis mollibus primum agebantur. nec deerant
praemia, quibus ad scribendum doctorum prouocarentur ingenia; sed et ac-
toribus munera offerebantur, quo libentius iucundo uocis flexu ad dul-
cedinem commendationis uterentur; caper namque pro dono his dabatur,
quia animal uitibus noxium habebatur. a quo etiam tragoediae nomen ex-
ortum est.

[At first they sang their songs in grassy meadows. And there was no lack of
prizes to incite the wits of the more learned to writing. And gifts were offered to the actors to encourage them freely to use pleasing modulations of
voice to gain sweet commendation. A goat [tragos] was given to them as a
reward, because the animal was considered an enemy of vineyards. From this
custom the name "tragedy" arose.][29]

Similar etymologies appear in the encyclopedic works of Isidore of Seville
in the seventh century, Vincent of Beauvais in the thirteenth, and others,[30]
and in Chaucer's period are repeated by Nicholas Trivet and Dante, among

others. One use of this etymology attributed to Dante (in the *Letter to Can Grande*) is representative: "et dicitur propter hoc a 'tragos' quod est hircus et 'oda' quasi 'cantus hircinus', id est fetidus ad modum hirci; ut patet per Senecam in suis tragediis" [And tragedy is so called from *tragos,* a goat, and *oda;* as it were a 'goat-song,' that is to say foul like a goat, as appears from the tragedies of Seneca].[31] Tragedy is now foul because of its unhappy ending, an etymology we might do well to recall when reading the Pardoner's encounter with the Host at the end of *The Pardoner's Tale:* Harry Bailly's accusation of foulness, with all its erotic implications, causes the Pardoner's tragic downfall. The Pardoner's goat-songs thus associate him from the very beginning with "tragedy" (different though the medieval conception of that genre obviously is from the classical one). But what has any of this to do with gender?

Equally well known to the Middle Ages was the theory that tragedy itself originated in the worship of Dionysus (also known as Bacchus or Liber); in fact, the passage in which Evanthius etymologizes "tragedy" as "goat-song" begins with a reference to Bacchus: "namque incensis iam altaribus et admoto hirco id genus carminis, quod sacer chorus reddebat Libero patri, tragoedia dicebatur" [The sort of song which the sacred chorus offered to Father Bacchus when the altars had been kindled and the sacrificial goat brought in was called tragedy].[32] (The etymology quoted above follows immediately.) As before, Donatus offers a more elaborate version of this history, but again draws the connection with the worship of Bacchus, this time following the "goat-song" etymology:

qui lusus cum per artifices in honorem Liberi patris agerentur, etiam ipsi comoediarum tragoediarumque scriptores huius dei uelut praesens numen colere uenerarique coeperunt. cuius rei probabilis ratio exstitit. ita enim carmina incohata proferebantur, ut per ea laudes eius et facta gloriosa celebrari proferrique constaret.

[Since these revels were performed at ceremonies in honor of Father Bacchus, the writers of tragedy and comedy began to worship and venerate the spirit of this god as though he were present. This is the probable explanation of the matter: these primitive songs were written for the purpose of setting forth and celebrating the fame and glorious deeds of Bacchus.][33]

As in the case of the "goat-song" etymology, this quasi-historical account of the origins of tragedy in the worship of Bacchus is repeated by various later authors.[34] If the Pardoner's voice and ultimate fate in *The Canterbury Tales* associate him with tragedy, then I would also like to point out that they associate him with the worship of Dionysus or Bacchus, god of tragedy—and of wine, an association reinforced by the Pardoner's often noted fondness for alcohol (as in his *Introduction*): "'But first,' quod he, 'heere at this alestake / I wol bothe drynke and eten of a cake'" (VI, 321–22).[35]

One version of Bacchus' story that Chaucer is likely to have known is that in Ovid's *Metamorphoses,* and it is here, at last, that we may find a myth of gender that is particularly relevant to the Pardoner. Ovid's Bacchus, like the Dionysus of Euripides (in *The Bacchae*), from whose story Ovid's seems ultimately to be derived, is associated with gender transgression from his earliest infancy: after the story of the new god's gestation in Jupiter's thigh and while he is being raised by the nymphs of Nysa, Ovid interrupts his story with that of the prophet Tiresias: "venus huic erat utraque nota" [for he had experienced love both as a man and as a woman].[36] This story of Tiresias' transsexuality, and the story of Narcissus that interrupts it in turn, eventually lead back to the story of Bacchus and his confrontation with Pentheus.

In that confrontation, the hypermasculine Pentheus consistently associates the worship of Bacchus with effeminacy, and specifically opposes that worship—in which men behave like women—to an unambiguous, martial form of masculinity. Effeminacy here is linked with both boyishness and drunkenness:

> aerane tantum
> aere repulsa valent et adunco tibia cornu
> et magicae fraudes, ut, quos non bellicus ensis,
> non tuba terruerit, non strictis agmina telis,
> femineae voces et mota insania vino
> obscenique greges et inania tympana vincant? . . .
> at nunc a puero Thebae capientur inermi,
> quem neque bella iuvant nec tela nec usus equorum,
> sed madidus murra crinis mollesque coronae
> purpuraque et pictis intextum vestibus aurum!

[Can brazen cymbals clashing, pipes with curving horns, trickery and magic have an effect so great that men who faced the swords of battle and heard its trumpet, undismayed, who were undaunted by the ranks of war with weapons drawn, should quail before wailing women and tinkling tambourines, drunken madmen and disgusting fanatics? . . . But now, Thebes will be taken by an unarmed boy, one who takes no pleasure in war, but delights in tresses dripping with myrrh, in fresh garlands and garments embroidered with purple and gold.][37]

Bacchus' priest Acoetes, too, describes the god as both effeminate and boyish in his account of the discovery of Bacchus:

"Adsumus en!" inquit sociorum primus Opheltes,
utque putat, praedam deserto nactus in agro,
virginea puerum ducit per litora forma.
ille mero somnoque gravis titubare videtur
vixque sequi.

["Here we are!" he cried, and came along the shore, bringing with him a
boy, as pretty as a girl. He had found him alone in a field, and had taken possession of this prize, as he thought. The boy, drowsy with sleep and wine,
seemed to stumble, and was scarcely able to follow.][38]

In the myth of Bacchus/Dionysus/Liber, then, we may find a possible literary antecedent for the drunken, effeminate, boyish—and goat-voiced—
Pardoner; in fact, in the following book, Ovid explicitly describes
Bacchus as simultaneously boyish and girlish: "Tu puer æternus, tu for-
mosissimus alto / conspiceris cælo; tibi, cum sine cornibus astas, / vir-
gineum caput est" [{H}e remains always a boy, the loveliest god in the
heights of heaven. When he appears before us, without his horns, his head
is like that of a young girl].[39] This myth, like the closely associated myth
of Tiresias, places a higher value on gender transgression than we might
expect: if Alan of Lille's grammatical metaphor condemns effeminacy,
Ovid's tales associate it with the sacred (both the god himself and the divine gift of prophecy), and with physical power: Pentheus learns that his
hypermasculine bellicosity is no match for the strength of Bacchus' specifically female followers when he is ultimately dismembered by the Maenads. Unlike that of Euripides, Ovid's version of the story does not place
a feminized Pentheus himself under the sway of Bacchus, but allows him
to remain a figure of exemplary masculinity destroyed by the feminine,
and by the effeminate.

    If the Pardoner's goat-song associates him with tragedy and hence with
Bacchus—and the similarities are undeniable—he emerges as a more dangerous and powerful figure than the grammatical metaphor alone would
allow. Myth and grammar can both be invoked to explain the Pardoner's
gender transgression, but it is the disjunction between the two visions that
is truly disturbing. Taken together, they show us a Pardoner who is both
weak and strong, both unnatural and a force of nature. As Susan Crane
writes, specifically with regard to Chaucer, the arbitrariness of gender itself means that "the sex of an author is not a completely reliable predictor
of a work's perceptions concerning gender. . . . The sex of an author fixes
discourse no more securely than sex fixes gender."[40] Thus the slippery
multiplicity of discourses on gender may prevent any author, even the most
patriarchal, from speaking about gender monophonically.

Even the myth of Bacchus itself seems to turn back on the Pardoner, for if the story of Pentheus associates him with the sacred power and danger of the effeminate god himself, another Ovidian tale, to be examined in chapter 6, places him in the role of the god's victim. I shall be arguing in that chapter that, alongside his association with Bacchus, the Pardoner, that dismembered singer, is also associated with another of the Maenads' victims, Orpheus.[41] The Pardoner is god and sacrificial victim both. It is this kind of discontinuous, contradictory, ambiguous characterization—his refusal of the ordering, normalizing function of the institution of gender identified by Lorber and Connell—that makes the Pardoner so fascinating and so troubling.

CHAPTER 2

THE PARDONER'S (OVER-)SEXED BODY

I wolde I hadde thy coillons in myn hond (VI, 952)

Of all the bodies and behaviors so meticulously described in *The Canterbury Tales,* and especially in the *General Prologue,* it is perhaps the Pardoner's that have aroused the most critical controversy, especially concerning the nature of his genitals, as in the line "I trowe he were a geldyng or a mare" (I, 691), and in the context of the other elements of his physical and behavioral description throughout the *Tales.* In a sense, most critics over the years seem to have wished, like Harry Bailly, that they could grasp the Pardoner's body, could hold his "coillons" in their hands. In this context, Glenn Burger's points about the Pardoner's conceptual instability are particularly helpful: rejecting the choice between Eugene Vance's "masculinist" and H. Marshall Leicester's and Carolyn Dinshaw's "feminist" hermeneutical models,[1] Burger uses the work of Jonathan Dollimore to reveal some of the ways in which "the Pardoner's destabilizing presence can provoke the kind of social and discursive dislocation that Dollimore calls 'discoherence.'"[2] Here is Dollimore's own definition:

> To borrow a now-obsolete seventeenth-century word, the dislocation which the critique aims for is not so much an incoherence as a discoherence—an incongruity verging on a meaningful contradiction. In the process of being made to discohere, meanings are returned to circulation, thereby becoming the more vulnerable to appropriation, transformation, and reincorporation in new configurations. Such in part are the processes by which the social is unmade and remade, disarticulated and rearticulated.
>
> The critique whose objective is discoherence further seeks to reveal and maybe to reactivate the contradictions which are effaced by ideology as an aspect of the control of meaning.[3]

Burger, like Dollimore, is primarily interested in the "discoherence" of sodomy as a critical force within *The Canterbury Tales* itself. But, deferring sodomy once again, insofar as that is possible, I would like to use the concept of discoherence to explore the contradictions regarding the Pardoner's body (considered in itself rather than in its practices) as they are expressed in the modern critical tradition, in the various medieval discourses of sex and gender upon which that tradition draws, and in Chaucer's own language about the Pardoner.

I do not intend to survey all of the scholarship on the subject, but I do wish to highlight certain contrasting moments in this debate in order to reveal the clash of discourses that have produced, and continue to produce, the Pardoner's sexed body. In doing so, I hope to challenge all critical attempts to fix the Pardoner's body, and hope further to render it discoherent, to reactivate the contradictions erased by the ideology of unitary discursive truth and its attempts to control meaning.

As early as 1926, Walter Clyde Curry, in the original edition of his influential book, *Chaucer and the Mediaeval Sciences,* found that the Pardoner as depicted in the *General Prologue* exhibits the symptoms that medieval medical science associated with the *eunuchus ex nativitate,* that is, with the born eunuch (as distinct from the *eunuchus qui castratus est,* the eunuch whose condition results from castration—this despite the narrator's specific use of the term "gelding").[4] Curry may be criticized for his reliance upon sources unlikely to have been familiar to Chaucer, especially the second-century Greek physiognomist Polemon Laodicensis, with whose portrait of a contemporary *eunuchus ex nativitate* Curry draws an extended comparison of the Pardoner's portrait in the *General Prologue.*[5] But, in fairness, Curry also adduces evidence close to Chaucer's own period, notably from the Middle English *Secreta Secretorum* (which Chaucer cites at the end of *The Canon's Yeoman's Tale* [VIII, 1446–47]) and from Trevisa's translation, contemporary with Chaucer, of Bartholomaeus Anglicus.

As evidence about the true nature of the Pardoner's body, however, even Curry's citations from these late medieval texts are open to question. Quoting the *Secreta Secretorum,* for instance, Curry notes that "ryst opyn eighyn and glysinge" may be read as betokening "a shameless man," and also cites this evidence regarding the voice: "tho that haue the voyce hei, smale and swete and plesaunt, bene neshe and haue lytill of manhode, and i-likened to women."[6] Curry thus takes the Pardoner's "glarynge eyen" (I, 684) and "smal" voice (I, 688) to denote a shameless effeminacy, which he also associates with the status of eunuch. Trevisa describes the physiognomical manifestations of the latter state, and they do seem applicable to the Pardoner: the Pardoner's thinning hair, "smal" voice, and beardlessness are indeed reminiscent of Trevisa's description of the eunuch, as quoted by Curry:

Also gelded men are not balde. . . . But in wymen and in gelded men other heer fallyth and faylyth. . . . And for febylnes and synewes ye voys of theum yt ben gelded is lyke ye voys of females. . . . And in lyke wyse men of colde and drye complexyon haue lytyll berdes, and therfore in men yt ben gelded growe noo berdes. For they haue loste the hote membre that sholde brede the hote humour and smoke, the matere of heer.[7]

The difficulties with Curry's use of such passages are fairly clear. In using the *Secreta Secretorum,* for instance, he assimilates effeminacy, not to mention shamelessness, to the status of eunuch all too unproblematically. As several more recent historians have noted, effeminacy was regularly perceived in the later Middle Ages as a sign of unauthorized gender, and hence class, transgression (male-male erotics being considered an aspect of gender transgression), and was therefore condemned, but not usually as a sign of any particular physical condition. At least one critic has even taken the Pardoner's effeminacy as a sign of excessive heterosexual lust, and hence of anatomical normality.[8] Medically speaking, Joan Cadden points out that for many medieval observers, effeminacy in men, including both physiognomical and behavioral features (like masculine behaviors in women), normally resulted from the placement of the fetus in the mother's womb, not from the absence of appropriate genitals.[9] Such medical evidence perhaps allows a more likely interpretation than Curry's of the *Secreta Secretorum*'s evidence.

Trevisa's translation of Bartholomaeus Anglicus, on the other hand, discusses eunuchs directly, and therefore provides better evidence for Curry's claims. But Curry describes the Pardoner as a *eunuchus ex nativitate,* and Trevisa, in every item Curry cites, refers to the eunuchs he is describing as "gelded men," that is, as examples of the *eunuchus qui castratus est,* which runs directly counter to Curry's main source, Polemon Laodicensis.[10] Castration was practiced in various cultural circumstances in the later Middle Ages for various reasons, most often as a cure for certain diseases and as a legal punishment for certain sexual offenses, sometimes including sodomy, but also including rape and bigamy.[11] Thus, the evidence that Curry cites that is closest to Chaucer may direct us toward at least two different ways of understanding the Pardoner in addition to the one Curry is promoting: he may be a *eunuchus ex nativitate,* but—merely according to the evidence Curry himself cites—he may also be an effeminate, but anatomically normal, man of the type Cadden describes; or he may be a castrated eunuch, as the source that is culturally closest to Chaucer, and even as Chaucer himself, in his use of the term "gelding," suggest.

My point here is not that Curry was wrong. Such critics as Robert P. Miller have influentially defended Curry's position on this matter, using the logic of patristic exegesis to deduce theological reasons in addition to the physiognomical ones for reading the Pardoner as a *eunuchus ex nativitate,* or more specifically as a figure for the *eunuchus non Dei.*[12] And even Cadden's work might conceivably be used in support of Curry's findings as well as in opposition to them. The medieval medical treatises she cites state that the womb is divided into seven cells; fetuses that develop in the three cells on the right will be born male, those in the three cells on the left will be born female, and those in the center cell will be born hermaphrodites. Furthermore, male fetuses closer to the hermaphroditic center will be born more effeminate, which does show an association of, or slippage between, fetal genital development and effeminate characteristics in later life[13] (another example of the medieval conflation of anatomical sex with gendered behaviors), though not, perhaps, in exactly the way Curry imagined.

Rather than claiming that Curry was wrong, then, I would say that his approach was wrongheaded in attempting to reduce and clarify the clash of medieval discourses concerning sexual anatomy. As in many other areas, in the realm of the body the Pardoner seems more like a site where the conflict of such discourses is made manifest than one where they are made to speak in unison, as Curry—and other critics taking other approaches— have tried to read him. If some physiognomies and patristic exegeses direct us toward an understanding of the Pardoner as a *eunuchus ex nativitate,* other physiognomies ask us to read him as a castrated eunuch, while denunciations of effeminacy as class and gender transgression (or as a sign of male-male erotics), as well as reproductive medical theories, may induce us to see him as anatomically normal, though effeminate or perhaps sodomitical. In other words, it is not only modern critical discourses, but the various medieval discourses of gender, too, that, taken together, render the Pardoner discoherent in Dollimore's sense. So does Chaucer's own language about the Pardoner.

For Curry's is not the only reading of the Pardoner's body to have been proposed over the years. While critics such as Miller and G. G. Sedgewick more or less completely accepted his reading and used it as a basis for their own interpretations of the Pardoner, others, citing different sources than those cited by Curry, and focusing on different passages of *The Canterbury Tales,* have arrived at quite different understandings of the Pardoner's body. Recall that Chaucer's use, in the *General Prologue,* of several mutually exclusive terms to describe the Pardoner's gender identity renders it semantically ambiguous. So do the individual terms themselves: Chaucer himself, as well as the wide variety of competing discourses upon which he seems to have drawn, is responsible for these critical disagreements.

Thus, if Chaucer describes the Pardoner in part as a *eunuchus ex nativitate* while the term "geldyng" in its primary meaning says that he has been castrated, portions of the physical description and the narrator's term apparently used to confirm it are not quite a match: there is some slippage as the description moves from an enumeration of symptoms describing a born eunuch to a word suggesting a castrated eunuch. Even odder, while Monica McAlpine demonstrated that the term "mare" could figuratively be used to imply receptive male homoeroticism, in its primary, nonfigurative meaning it refers to the anatomically female.[14] At least one critic, Beryl Rowland, notoriously seized on the disjunction between the Pardoner's masculine and feminine characteristics, and concluded that the Pardoner is actually a hermaphrodite, specifically "a testicular pseudo-hermaphrodite of the feminine type."[15]

As Dinshaw notes, this description has regularly been ridiculed since its original publication in 1964,[16] in part because Rowland relied on a modern medical text in making her analysis (she got the specific diagnosis just quoted from the 1956 *Price's Textbook of the Practice of Medicine*).[17] Like Curry's, her evidence was thus originally drawn in part from the wrong period to be historically plausible. But also like Curry's, such evidence forms only one, in Rowland's case quite minor, portion of her argument. Her major argument is drawn from her own field of medieval animal lore, and from plausible sources ranging from Aristotle to the late Middle Ages: the comparison of the Pardoner's eyes to those of a hare (I, 684), as well as that of his voice to a goat's (I, 688), remind us that both animals were believed to be hermaphroditic, and the constellation of these details with the Pardoner's beardlessness and long hair lead to such a diagnosis for the Pardoner as well.

Less frequently quoted, perhaps because it is less easy to ridicule, is Rowland's later (1979) defense of her claim, in which not only animal lore, but various other classical, patristic, and medieval sources are shown to support it, and which insists that the physical doubleness of the hermaphrodite represents as well a moral or spiritual duplicity consistent with the Pardoner's behavior.[18] Rowland at times comes very close to perceiving the disjunctive clash of Chaucerian discourses for which I am arguing here. She points out that Curry's diagnosis fails to take the Pardoner's behavior elsewhere in *The Canterbury Tales* into account: "his wenching, lechery, marital ambitions, and association with the Summoner."[19] She also notices the discrepancies in Chaucer's own language, and criticizes earlier critics for assuming that "gelding" and "mare" amount to the same thing.[20] But in the end she, too, repeatedly insists on foreclosing all readings other than her own hermaphroditic one. And her arguments for doing so are weak in the same ways as are the arguments of the critics to whom she is responding: she too ultimately reduces the quite different connotations of "gelding" and "mare" to a single meaning, eliding the presence of castration in "gelding" in favor of the lustful, feminine implications of "mare."[21] She is also content to explain away the references to the Pardoner's "marital ambitions" as "the typical desire of the deviate to conform to the sex in which he has been reared" despite his being "physically impotent,"[22] an ahistorical refusal to take Chaucer's contradictions seriously. Rowland's animal lore and medical and patristic sources add further elements to the discoherent clash of discourses I have been describing, but they do not succeed in making Chaucer speak univocally of the Pardoner any more than Curry's arguments did.

The possibility that the Pardoner is anatomically "normal" has had its defenders as well. Both C. David Benson and Richard Firth Green are primarily interested in countering critics who link the Pardoner to sodomy, but both also make claims about his anatomy in order to do so. Benson presents his points quite tentatively, arguing against Curry, Rowland, McAlpine, and others in order to emphasize, somewhat along the lines I have been arguing here, that "Chaucer throws out several hints, but he does not define. He may have aroused our suspicions, but he does not indicate any exact condition that can be used as a sure foundation on which to build an interpretation."[23] Nevertheless, Benson concludes his essay by referring to those moments later in *The Canterbury Tales* that hint at anatomical normality for the Pardoner: "Despite suggestions of sexual abnormality in his portrait, other information in the rest of the *Canterbury Tales*—such as the Pardoner's announcement to the Wife of Bath that he is thinking of marriage (D 166–68), his claim to have a wench in every town (C 453), and even the Host's threat to cut off his 'coillons' (C 951–55)—suggest a more ordinary sexual life, forcing those who suggest that the Pardoner does have a sexual secret to read these passages ironically."[24] The notion that Chaucer—whose commitment to a pervasive irony is precisely what makes all such critical discussions necessary in the first place—should *not* be read ironically is hardly convincing. But Benson is correct to point out the discrepancy between what is implied about the Pardoner's body in the *General Prologue* and what is hinted about his erotic practices elsewhere: this is a case in which the two do not seem to speak univocally. The problem, however, is not that Chaucer provides too little information, as Benson would have it. Rather, he provides too much: the Pardoner's gender identity signifies in too many ways.

Benson also cites as evidence for the Pardoner's normality the "Canterbury Interlude" or prologue to *The Tale of Beryn,* a spurious continuation of the *Tales* found only in the Northumberland manuscript, in which the Pardoner tries to seduce a barmaid named Kit.[25] I shall return to this fascinating text in the conclusion, and will show that it represents a considerably more complex response to Chaucer's Pardoner than Benson allows;

at this point, it is necessary only to point out that this seduction is a miserable failure, and that it hinges on a symbolic contest for the phallus—a contest the Pardoner loses.

Nevertheless, Richard Firth Green also cited this spurious text as "evidence" for "the sexual normality of Chaucer's Pardoner" in an essay of that title published alongside Benson's in 1982.[26] The title is perhaps an overstatement, as much of Green's essay is devoted to an analysis of the Pardoner's effeminacy. In his view, it is caused by excessive heterosexual lust, which in turn implies a normative male anatomy. Ironically, Green, like Curry, cites evidence from both the wrong period (Sidney, Lydgate), and the *Secreta Secretorum:* desire for women "makith a man oft femynyne."[27] He also quotes contemporary literary sources, most convincingly Gower's use of the story of Sardanapalus, who, in the *Confessio Amantis,* becomes "womannyssh" because of his desire for women.[28] If male effeminacy does signal heterosexual lust, and if that in turn signifies a normative male anatomy, then the Pardoner may be read as unequivocally male, as Green reads him.

But such a reading comes at the expense of ignoring all of the evidence to the contrary adduced earlier. Like so many other critics who attempt to reduce the Pardoner's body to a univocal reading, ultimately Green only adds further evidence for its conceptual "discoherence": the Pardoner is anatomically a "normal" man, according to literary evidence and the critics who find it convincing, as well as to certain portions of *The Canterbury Tales; and* a hermaphrodite, according to the medical evidence, animal lore, etc., that Rowland cites, and according to the *General Prologue; and* a *eunuchus ex nativitate,* according to other medical evidence and the patristic sources that convinced Curry, Miller, and others; *and* castrated, as suggested by Trevisa and legal discourse as well as the literal meaning of Chaucer's terminology. He is also both excessively heterosexual and a sodomite. Like the medieval evidence, the modern critical positions derived from it are discursively fragmentary and contradictory, and the fictional body these discourses produce is as unstable and discoherent as they are.

We might, then, go so far as to say that the Pardoner's description tends to dissolve sexual difference: he problematizes the very concept of sexual dimorphism because he makes it so difficult to decide where one sex begins and the other leaves off. Competing bodies of discourse on the body serve not to define, but to overdetermine, anatomy itself. That such discoherence remains sedimented in the language of gender is demonstrated by twentieth-century feminist theorists like Monique Wittig; she claims that not only gender, but sex itself, is not a natural category, but is instead a linguistically constructed and political one. Thus the two terms "gender" and "sex" perhaps cannot be as easily separated as I have been trying to do:

... the concept of difference between the sexes ontologically constitutes
women into different/others. . . . This ontological characteristic of the difference between the sexes affects all the concepts which are part of the same
conglomerate. But for us there is no such thing as being-woman or being-
man. "Man" and "woman" are political concepts of opposition, and the cop-
ula which dialectically unites them is, at the same time, the one which
abolishes them. It is the class struggle between women and men which will
abolish men and women. The concept of difference has nothing ontological about it. It is only the way that the masters interpret a historical situation of domination.[29]

A similar blurring of boundaries between nature and culture, sex and
gender, masculine and feminine, and even male and female, also occurs in
the previously discussed medieval tradition, represented by Alan of Lille's
Complaint of Nature, in which the Latin grammatical system and the medieval sex/gender system stand in for each other.[30] Like Wittig, Alan draws
little or no distinction between gender and sex: for him, to behave like a
woman is to become a woman, or perhaps a hermaphrodite. And, most significantly, sexed bodies, including the hermaphrodite's, are for both Alan
and Wittig as much linguistic constructions as they are physical ones; as
Wittig famously puts it, "[l]anguage casts sheaves of reality upon the social
body, stamping it and violently shaping it."[31] The violation of linguistic
rules thus implies the reconfiguration of bodies as well.

If we situate the Pardoner in this tradition, then he may, like the linguistic hermaphrodites Alan describes, be seen as occupying a border territory not only between the masculine and feminine genders created in
discourse, but also, and as the inevitable concomitant of this linguistic ambiguity, between the male and female anatomical sexes. The language used
to describe the Pardoner—in which the binaries not only of "homosex-
ual/heterosexual" and "masculine/feminine" but of "male/female" as well
are blurred to the point of erasure—may thus seem, from this perspective,
to anticipate Wittig's call for the abolition of the supposedly "natural" category of bodily sex.

For Wittig, such an ambiguity or failure to draw the conventional distinctions would be liberating and, as we might expect, it is a liberation to
be pursued in language. Rather than celebrating sexual difference, and
working toward a "different but equal" status for the two sexes (as other
feminist thinkers such as Irigaray have recently done[32]), Wittig more radically declares that difference necessarily includes hierarchical domination,
and proposes a culture of sameness to take its place, one that can come into
being only through the abolition of difference itself. Alan of Lille, in his
very attempt to promote the concept of Nature's distinctions (natural sex
and natural gender both), also reveals some of the ways in which such an

abolition might be accomplished in language, as Chaucer does in his adaptation of such procedures to his own discourses.

Needless to say, neither Alan nor Chaucer would approve of such an abolition. But, as Foucault maintains, every discourse of power includes the possibility of its own undoing: "in the relations of power, there is necessarily the possibility of resistance, for if there were no possibility of resistance,—of violent resistance, of escape, of ruse, of strategies that reverse the situation—there would be no relations of power."[33] Alan's and Chaucer's very attempts to police and maintain the boundaries discursively thus also demonstrate the possibilities of doing away with them, possibilities that remain historically embedded or sedimented in the discourses of sex and gender, only to emerge more positively in a period when it is possible to deconstruct those boundaries.

If we think of the Pardoner as blurring the boundaries of sexual dimorphism, it may be time to resurrect certain aspects of Rowland's diagnosis of hermaphroditism as suggestive of multiple possibilities for the Pardoner's sex, gender, and/or sexual practices—though not her insistence that it must preclude other possibilities—especially given Alan of Lille's association of "hermaphrodites" with a transgression that is both bodily and discursive, and Chaucer's knowledge of Alan's text. In both cases, multiple linguistic constructions can be assimilated to multiple bodily sexes. Rowland's reading claims a double nature for the Pardoner: the hermaphrodite partakes equally of the male and the female, according to medieval sources including Albertus Magnus, the *Ovide moralisé* and several others.[34] Chaucer's language, in which the masculine pronoun "he" is quickly modified by terms that connote both a neuter and a feminine, or even female, status, like Alan's, thus does not exclude the female, but rather includes it— hermaphroditically—as a possibility along with the male. The Pardoner is not only double but, like Irigaray's "woman," multiple.

The case of the nineteenth-century hermaphrodite Herculine Barbin as analyzed, influentially, by Michel Foucault, lends credence to such claims: Herculine's body signifies sex as equivocally as Chaucer's description of the Pardoner signifies gender, and is regarded as male and as female at different points in her/his life. But Foucault also uses her/his case to make a questionable claim for historical variation in the cultural constructions of the hermaphrodite:

> In the Middle Ages, the rules of both canon and civil law were very clear on this point: the designation "hermaphrodite" was given to those in whom the two sexes were juxtaposed, in proportions that might be variable. In these cases, it was the role of the father or godfather (thus of those who "named" the child) to determine at the time of baptism which sex was

going to be retained. . . . But later, on the threshold of adulthood, when the
time came for them to marry, hermaphrodites were free to decide for themselves if they wished to go on being of the sex which had been assigned to
them, or if they preferred the other. . . . Changes of option, not the anatomical mixture of the sexes, were what gave rise to most of the condemnations
of hermaphrodites that survive in France for the period of the Middle Ages
and the Renaissance.[35]

Foucault, as Judith Butler points out, "is clearly trying to show how an hermaphroditic or intersexed body implicitly exposes and refutes the regula-
tive strategies of sexual categorization."[36] And he does so by suggesting
that such categorization might be less strict in the Middle Ages than in the
modern world.[37]

Foucault's historical pronouncements, however, are not always trustworthy. Historians provide a considerably more complex picture of medieval attitudes toward hermaphrodites. Cadden, for instance, finds that
such relatively benign medieval representations of hermaphrodites are "the
exception rather than the rule,"[38] and demonstrates that religious and social, as well as scientific, thought was more likely to condemn hermaphrodites or to assimilate their condition to more rigid gender distinctions.
Albertus Magnus, for example, recognized the hermaphrodite's potential
for an unmoored gender identity: "tamen aliquando etiam complexio
cordis ita media est quod vix discerni potest quis sexuum praevaleat"
[however, sometimes even the complexion of the heart is so intermediate
that it is scarcely possible to discern which of the sexes should prevail].[39]
The typical medieval response to such an intermediate condition, however, was not as neutral as Foucault would have it. "Such breaches of the
ordinary pattern of things commonly elicited two types of response. First,
and more generally, hermaphrodites were pejoratively described as rebellious or disruptive. Second, and more subtly, the traits and behaviors of the
individuals in question were at once identified and suppressed by attempts
to reduce them to permutations of the conventional categories of masculine and feminine. Attributes that did not fit the accepted range known as
'feminine' were necessarily 'masculine,' and vice versa."[40] Those who cannot be reduced to sexual dimorphs are condemned, like the Pardoner, as
disruptive. In other words, if Herculine Barbin radically calls the very notion of sexual dimorphism itself into question in the nineteenth century,
the same might be said of the Pardoner in the fourteenth.

Since most discussions of this character agree that his body is marked
by the feminine if not the anatomically female, it also may not be amiss to
allow the term "mare" to retain its nonfigurative meaning. This possibility

would seem to be another aspect of the passages from Alan's *Complaint of Nature* cited previously, in which non-normative men are in some sense women. And the social disruption such ambiguities of sex and gender create become most apparent in the Pardoner's encounter with the Host at the end of *The Pardoner's Tale,* as we shall see in part II.

This is to say that, in the Middle Ages as in the twentieth century, biology itself is political, as recent feminist scientists have insisted. Butler poses the problem succinctly: "One question that feminists have raised, then, is whether the discourse which figures the action of construction as a kind of imprinting or imposition is not tacitly masculinist, whereas the figure of the passive surface, awaiting that penetrating act whereby meaning is endowed, is not tacitly or—perhaps—quite obviously feminine. Is sex to gender as feminine is to masculine?"[41] Has the body itself, sex, as distinct from its cultural meanings or gender, traditionally been assimilated to the feminine or female? If we do agree with Bynum that in the Middle Ages, "the weight of the Western tradition had long told women that physicality was particularly their problem,"[42] the answer would be "yes."

Haraway has described the manner in which feminist scientists have faulted the modern discourse of scientific truth, finding that such processes as the medieval symbolization that Bynum identifies remain embedded or sedimented in it: "bad science did not emerge accidentally, but systematically—and further, *must* continue to emerge, no matter how much individual scientists try to do good science on sex and gender. Facts are theory-laden; theories are value-laden; values are history-laden. And the history in this case makes it impossible for any researcher to step far enough away from daily, lived dominations of gender to study gender with any authority. The very constitution of gender and sex as objects of study is part of the reproduction of the problem. . . ."[43] Other historians of science generalize the problem from women to all "deviant bodies," those which, like the Pardoner's, are not fully male; one recent volume announces itself as "an effort both to efface 'normal' and 'healthy' bodies as fictions of science, and to document the subversiveness and resistances of 'deviant' bodies. In demonstrating that the notion of normalcy is parasitic to the construction of deviance, we recognize that systems of binary classification work in particularly oppressive ways to subjugate those classified as deviant. Yet we would like to leave readers with a reminder that no one is free from the powerful and haunting effects of discipline and subjectification that binary classifications impose."[44]

The Pardoner, not only in his apparent incorporation of the female, but in all his forms of deviance from the normatively male, exemplifies the notions of "normal" and "healthy" precisely in his deviation from them. The clash of medical, theological, juridical, grammatical, and literary discourses produces this deviant body even as each discourse, like the modern critical discourses drawing on them, attempts to normalize it by bringing it back within a system of binary classification. Both the normalization and the possibility of resistance to it are sedimented in modern discourses of sex such as those discussed in this book.

CHAPTER 3

THE PARDONER'S DIFFERENT
EROTIC PRACTICES

This Somonour bar to hym a stif burdoun (I, 673)

The Pardoner has traditionally been seen as the most sinful or "abandoned"[1] of all of Chaucer's pilgrims, the "one lost soul"[2] in the Canterbury group, to use an often-repeated critical formula. At least until quite
recently, this moral status has been regularly, though not universally, associated not only with the Pardoner's unorthodox body, but also with an unorthodox sexuality. The Pardoner's physical description in the *General
Prologue* allows him an effeminate, but still ambiguous, gender identity, and
ever since Walter Clyde Curry's analysis of the medical details of this description,[3] its details have typically been taken to imply that he is some sort
of eunuch. In addition to this apparent status as a eunuch, the Pardoner has
also been more problematically regarded as "homosexual," and the moral
condemnation of his "homosexuality" has been assigned considerable thematic importance by those critics who accept it. According to one such
critic, for instance, the Pardoner attempts to divert the other pilgrims from
the true purpose of their journey, and his "diversionary malfeasance gives
thematic significance to his unsavory relationship with the Summoner."[4]

Arguments for the Pardoner's "homosexuality" have been supported
with reference to two specific lines in the *General Prologue*: in one, the narrator says "I trowe he were a geldyng or a mare" (I, 691), "mare" in this
reading figuring sexual receptivity; in the other, which describes his
singing of a popular love song, the narrator informs us that another male
pilgrim, the Summoner, "bar to hym a stif burdoun" (I, 673), "bore a stiff
burden to him," which literally means that the Summoner sang the bass
line to the Pardoner's melody, but that has been taken by some as
metaphorically hinting at homoerotic relations between the two men.[5]

I am placing the terms "homosexual" and "homosexuality" in quotation marks because, as we all know by now, they are modern terms that do not seem to correspond to any medieval concept. They remain in use among medievalists, however, because there is no really satisfactory medieval term to use in their place, for reasons discussed later in this chapter. I will try to confine myself to the cumbersome, but perhaps more accurate, terms "same-sex desire," "male-male eroticism," and so on, when referring to medieval texts (as opposed to modern critics), although the Pardoner is such a slippery figure as to call even the meaning of such apparently neutral terms into question.

Not only do some scholars reject the identification of the Pardoner as "homosexual," however; many also reject the notion that Chaucer uses this figure to represent same-sex desire regardless of historical construction or terminology. I therefore take as my starting point for this chapter the odd discomfort exhibited by some Chaucerian scholars when dealing with the possibility that the portrait of the Pardoner in the *General Prologue* to *The Canterbury Tales* implies a "homosexual" relationship between the Pardoner and the Summoner. This view was advanced, not originally (that distinction probably belongs to Muriel Bowden),[6] but perhaps most influentially in Monica McAlpine's 1980 *PMLA* article.[7] While McAlpine uses the term "homosexuality," she specifically argues against the possibility that the modern concept of a homosexual *identity* would have been comprehensible to a medieval audience,[8] and her argument about the Pardoner's erotic *practices* remains convincing to many readers, especially—and perhaps surprisingly, given Chaucer's largely unsympathetic portrayal of him—to gay and antihomophobic readers such as Steven F. Kruger. I agree with Kruger's interesting recent *Exemplaria* article that "we need to show how the Pardoner's challenge to medieval heterosexist notions of signification—and Chaucer's anxiety about that challenge—lay bare the constructed nature of those notions."[9]

Briefly, McAlpine centers her reading on the narrator's line summing up the Pardoner, "I trowe he were a geldyng or a mare." She adduces evidence from Walter of Chatillôn suggesting that a late medieval audience could have perceived this use of the term "mare" as a sign that the Pardoner engages in homoerotic practices, and goes on to make a convincing argument that the term's implication of effeminacy would also have signaled such practices to Chaucer's readers.[10]

Influential though McAlpine's reading of this character has undoubtedly been, it has also produced a profound resistance from a surprisingly wide range of medievalists. Early responses to McAlpine's work (such as C. David Benson's)[11] asserted that the Pardoner, though effeminate, should be read as a heterosexual. As we have seen, perhaps the most extreme such re-

sponse was Richard Firth Green's essay entitled "The Sexual Normality of
Chaucer's Pardoner"[12]—a title that seems little short of bizarre given the
narrator's description of this pilgrim as seeming to be either a gelding or
a mare. Green's essay would seem to require, at the very least, a definition
of "sexual normality" so broad as to be meaningless—one that could include at least the appearance of castration, for instance. It does not require
a great stretch of the imagination, or any special pleading, to find in such
readings a kind of institutionalized homophobia, or at any rate a heterosexist attempt, conscious or unconscious, to erase any queer sexuality, homosexual or otherwise, from scholarly consideration—even if such
sexuality is depicted critically.

Even criticism that does not simply erase same-sex erotics from its discussion of the Pardoner often exhibits difficulty in asserting it, as another
example will illustrate. Melvin Storm's 1982 article on the Pardoner seems
forthrightly and good-naturedly (and no doubt unconsciously) heterosexist in its assumptions, especially in its abstract's characterization of the Pardoner's "unsavory" relationship with the Summoner, cited above. What
looks like homophobia does not lead to the erasure of same-sex erotics
from the essay in question, however; this article crucially depends on es-
tablishing the existence of such a relationship in order to make its argument about the congruence of physical and spiritual "sterility."
Nevertheless, Storm's language betrays a certain discomfort with the very
argument he is committed to making. He also finds that the Pardoner's
"sexuality, to put it gently, is ambiguous" and cannot decide whether this
ambiguous sexuality is "perverse or merely lacking"[13]; that is, he accepts
the Pardoner as eunuch ("merely lacking") but cannot decide whether
"perverse" homoerotic practices are also at issue.

This passage leads into a lengthy discussion of the "stif burdoun" line
and its implications for the Pardoner's erotic relationship with the Summoner, "if there is one."[14] Why is this critic so tentative about making an
argument crucial to the very point of his essay? It is worth noting that
even an uncloseted gay medievalist like Donald R. Howard, for instance
in *The Idea of the Canterbury Tales,* could seem reluctant to allow the possibility that such a relationship is being depicted: the erotic relationship
between the Pardoner and the Summoner, to quote Howard, "is at best a
faint suspicion that passes quickly in and out of the text, as it should pass
in and out of our thoughts."[15] We need to ask, then, why both heterosexist and some consciously antihomophobic critics seem to share this reluctance to accept homoerotic sexual practices as a possibility for the
Pardoner. Why has it been so much easier to accept him as a "geldyng"
than as a "mare" in McAlpine's sense? Heterosexism, or at least modern
academic heterosexism, is not the whole story; it might be more accurate

to say that this modern academic homophobia reflects, or sediments, some of the specific ways in which the later Middle Ages constructed same-sex erotics. I shall be investigating two aspects of this construction in particular: the internal contradictions in the medieval conceptualization of sodomy, and its preterition.

Michel Foucault, famously, described sodomy as "that utterly confused category,"[16] and recent social historians, as well as historians of religion, medicine, and literature, have found plenty of evidence that it was, if anything, even more confused in the Middle Ages. Cadden's work on gender issues in medieval medicine, for instance, shows that while most medical texts were content to condemn same-sex erotic practices by attributing undesirable personal characteristics (lust, deceit) to those who indulged in them, the one writer who addresses sodomy as a medical condition in some detail actually presents two different, and contradictory, etiologies for it.[17] Peter of Abano is remarkably clinical in his description of the various ways in which men perform the acts under consideration: "quidam exercent manu fricando virgam. Alii puerorum inter cossas confricatione. . . . Alii autem fricationem faciendo circa anum et virgam in ipsum imponendo" [some . . . by rubbing the penis with the hand; others by rubbing between the thighs of boys . . . others by making friction around the anus and by putting the penis in it].[18] Peter considers the etiology of this behavior purely anatomical, stemming from the blockage or misdirection of the vessels that carry semen; Cadden states that Peter sees such behavior as "natural *for these individuals,* in the sense that the disposition of their pores and vessels is innate."[19] Sodomy in this sense is a condition that might be corrected surgically.[20]

But even so, Peter also—in the very same passage, in fact—passes a moral judgment that seems unwarranted if he is describing a purely medical condition, referring to the above-mentioned practices as "illud nephandum opus sodomiticum" [the wicked act of sodomy].[21] And he later, according to Cadden, goes on to provide a second etiology, this time moral rather than anatomical: "[Peter of Abano] identified a second group of men with the sexual sensibilities and appetites he has been describing: those who are not born that way but who come to it 'on account of depraved and filthy habit—such are sodomites.'"These sodomites are damned by their sin.[22] On the one hand, those who engage in these erotic practices are sinners; on the other hand, those who engage in the same practices are sick, and Peter "does not treat them as blameworthy"[23]—though even in this case, the acts themselves are wicked. Medical and religious language here seem to cancel each other out; coexisting side by side in the same text, they render sodomy as a concept virtually incomprehensible, certainly discontinuous and self-contradictory.

Mark D. Jordan has made a similar point about Albertus Magnus' work on sodomy, which in appropriating ancient sources combines medicine with moral theology:

> The moral use of Aristotelian natural history must point up the persistent inconsistency in Albert. The moral use is extraordinarily selective. It requires not only a rewriting of some pages in Aristotle; it requires the suppression of whole topics in the natural history of medicine. There is in Albert the Great's texts on Sodomy a series of dissociations by which he refuses to engage the analyses of same-sex copulation in his own scientific or medical authorities, and this despite his regular appropriation of their teaching on other topics.[24]

The very language of medieval theology, even unallied with medicine, is, as Jordan demonstrates, conceptually unstable where sodomy is concerned. He credits Peter Damian with the invention of the later Middle Ages' conventional terminology of sodomy in his well-known eleventh-century *Book of Gomorrah*. Like the medical texts, Damian's is explicit about the different manners in which men can engage in the erotic practices under discussion: "Alii siquidem semetipsos polluunt, alii sibi invicem inter se manibus virilia contrectantes inquinantur, alii inter femora, alii fornicantur in terga" [There are some who pollute themselves; there are others who befoul one another by mutually handling their genitals; others still who fornicate between the thighs; and others who do so from the rear].[25] As in the medical texts, however, despite the clarity with which these acts are described—and the ferocity with which Damian denounces them—their moral status remains uncertain. Much of the *Book of Gomorrah*, in fact, is devoted to Damian's attempt to refute what he regards as the excessively lenient treatment of sodomy by earlier writers, especially in the penitential canons, which Damian himself finds contradictory: "Quibus ergo canonibus, quibus patrum decretis ludibria ista conveniant, quae a semetipsis tam dissona et velut cornuta fronte resultant? Quaeque semetipsa convellunt, quibus auctoritatibus fulciantur?" [With which canons or decrees of the Fathers do these ridiculous ordinances agree, in that they are so self-contradictory and leap about like horn-headed creatures? If they do violence to one another, by which authorities will they be supported?].[26] In other words, the handbooks of penance themselves render the moral status of sodomy undecidable, and Damian presents his condemnations both of sodomy itself and of the excessive leniency with which he claims it has been treated as an attempt to restore a single, univocal, "correct" understanding of this sin. But as Jordan points out, Damian's own argument is as contradictory as those of the texts he condemns: although addressed to sodomites

as an exhortation to repent and abandon their sin, his book's ferocity simultaneously, and contradictorily, declares sodomy a sin that cannot be repented: "This conception violates the fundamental Christian teaching
about sins of the flesh, namely, that they are always repentable. To conceive
of a fleshly sin that cannot be repented is to set in motion an interminable
dialectic. The dialectic can be stopped only by admitting that what has been
categorized as an unrepentable fleshly sin is either not a sin or not fleshly."[27]
For Jordan, this "fundamental paradox" at the root of medieval theological
conceptions of sodomy continues to disrupt medieval theological thinking
about this category into Chaucer's period, and into our own. Legally,
sodomy as a category became more "utterly confused" than ever, Damian's
limited definition being expanded in the late Middle Ages to include "any
and all practices . . . considered unnatural, including masturbation, mutual
masturbation, oral sex, and anal sex, either homosexual or heterosexual."[28]

Recently, Elizabeth B. Keiser has demonstrated the unstable, self-
contradictory ways in which male-male erotic practices were conceptual-
ized in Chaucer's period, especially as appropriated by Chaucer's
contemporary, the *Pearl*-poet. Her consideration of another poem usually
attributed to him, *Cleanness,* claims that it lacks "theopoetic coherence" because of the incoherence of these concepts themselves, for instance as regards pleasure. Keiser shows (as Jordan does also) that to some extent St.
Thomas Aquinas legitimizes pleasure in human relations: "he provides a cogent legitimation of the abundance of pleasure in a well-tempered sex act
and even defends passion so intense that it must extinguish for a time the
light of reason."[29] The author of *Cleanness* goes further than Aquinas,
uniquely legitimizing mutual pleasure rather than procreation as the proper
end of heterosexual intercourse in his praise of "the play of paramours."[30]

And yet neither Aquinas nor the author of *Cleanness* is able to take the
logical next step of suggesting that, if sexual pleasure is legitimate and even
the proper goal of intercourse between men and women, there is no
longer any reason to condemn same-sex erotic pleasure. Instead, both writers categorize this form of pleasure as uniquely sinful: according to John
Boswell, "Aquinas subtly but definitively transferred [homosexual behav-
ior] from its former position among sins of excess or wantonness to a new
and singular degree of enormity among the types of behavior most feared
by the common people and most severely repressed by the church."[31] The
Cleanness poet, too, in his virulent attacks on male-male eroticism, exemplifies this contradiction, as Keiser eloquently argues: "Can a poet capable
of such an extraordinary breakthrough about the legitimacy of pleasure in
one kind of gratuitous sexual activity not see that it applies equally to the
other? And why is he not only unable to see it but actually seems to need
the rejection of the other in order to achieve the breakthrough on the

first—so that the homophobia whose very basis he has just exploded seems necessary to the dynamic of his affirmation of heterosexual pleasures."[32] The rejection of same-sex eroticism is, thus, now based on a contradiction, like the medieval concept of sodomy itself.

The problem is only exacerbated by a second, closely related medieval phenomenon, the reluctance directly to discuss or describe "unnatural" erotic practices at all. One of the earliest modern treatments of same-sex eroticism in the Middle Ages called it "the unmentionable vice,"[33] and for some medieval discourses, at least, this description seems largely correct.

While the medical discourse mentioned above, and such virulent attacks on sodomy as Peter Damian's, describe these practices in clinical detail, equally powerful if not more so is the tradition of veiling them in a cloak of secrecy or silence. Both Jordan and Keiser have discussed the linguistic veiling of sodomy—which often may not even be named, but is referred to as "the sin against nature"—in some detail. Jordan, for example, cites the treatises on confession appearing around the time that the Fourth Latern Council specified annual confession (1215), which commonly cite a traditional etymology that makes "Sodom" mean "mute," because it is a sin that should not be spoken.[34] Jordan quotes, among several other examples, Paul of Hungary's paradoxical recommendations that this sin must be confessed, yet is at the same time so horrible that it should not be spoken: "The sin against nature cannot be forgiven anyone unless it is confessed by name, and yet its acts are so bestial that they can hardly be named. As Haymo of Auxerre says, they are left unnamed even by nature. Not to speak them is to entomb oneself in hell, and yet nature itself seems to abhor the speaking."[35] Silence on the subject of same-sex eroticism is thus another aspect, or even result, of its paradoxical medieval construction. And it leads to a further paradox: "The fear of Sodomy ends up by undoing the pretense of spiritual care for Sodomites. Their sin cannot be spoken plainly. It cannot be preached against. It cannot be broached even with the confession except with utmost indirection. . . . Incoherent fear of sin has taken away the voice of confessors and preachers."[36] P. L. Heyworth points out that even vaguer formulas referring to "things 'of which it is best to say nothing'" (what Heyworth calls "the *tacenda*-formula") quickly came to substitute for the already vague "vice against nature."[37]

Keiser addresses the problem of sodomy as unmentionable vice with regard specifically to the fourteenth century in her analysis of *Cleanness* and its common circumlocution "filth of the flesh." She follows Heyworth in pointing out that the injunctions against naming sodomy can be derived from St. Paul's reference to "the unspeakable vice" in Ephesians 5:3–12 and its conventional connection with the story of Sodom and Gomorrah.[38]

Chaucer himself participates in this refusal to name same-sex eroticism, not only in his ambiguous construction of the Pardoner's erotic practices, but even in the Pardoner's own comments on confession and penance in his *Prologue:* "If any wight be in this chirche now / That hath doon synne horrible, that he / Dar nat, for shame, of it yshryven be, / Or any womman, be she yong or old, / That hat ymaked hir housbonde cokewold, / Swich folk shal have no power ne no grace / To offren to my relikes in this place" (VI, 378–84). Of course, the Pardoner has no intention of letting potential contributions slip away; this exhortation is instead designed to lure further offerings from those who fear that a refusal might brand them as adulterous wives or "horrible" sinners. The emphasis is not on the sin, but on the admission of it, and the suggestion that this horrible sin actually cannot be shriven and even cancels the power of holy relics places the Pardoner in the tradition identified by Jordan.

Chaucer's Parson also belongs in this tradition; the "synne horrible" is given somewhat more space in *The Parson's Tale,* itself a treatise on penance and confession. Speaking of the various subcategories or "speces" of the sin of lechery (*luxuria*), the Parson says: "The fifthe spece is thilke abhomynable synne, of which that no man unnethe oghte speke ne write; nathelees it is openly rehersed in holy writ. / This cursednesse doon men and wommen in diverse entente and in diverse manere; but though that hooly writ speke of horrible synne, certes hooly writ may nat been defouled, namoore than the sonne that shyneth on the mixne" (X, 909–10). The Parson seems, oddly, more concerned that the Bible's audacity in openly mentioning this unnamed horrible sin might call the authority of Holy Scripture into question than with the sin itself. This unmentionable sin apparently has the paradoxical power, if named, of calling the propriety of God's word itself into question. Thus it is this potentially subversive power of naming, rather than the act itself, that must be addressed here; the Parson's anxiety centers on language about the sin rather than the sin itself.

In some sense, the sin and the language about it are coextensive, and the manner in which their identity is established may be illuminated by returning once more to Alan of Lille and his *Complaint of Nature,* which constructs same-sex eroticism not as an essential "homosexuality" or even "sodomy," but rather, as we have seen, in a set of ambiguous linguistic relations. It should be noted that Alan, like the Pardoner and the Parson, counsels silence on the subject of sodomy, in his *Liber poenitentialis.* Jordan notes that Alan "says quite plainly that the confessor is not to inquire into the details of illicit coitus, including the sins against nature. To do so is to give occasion for sin."[39] In *The Complaint of Nature* he goes into greater, though perhaps no more explicit, detail. In the *Complaint,* too, Nature declares that sodomy must not be discussed directly: "In sequenti tamen trac-

tatu, ne locutionis cacephaton lectorum offendat auditum uel in ore uirginali locum collocet turpitudo, predictis uiciorum monstris euphonia
orationis uolo pallium elargiri" [In the following disquisition, however, it
is my intention to contribute a mantle of fair-sounding words to the
above-mentioned monsters of vice to prevent a poor quality of diction
from offending the ears of readers or anything foul finding a place on a
maiden's lips].[40]

Hence the elaboration of the grammatical metaphor rather than a clinical discussion of sodomy like those found in some medical or theological
texts. In one passage of the *Complaint,* Alan imagines sodomy not merely
as an improper use of language, such as a figure of speech (technically improper because it names its object by what it is not), but as an unforgivable error in grammatical gender. Nature says:

Cum enim masculinum genus suum femininum exigentia habitudinis genialis adsciscat, si eorundem generum constructio anomale celebretur, ut
res eiusdem sexus sibi inuicem construantur, illa equidem constructio nec
euocationis remedio uel conceptionis suffragio apud me ueniam poterit
promereri. Si enim genus masculinum genus consimile quadam irrationabilis rationis deposcat iniuria nulla figure honestate illa constructionis
iunctura uicium poterit excusare sed inexcusabili soloecismi monstruositate turpabitur.

[Since, by the demands of the conditions necessary for reproduction, the
masculine joins the feminine to itself, if an irregular combination of members of the same sex should come into common practice, so that appurtenances of the same sex should be mutually connected, that combination
would never be able to gain acceptance from me either as a means of procreation or as an aid to conception. For if the masculine gender, by a certain violence of unreasonable reason, should call for a gender entirely similar
to itself, this bond and union will not be able to defend the flaw as any kind
of graceful figure but will bear the stain of an outlandish and unpardonable
solecism.][41]

We may find here a description both of sodomy and of gender confusion
that is itself admirably confused (Alan's translator calls this passage
"strained,"[42] and it is impossible to disagree). The notion that gender transgression and the sodomitical acts it signifies are "unpardonable" flaws, both
linguistic and moral, is clear enough. Sodomy is thus represented as an "unnatural" confusion in language, which for Alan should in its natural state
signify directly and unambiguously. If same-sex erotic practices are to be
seen as the equivalent of language that cannot signify correctly, it is not
surprising that sodomy becomes that which cannot be spoken or written

directly; sodomy disrupts language itself as a signifying system, and therefore cannot be unambiguously signified.

But exactly what, grammatically, is being condemned? After all, masculine nouns do, in fact, "call for" masculine adjectives. The metaphor is thus
uncomfortably "strained" because the grammatical structure of language
itself is, in the terms Alan sets up, sodomitical. The confused category of
sodomy cannot be discussed directly, but also subverts Alan's own attempt
to discuss, and condemn, it indirectly.[43] For Chaucer, then, as a reader of
Alan of Lille, sodomy is constructed in language rather than bodies, language that by its very nature cannot be definitive. Language about sodomy
cannot be directly referential because sodomy is precisely that which destabilizes language.

Keiser discusses the hermeneutic problems such medieval injunctions
and circumlocutions create for the modern reader:

> Something resembling the medieval reluctance to speak of same-sex eroti-
> cism has until recently characterized most modern critical discourse about
> [Cleanness]. The predominant approach to Cleanness translates its sexual
> themes into more abstract meanings. . . . Yet by translating sodomy into its
> more general categories of sin, such as lust or pride, or into its exegetically
> conventional equivalents (idolatry or sacrilege, sterile speech of false teach-
> ing and bad preaching), we miss what Cleanness has to teach us about the
> theopoetic logic of both homophobia and heterosexism, not only in the late
> Middle Ages but in the cultural legacy we have inherited from that forma-
> tive period.[44]

And yet it is the text itself that encourages such translations from one register of meaning to another, in its very refusal to speak directly of the "unmentionable" vice. As Keiser insists, medieval "homophobia" is embedded
or sedimented in modern homophobia; but it is equally important to note
that medieval silence and circumlocution are also embedded in their modern equivalents.

Academic homophobia may thus be regarded as responding to language
as much as to bodies and acts. This contradictory, unstable, incoherent, and
even silent medieval construction of same-sex erotic practices necessarily
renders any modern attempt to discuss it, or to find evidence of it in literary texts, especially in the later Middle Ages, highly problematic. A text
may look "queer" to us, but this impression is nearly impossible to pin
down more exactly, given the incoherence of the very concepts we are
looking for. How can we find evidence of the existence of a concept as ill-
defined as same-sex desire has become in all these categories (medical, theological, legal, and literary) by Chaucer's period? One might argue that the
modern academic (in some cases heterosexist) reluctance to find evidence

of same-sex desire in the Pardoner's portrait to some extent is a sedimentation of the medieval "homophobia" that makes this unstable concept so difficult to represent. The incoherent medieval ways of conceptualizing same-sex desire thus produce, and are embedded in, the ambiguity and multiplicity of modern responses to the Pardoner. They also call into question the very nature of evidence in the construction of a scholarly argument, as discussed in the introduction to this book.

Eve Kosofsky Sedgwick has pointed out the vexed relationship between language and same-sex erotics that extends both further back and further forward in history than the late Middle Ages; she cites two widely separated moments in its history: "St. Paul's routinely reproduced and reworked denomination of sodomy as the crime whose name is not to be uttered, hence whose accessibility to knowledge is uniquely preterited," and Lord Alfred Douglas' famous reference to "the Love that dare not speak its name."[45] We can now, perhaps, specify a few more moments in the history of this theme: the construction of sodomy as that which cannot signify directly or be directly signified finds specific historical variations in Alan of Lille's twelfth-century Latin grammatical metaphors, in Chaucer's ambiguous fourteenth-century semantics, and perhaps in twentieth-century critical practice as well, including the heterosexist responses to McAlpine's essay.

Not only the Pardoner's gender, but his sexuality, too, is thus plural or undecidable in ways similar to those described by Irigaray. While an anal passivity in relation to the active Summoner is implied in the "stif burdoun" passage, the Pardoner also represents himself as sexually active in his dialogue with the Wife of Bath during her *Prologue:* "Up stirte the Pardoner, and that anon; / 'Now, dame,' quod he, 'by God and by Seint John! / Ye been a noble prechour in this cas. / I was aboute to wedde a wyf; allas! / What sholde I bye it on my flessh so deere? / Yet hadde I levere wedde no wyf to-yeere!'" (III, 163–68). The Pardoner here (and elsewhere) claims "heterosexual" status as a potential husband—and one who imagines himself not only as different from, but in conflict with, women—in addition to, or instead of, the homoerotic practices implied in the *General Prologue.* Thus it is not only within the *General Prologue's* description that the Pardoner appears as plural in his sexuality, but also in the relation between that description and his other appearances in the text as a whole.

Erotic practices may be considered an aspect of gender, that is, as one of the means through which gender is displayed: ideally, anatomical sex (he "should" be male), cultural gender (he "should" be masculine), and erotic practice (he "should" demonstrate maleness and masculinity through erotic acts with the other sex) all march together, signifying univocally. Again like Irigaray's "woman," however, throughout *The Canterbury Tales* the Pardoner, in failing to achieve such univocity, represents a "mystery" "in a culture claiming to count everything, to number everything by units, to inventory everything as individualities. *She is neither one nor two.* Rigorously speaking, she cannot be identified either as one person, or as two. She resists all adequate definition."[46] For Irigaray, to disrupt gender is to disrupt discourse, and vice-versa. So too, "homosexuality," including male homosexuality, represents a subversion of the symbolic order of language: "The 'other' homosexual relations, masculine ones, are just as subversive, so they too are forbidden. *Because they openly interpret the law according to which society operates,* they threaten in fact to shift the horizon of that law. . . . Once the penis itself becomes merely a means to pleasure, pleasure among men, *the phallus loses its power.*"[47] The Symbolic is the order of language that imposes its rules on bodies: it constructs gender as a set of proper relations among anatomy, behavior, desire, etc., that must all signify in the same way. Like Alan's grammatical "barbarisms," the "heterogeneous" (in Kristeva's sense) Pardoner fails to conform to this linguistic order; the non-sense of the language used to describe him signifies an improper plurality of possible gender relations. As Butler suggests, "the very notion of 'the person' is called into question by the cultural emergence of those 'incoherent' or 'discontinuous' gendered beings who appear to be persons but who fail to conform to the gendered norms of cultural intelligibility by which persons are defined."[48]

Wittig ultimately asserts that the lesbian perspective abolishes the categories of sex altogether: "What is woman? . . . Frankly, it is a problem that the lesbians do not have because of a change in perspective, and it would be incorrect to say that lesbians associate, make love, live with women, for 'woman' has meaning only in heterosexual systems of thought and heterosexual economic systems. Lesbians are not women."[49] Butler asks the pertinent question here, wondering whether, if the lesbian perspective abolishes the category of woman, *anyone* can become a lesbian.[50] If sex, like gender, is a social, indeed political, construct, as Wittig argues, the answer would have to be yes; if in this sense lesbians are not women, having abolished the categories of sex, perhaps any subject whose relation to categories of erotic practice is similarly unstable—the Pardoner, for instance—is in that sense a lesbian. While such an assertion may seem to mean that the term "lesbian" no longer has any meaning at all, even a less radical understanding than Wittig's might find the suggestion of female same-sex desire in the Pardoner's description: if we regard him from the perspective of the feminized sex and gender status examined in the previous two chapters, and of his professed desire for women noted above, "lesbian" may seem the most appropriate designation for him.

I have been striving for a language as startling as Wittig's, but I hope it serves here as more than just a clever effect. That declaring the Pardoner a lesbian is even possible should serve to demonstrate just how "utterly confused" not only sodomy, but all medieval categories of sex, gender, and erotic practice are, especially when brought together in a single figure. The Host and the Knight—and Chaucer—may repudiate the Pardoner and the confusion of categories he represents; but we should also note that Chaucer's depiction of him only brings a bit closer to the surface his culture's anxieties about these categories themselves. The following chapters will examine some of the intricacies with which all these categories are deployed and interrogated in *The Canterbury Tales*.

PART II

READINGS: BODIES, VOICES, TEXTS

Ellesmere Chaucer, The Pardoner. *Reproduced by permission of* The Huntington Library, San Marino, CA (EL 26 C9 f. 138r).

CHAPTER 4

THE PARDONER UNVEILED

For in his male he hadde a pilwe-beer
Which that he seyde was Oure Lady veyl (I, 695)

The dust jacket on my hardcover copy of David F. Greenberg's book *The Construction of Homosexuality*[1] features a drawing by Dennis Anderson of two figures, shown from the shoulders up against a vaguely modern urban background; one figure has its (his? her?) hand around the other's shoulder. The most striking aspect of the drawing is that both heads are heavily veiled in white cloths like pillowcases, whose folds, loosely clinging to their features, both reveal that there are invisible faces underneath the veils, and conceal what those faces look like. I notice that current paperback reprints of this book have an entirely different cover; perhaps this mysterious drawing puzzled other readers as much as it does me. Given the book's topic, is it meant to suggest that there is an authentic face of homosexuality whose true nature is hidden by the veil of social construction, and that the relationships of gay people, more than others, are mediated by these social veils? Or have the veils actually made the depicted encounter possible, allowing the two figures to recognize their similarities in structure (or construction) as more important than their differences in detail? Gender itself seems to be at issue here as well: the veils prevent us from identifying the two figures as male or female, and perhaps this gender ambiguity, too, is to be seen as a component in "the construction of homosexuality."

The Vernicle

The veil as a metaphor for that which both conceals and reveals has a long rhetorical history, especially in the Middle Ages, and Marjorie Garber has demonstrated the veil's historical association with the crossing of gender (and other) boundaries as well.[2] Dennis Anderson's drawing can thus be regarded as a late example of both metaphorical uses of the veil, and in this chapter I shall examine a hitherto neglected medieval point on the same historical continuum: Chaucer's description of the Pardoner's veils in the *General Prologue* to *The Canterbury Tales.*

The Pardoner, while ostensibly male, is also, as we have seen, a figure of fluid gender, erotic practice, and even sex; his body and behavior gesture toward a variety of incompatible identities without fully conforming to any. Chaucer's language, continuously oscillating among these various possibilities for the Pardoner, suggests less a stable, finished gender identity than one that is perpetually under construction. The Pardoner's veils, like those in Anderson's drawing, can be construed as metaphors for this fluid construction of gender: veiling is crucial to the construction of the Pardoner's ambiguous masculinity. His veils, as multivalent gender signs and also as signs in themselves of multivalent signification, provide a useful point of entry into the question of just how this gender identity is endlessly constructed and reconstructed.

The Pardoner's masculinity has heretofore been largely taken for granted: while a wide variety of explanations has been offered for his deviations from this supposed norm, the construction of his masculinity itself has received little attention, as is demonstrated by the large amount of commentary attracted by the controversial line in which the narrator of the *General Prologue* declares of the Pardoner, "I trowe he were a geldyng or a mare" (I, 691). Almost every word in this line has received special attention from scholars: "I trowe" as expressing either the narrator's belief or the uncertainty of his judgment, the subjunctive "were" as reinforcing the air of doubt, "a geldyng" as a reference to the Pardoner's presumed state of eunuchry, "or" as implying the narrator's indecision, "a mare" as suggesting homosexuality or hermaphroditism.[3] The only word in this line whose meaning has been virtually taken for granted is the masculine pronoun "he"; this chapter may be seen as an investigation into how such a problematic character as the Pardoner assumes this unexamined masculinity.

The Pardoner is not alone in this problematic assumption of the masculine pronoun[4]; according to Homi K. Bhabha, "'He,' that ubiquitous male member, is the masculinist signifier writ large—the pronoun of the invisible man; the subject of the surveillant, sexual order; the object of humanity personified. It must be our aim not to deny or disavow masculinity, but to disturb its manifest destiny—to draw attention to it as a prosthetic reality—a 'prefixing' of the rules of gender and sexuality; an appendix or addition, that willy-nilly, supplements and suspends a 'lack-in-being.'"[5] The veils associated with the Pardoner may thus prove a useful tool not only in exploring masculinity as a social construction, performance, or masquerade in *The Canterbury Tales,* but as an epitome of Western masculinist culture: the Pardoner, an anomaly in medieval culture, may be universalized in postmodern analysis. To this end I shall attempt an unveiling of the Pardoner and his phallic authority—an investigation of his discursive "male member"—in order to render the "invisible man" beneath the veils somewhat more visible.

The first of the Pardoner's veils mentioned in the *General Prologue* might better be termed a *representation* of a veil: "A vernycle hadde he sowed upon his cappe" (I, 685). This "vernycle," or vernicle, is one of the badges worn by those who had made a pilgrimage to Rome, and represents the original cloth, supposedly belonging to St. Veronica, on which, according to her legend, an image of Christ's countenance was miraculously imprinted. The vernicle was thus a representation of the face of Jesus as it appeared on this miraculous cloth; it is clearly visible in the Ellesmere manuscript's miniature portrait of the Pardoner.

Different versions of Veronica's legend describe the original of the vernicle in various ways: in the *Legenda aurea,* for instance, it is merely a piece of linen on which Veronica intended to have Jesus' portrait painted until the miracle provided her with a better image.[6] Some later adaptations of her legend suggest that the cloth was Veronica's handkerchief, and that she used it to wipe Jesus' face on the road to Calvary. A persistent version of the story, however, that appears both in the early *Mors Pilati*[7] and in Chaucer's period, describes Veronica's cloth specifically as a veil;[8] the Middle English *Siege of Jerusalem,* for example, dated to the last decade of the fourteenth century,[9] is quite clear: "& þat worliche wif, þat arst was ynempned, / Haþ his visage in hir veil, Veronyk o hatte, / Peynted priuely & playn, þat no poynt wanteþ; / For loue he left hit hir til hir lyues ende."[10]

This veil would appear to be at odds with the traditional metaphor of the veil as it occurs, for example, in medieval rhetorical theory, where it is commonly used to describe the figure of allegory, both theological and poetic. This metaphorical use of the veil originates in St. Paul's reading of the veil of Moses: "And not as Moses put a veil upon his face, that the children of Israel might not steadfastly look on the face of that which is made void. But their senses were made dull. For, until this present day, the selfsame veil, in the reading of the old testament, remaineth not taken away (because in Christ it is made void). But even until this day, when Moses is read, the veil is upon their heart. But when they shall be converted to the Lord, the veil shall be taken away."[11] Those who read the Old Testament only literally see the veil, but not the truth concealed beneath it; only the Christian reading of Scripture can remove the veil of allegory and reveal the spiritual truths beyond the literal level. The veil, in other words, is a figure for a figure, deferring proper interpretation until Christian enlightenment allows direct, unmediated knowledge of the truth.

St. Augustine's account of his own conversion in the *Confessions* 6.4 gives a similar reading of the veil, when St. Ambrose reveals the hidden truth of Scripture to him: "cum ea, quae ad litteram perversitatem docere videbantur, remoto mystico velamento spiritaliter aperiret" [those things which taken according to the letter seemed to teach perverse doctrines, he spiritually laid open to us, having taken off the veil of the mystery].[12] The *Glossa ordinaria* expands the meaning of the veil to include the literal level of Scripture generally, not just of the Old Testament, in its discussion of the wedding at Cana.[13] In Chaucer's period, secular allegory, too, was described as a fictional veil concealing spiritual truth, for instance in the commentaries on classical authors by Theodulphus of Orléans, Bernardus Silvestris, Boccaccio, and Petrarch.[14] Boccaccio notes, for instance, that Virgil wrote "sub fabuloso velamine" [beneath the superficial veil of myth].[15] All of these veils are figures for concealment and mediation, for the deferral of truth pending proper interpretation.

At the same time, to the Christian interpreter, the veil does not merely conceal, but reveals the presence of a hidden truth; from this perspective, the veil actually protects spiritual mysteries from the prying eyes of the uninitiated while allowing enlightened interpreters to perceive their outlines. The veil in this reading represents a readable code for those in the know; others won't even notice the presence of such a code, much less be able to interpret it: For Robert Grosseteste, "somehow the sacred veils, to some, are manifestations of the thing veiled under them, but to others they are concealments."[16] This revealing function of the veil, too, is extended to secular literature by the fourteenth century, as in Boccaccio's defense of the classical poets: "si sub velamento fabuloso sapidum comperiatur aliquid, non erit supervacaneum fabulas edidisse" [If, then, sense is revealed under the veil of fiction, the composition of fiction is not idle nonsense].[17]

The vernicle, on the other hand, is a veil that seems to function in a rather different way: it neither conceals nor encodes, but instead provides direct, unmediated access to the Logos, the bodily visage of Christ, God's word embodied. It is important to remember that the original veil of Veronica is not imagined merely as an image or representation, but as a true icon;[18] indeed, *vera icon* is a medieval etymology for "Veronica," from which the term "vernicle" is derived.[19] This is a veil that does not perform the usual functions of veiling: the veil of Veronica actually carries the Truth, the miracle of God's presence, on its surface rather than covering it up. It neither defers ultimate meaning nor encourages the enlightened reader to interpret, but displays truth itself for direct apprehension.

For medieval defenders of the icon, its power is the power of the Incarnation, which, as Marie-José Baudinet has suggested in her analysis of Nicephorus the Patriarch's *Antirrhetic II*, is also associated with the mother of Christ: "The first icon came into being at the moment of the Annunciation, when Mary received the Word that she had been chosen as the abode of infinity. The icon, in turn, produces the implantation of the Word within the virginal frame—the uterine Chora traversed by divine breath and confirmed by the harbinger's voice that institutes the device of homonymy. The work of the Holy Spirit is a fecundating voice that, in turn, guarantees the icon's fecundity."[20] The fecundity of the icon is the fecundity of the Mother of God.

It is worth pointing out that Veronica's veil was itself veiled during the Middle Ages; it hung in the Chapel of Veronica at St. Peter's in Rome, and as James F. Rhodes (citing Giraldus Cambrensis) writes, "usually the cloth remained in the Chapel under a protective covering, but . . . the veil proved so popular that it was frequently given public displays with its covering removed, most often on feast days or as a climax to the journey made by so many pilgrims during the mass pilgrimages of the late Middle Ages."[21] The original vernicle here functions not as the concealing or encoding veil, but is itself the spiritual truth hidden beneath a different veil; it is the second, outer veil, the one covering the vernicle, that, by suggesting what it conceals, inflames the pilgrims' desire to behold this truth "face to face."

Individual vernicles like the one worn by the Pardoner, then, may be only representations of the original veil, but they can be traced back to this originary truth. In itself, the Pardoner's vernicle is only one link in a chain of signifiers, but this chain is not endless: it finds its endpoint, and its signification comes finally to rest, in the transcendental signifier, the Logos in its full presence. The Pardoner, by wearing the vernicle, inserts himself into this chain, thereby implying that his own authenticity is guaranteed by its relation to the Logos. It is therefore not surprising that the Pardoner derives his professional identity and the respect of his villagers/victims (and, he hopes, of the other pilgrims) from his service to the Church's phallic power, because this power is also derived from the Logos, through the medium of Marian fecundity. The icon may originate with Mary/Mother, but the Church/Father appropriates its power, making the Church comparable in the Middle Ages to Bhabha's phallic nation: "The instinct for respect—central to the civic responsibility for the *service* of nation-building—comes from the Father's sternness, which is an effect of his 'peripheral' position in the family: 'This is the natural love of the child for the father, not as the guardian of his sensuous well-being, but as the mirror from which his own self-worth or worthlessness is reflected for him.'"[22] The Pardoner's service not to the nation but to the Church, reflected in the vernicle, allows his assumption of its phallic authority.

Our Lady's Veil

In twentieth-century feminist theory, the Logos is associated, if not equated, with the phallus, as is suggested by the term "phallogocentrism," coined by Jacques Derrida[23] and quickly adopted in deconstructive feminist discourse. According to Carolyn Burke, Derrida's term "implies that psychoanalytic discourse is guilty of identifying the phallus with the Logos as transcendent and, therefore, unexamined (and unexaminable) grounds of signification, of assigning meaning . . . when it puts the phallus in the central position as a kind of Logos, as the 'signifier of all signifiers.'"[24] The Logos, of course, is not only signifier, but also signified. In this sense, the phallus and the Logos are simply two versions of this same transcendental signifier, now perceived as the illusion or fantasy of an ultimate, prescriptive, and oppressive authority—gendered masculine; indeed, the masculine is the transcendental signified of the phallic signifier. Modern psychoanalysis is seen here as theorizing signification in a manner comparable to that of medieval rhetoric: both ground meaning in the transcendental signified, whether Logos or phallus. We may find a similar connection in *The Canterbury Tales* by examining the Pardoner's second veil described in the *General Prologue,* one of the false relics he carries with him to deceive ignorant villagers: "For in his male he hadde a pilwe-beer, / Which that he seyde was Oure Lady veyl" (I, 694–95).

This veil, too, is only a representation, but of a distinctly different sort than the vernicle. Not only is this pillowcase a false representation of Mary's veil (in contrast to the vernicle, which as icon is supposed to reproduce the true fecundity of Mother Mary), but what it conceals emphasizes even more starkly the contrast between the body of Christ and the Pardoner's body, a contrast that has already been implied by the immediate juxtaposition of their two faces earlier in the Pardoner's *General Prologue* portrait: "Swiche glarynge eyen hadde he as an hare. / A vernycle hadde he sowed upon his cappe" (I, 684–85). The Pardoner's "glaring eyes" are here distinguished from the serene face of Christ directly above them on his cap (the Ellesmere miniature confirms that this vernicle depicts a calm, not a suffering, Jesus), and the contrast implies differences beyond those of facial expression. The reference to the hare, supposed in medieval lore to be hermaphroditic and associated with sodomy as well,[25] is another of the details in the description of the Pardoner that hint at gender ambiguity and at an ambiguity concerning the nature of his anatomical sex.

If, then, the vernicle represents a unitary, phallogocentric truth that finds its ultimate authority in the body of Christ, the Pardoner appears to represent the opposite: neither clearly male nor clearly female, indeterminate in gender and in erotic practice as well as in anatomical makeup, his fragmented gender identity and possibly dismembered body are without authority and hence excluded from the unambiguous truth of the vernicle. Barred by Chaucer's language from participation in the Logos, as a possible eunuch he can lay no clear-cut claim to the phallus, either. The importance of the second veil (along with the other supposed relics) is that it allows the potential rhetorical construction of a masculine role from this mass of ambiguous details. As a kind of costume or drag, the veil also demonstrates that this masculinity is only a role, never achieved but only assumed.

What is it that this supposed veil covers? It is carried, significantly, in a "male," apparently the same "walet" or traveler's bag in which the Pardoner carries his pardons "biforn hym in his lappe" (I, 686).[26] "Lappe" may be glossed (as in *The Riverside Chaucer*) as a fold or pocket in the Pardoner's clothing, but given its position "biforn hym" as he rides horseback and its description as "his lappe," it makes more sense to read it as "lap" in the modern sense.[27] And while "male" itself is an unambiguous noun meaning "bag" here, it may also carry overtones of the modern noun or adjective "male" (i.e., the opposite of "female"): the *Oxford English Dictionary* (s.v. "male") lists a number of occurrences contemporary with Chaucer for this sense of the term (the *Middle English Dictionary*, s.v. "male," gives 1382 as its earliest occurrence in this sense), and several critics have also pointed out the common metaphorical link drawn in the Middle Ages between the traveler's bag and the testicles.[28]

For it is the Pardoner's testicles, the organs that, etymologically, "testify" to one's masculinity, which are at issue here. While it is unclear exactly which sex organs the Pardoner may lack (*pace* Irigaray, the male sex anatomically *n'en est pas un* either), his final encounter with the Host at the end of *The Pardoner's Tale* implies that the other pilgrims identify the nature of his possible lack with his "coillons"; as the Host says, "I wolde I hadde thy coillons in myn hond / In stide of relikes or of seintuarie. / Lat kutte hem of, I wol thee helpe hem carie; / They shul be shryned in an hogges toord!" (VI, 952–55). The Pardoner's furious silence here also allows us to read the testicles as his specific point of vulnerability.[29]

Jacques Lacan reminds us that the phallus is not identical with the penis, but "symbolizes" it: "In Freudian doctrine, the phallus is not a phantasy, if by that we mean an imaginary effect. Nor is it as such an object . . . in the sense that this term tends to accentuate the reality pertaining in a relation. It is even less the organ, penis or clitoris, that it symbolizes."[30] In the case of the Pardoner, the symbolic function of the phallus seems to be associated with the testicles rather than the penis, precisely because they are (possibly) what he (possibly) lacks. While the various suggestions of castration, then, might seem to place the Pardoner outside the boundaries of phallogocentric discourse, preventing any identification with the divine truth represented by the vernicle, the threat of castration is necessary to the transformation of penis (or testicles) into phallus, as Jean-Joseph Goux's reading of the Osiris myth (a myth well known to the Middle Ages) demonstrates. The dismembered body of Osiris is reassembled, but his penis cannot be found; Isis therefore fabricates a simulacrum of it and demands that it be honored. "The phallus is a fabrication. It is a constructed model. It is an artifact that simulates what is missing, at the same time rendering it sacred and larger than life to make it a cult object."[31] Only the threat of castration, the disappearance, can raise the physical genitals to the symbolic level of the phallus.[32]

Lacan can also assist in our reading of the second veil as that which also allows the potential for the Pardoner's identification with the Logos. As he suggests in "The Signification of the Phallus," the phallus "can play its role only when veiled, that is to say, as itself a sign of the latency with which any signifiable is struck, when it is raised (aufgehoben) to the function of the signifier. The phallus is the signifier of this Aufhebung itself, which it inaugurates (initiates) by its disappearance."[33] It is the disappearance of the phallus that makes it a signifier: not its mere absence, but its disappearance beneath a veil, that which may suggest presence without fully revealing it. Neither clear presence nor mere absence allows the phallus to "play its role," but veiling (the simultaneous concealment and revelation familiar from medieval rhetorical theory) does so. The Lacanian veil can be understood as a better analogue of the medieval rhetorical figure of the veil than can the vernicle, whose immediate manifestation of the Logos allows direct access rather than signification. The Pardoner's second veil, like the cloth covering Veronica's veil rather than the original vernicle itself, increases, or even creates, the significance of the phallus/Logos that it conceals.

Jean Baudrillard's work on the simulacrum is useful in this context. He emphasizes the distinction to be drawn between pretense and simulation: "pretending, or dissimulating, leaves the principle of reality intact: the difference is always clear, it is simply masked, whereas simulation threatens the difference between the 'true' and the 'false,' the 'real' and the 'imaginary.'"[34] The Pardoner too threatens these distinctions: he is neither "masculine" nor "not masculine," his phallus is neither "true" nor "false" in Baudrillard's terms. His masculinity, then, is neither the real thing nor a pretense, but a simulacrum, a copy for which there is no original, but that dangerously

takes the place of an original and is thus in some sense "true," though it is
obviously also to be distinguished from the "vera icon." It is not a representation, and "not unreal, but a simulacrum, that is to say never exchanged
for the real, but exchanged for itself, in an uninterrupted circuit without
reference or circumference."[35]

Garber's discussion of the veil in terms of gender ambiguity draws on
another aspect of Lacan's discussion of the veiled phallus: "the 'to seem' that
replaces the 'to have' in Lacan's trajectory of desire."[36] She refers to Lacan's
description of "the intervention of a 'to seem' that replaces the 'to have' . . .
which has the effect of projecting in their entirety the ideal or typical manifestations of the behaviour of each sex, including the act of copulation itself, into the comedy."[37] Only the veiling of the phallus can have this effect
of seeming; thus the "typical manifestations of the behaviour of each sex"
are projected by the veiling itself. Gender (not anatomical sex but its ideal
manifestation) is constructed behind the veil. Or, more precisely, gender is
always under construction behind the veil, projected as an ideal to be ap-
proached rather than achieved. Goux maintains "that the (masculine) subject is only erected under threat, that his identity, which seems to promise
[him] security, is only an indemnity which must always be paid, the cost of
a debt, the counterpart of an obscure sacrifice that leaves its traces some-
where. . . ."[38]

Goux's, Garber's, and Lacan's observations can thus be used to gender
Baudrillard's notion of the simulacrum, the copy with no original, which
is therefore neither true nor false. Gender itself is here conceived as a simulacrum. Or as a prosthesis; as Bhabha puts it, "[a]ttempts at defining the
'subject' of masculinity unfailingly reveal what I have called its prosthetic
process."[39] The prosthesis is also a kind of simulacrum, a copy of, or replacement for, something that is not there to begin with.

We may observe this process in the Pardoner's case. As Dinshaw has
brilliantly and painstakingly shown, the Pardoner's bulls and relics, including the supposed veil of Our Lady, are transmuted into fetishes, part-ob-
jects that both substitute for what is lacking and simultaneously signify lack
itself.[40] Again like the veil of allegory, the fetish both conceals and reveals,
though what it conceals and reveals is absence rather than the presence of
the Logos, specifically the mother's lack of a phallus and hence the possibility of castration.

Related to this aspect of the fetish, and more important for our purposes, is its social function: the fetish does not satisfy desire, but rather, in
Lacan's terms, reifies "the desire of the Other:"[41] "The infant's main means
of obtaining satisfaction is by identifying himself with the mother's object
of desire. . . . He informs the mother that he can make up to her what she
lacks, and he will be, as it were, the 'metonymy' of the phallus, replacing

the desired phallus by himself. It is around this lure that the fetishist artic-
ulates his relation to his fetishistic objects. . . ."[42]

The fetish, then, represents an attempt to identify with that which is
desired by the Other, the absent or hidden phallus. Because metonymy
is not identity, such representations cannot achieve the status of true
icon like the vernicle. This attempted identification is therefore bound
to fail, and its failure requires another attempt; rather than coming to
rest in the transcendental signified, these veiled representations demand
endless repetition.

The Pardoner is described in the *General Prologue* as attempting to incite this kind of fetishistic desire in his various audiences. The ignorant
villagers to whom he sells his wares must be made to desire what he has
to offer, his relics and pardons; only through their desire can his fetish-ob-
jects be identified with the phallus: "But with thise relikes, whan that he
fond / A povre person dwellynge upon lond, / Upon a day he gat hym
moore moneye / Than that the person gat in monthes tweye; / And thus,
with feyned flaterye and japes, / He made the person and the peple his
apes" (I, 701–06). A more detailed description of how the Pardoner uses
the relics to create this desire of the Other appears in his own prologue
(VI, 329–88), and includes a variety of methods. One is simple visual display: "Thanne shewe I forth my longe cristal stones, / Ycrammed ful of
cloutes and of bones—/ Relikes been they, as wenen they echoon" (VI,
347–49). Like the display of the vernicle taken from its covering, the unveiling of the relics creates desire in the audience. Another method is the
promise of various magical properties supposedly associated with the
relics: they turn well water into a miraculous healing substance (with the
immersion of a patriarch's, or "holy Jew's," sheep-bone) and cure jealousy,
for instance (VI, 351–71). The relics can also be used to blackmail the
congregation into making an offering (in the passage obliquely referring
to sodomy): "If any wight be in this chirche now / That hath doon synne
horrible, that he / Dar nat, for shame, of it yshryven be, / Or any womman, be she yong or old, / That hath ymaked hir housbonde cokewold, /
Swich folk shal have no power ne no grace / To offren to my relikes in
this place" (VI, 378–84). The relics are a source of power or potency; they
also have the ability to remove or destroy the villagers' power. And since
the power in question is only the power to offer wealth to the Pardoner,
he leaves them in the unenviable position of either giving up their own
relation to the ultimate source of potency and grace, or giving up their
money to the Pardoner.

Most importantly, the Pardoner creates desire through an appeal to a
primitive capitalism, offering a good return on the villagers' initial investment in the relics' potency:

If that the good-man that the beestes oweth
Wol every wyke, er that the cok hym croweth,
Fastynge, drynken of this welle a draughte,
As thilke hooly Jew oure eldres taughte,
His beestes and his stoor shal multiplie. . . .
Heere is a miteyn eek, that ye may se.
He that his hand wol putte in this mitayn,
He shal have multipliyng of his grayn,
Whan he hath sowen, be it whete or otes,
So that he offre pens, or elles grotes. (VI, 361–65, 372–76)

The investment of "pens, or elles grotes" is to result in the multiplication, not of money, but of the farmers' productivity; the circulation of the relics will supposedly provide an investment opportunity in which monetary capital is transformed into surplus merchandise. But it is all a "gaude" (VI, 389): the Pardoner in reality generates only wealth for himself based on no real product at all, a fact with implications for the status of his supposed authority as well.

The point, in any case, is clear: the fetishes have value insofar as they are desired by others, for whatever reason. The supposed veil and the other false relics create that desire, which in turn grants the Pardoner not only a comfortable living, but the ability to project a potent gender identity too: the authority that comes with access to the Logos. That this identity is phallic as well also seems clear from the sharpening, piercing, stretching, and stinging imagery associated with his verbal authority over the audience of villagers in both the *General Prologue* and *The Pardoner's Prologue*: "He moste preche and wel affile his tonge" (I, 712); "Thanne peyne I me to strecche forth the nekke" (VI, 395); "Thanne wol I stynge hym with my tonge smerte" (VI, 413), etc.

For the Pardoner, at least, these "typical manifestations" of masculinity can be constructed only beneath the veil. The Pardoner's money and authority, the components of his phallogocentric identity, are derived from the villagers' desire; desire is constructed through the fetishized relics; the relics, including the veil itself, are fetishized in the veiling of the phallus. The Pardoner's masculinity is thus constructed in a chain of signifiers, but this chain, unlike that in which the vernicle takes its place, ends neither at the Logos nor at the phallus, but at the veil: at "seems" rather than definitive truth. Therefore, as the end of his *Tale* suggests, the Pardoner can never be satisfied; since he cannot achieve full, iconic identification with Logos or phallus, he must repeat his performance endlessly as a direct expression of anxiety about his own authenticity: "Or elles taketh pardoun as ye wende, / *Al newe and fressh at every miles ende,* / So that ye offren, *alwey newe and newe,* / Nobles or pens, whiche that be goode and trewe. /

It is an honour to everich that is heer / That ye mowe have a suffisant pardoneer . . ." (VI, 927–31; emphasis added). The emphasis on coins ("nobles or pens") may remind us of his *Prologue:* as the Pardoner moves from
a rural audience to the more sophisticated one composed of his fellow
pilgrims, he is also moving from an exchange of goods (the "moneie,
wolle, chese, and whete" he takes from a village's "povereste page" or
"povereste wydwe" [VI, 448–50] in addition to the "pens" and "grotes")
to a more purely monetary exchange, a move that Goux relates to the passage from the archaic phallus on ritual display to the modern veiled one.
The Pardoner's primitive capitalism thus appears as an early example of
Goux's "modern" phallus: "the analysis made of the passage from the archaic phallus to the classical and modern one evokes the emergence of a
monetary structure in exchange."[43] The audience of pilgrims is continually invited to manifest in money its desire for what the Pardoner supposedly has, in the vain hope that this constant repetition can reassure him
that he really is "suffisant." This anxiety is "a 'sign' of a danger implicit
in/on the threshold of identity, in between its claims to coherence and its
fears of dissolution,"[44] resulting in "a kind of neurotic 'acting out' of its
power and powerlessness."[45] Full identification—or identity—cannot be
achieved behind the veil, but is always under construction.

    For Lacan, as for Bhabha, this performative construction of masculinity
is not atypical: if the phallus is not an organ, whether or not the Pardoner
actually has "coillons" to be found beneath the veil is, as it were, immate-
rial, because the veil is necessary to the phallus as signifier. Unveiling always undoes the signification of the phallus: "This is why the demon of
Αἰδος (*Scham,* shame) arises at the very moment when, in the ancient
mysteries, the phallus is unveiled. . . ."[46]

    This shameful unveiling, too, and the concomitant destruction of the
signifier, can be observed in the Pardoner's case, in the famous scene that
concludes *The Pardoner's Tale.* Having tried, as now seems inevitable, to
create in the audience of pilgrims that same desire of the Other that he
usually successfully creates in his less sophisticated audiences of villagers,
the Pardoner attempts to assert his authority over them by inviting the
Host to kiss his supposed relics: "Com forth, sire Hoost, and offre first
anon, / And thou shalt kisse the relikes everychon, / Ye, for a grote! Unbokele anon thy purs" (VI, 943–45). The Host, however, refuses to grant
the Pardoner any part of his own phallogocentric authority, declines to
fetishize the relics, and verbally unveils the Pardoner's phallus instead:
"Thou woldest make me kisse thyn olde breech, / And swere it were a
relyk of a seint, / Though it were with thy fundement depeint! / But, by
the croys which that Seint Eleyne fond, / I wolde I hadde thy coillons in
myn hond / In stide of relikes or of seintuarie. / Lat kutte hem of, I wol

thee helpe hem carie; / They shal be shryned in an hogges toord!" (VI, 948–55). Critics have usually, and rightly (if somewhat contradictorily), emphasized both the threat of castration in these lines, and their direct reference to the Pardoner's presumably already missing "coillons," as the sources of his subsequent anger and silence. Following Calvin Thomas, one might also read this passage, in its emphasis on money and rectal filth, as the loss of the sublimated, sacred, ithyphallic superiority described by Goux in favor of an abjectly bodily status: "if the bodily in masculinity is encountered in all its rectal gravity, the specular mode by which others become shit is disrupted."[47]

I would also like to emphasize the threat of exposure or unveiling: the "coillons" are to be taken from beneath Our Lady's veil, carried publicly in a procession, and enshrined (like Veronica's veil?) for public display, even if only in a hog's turd. For Lacan, after all, the possibility of castration is essential to the construction of the phallic signifier, and the sexual organs themselves are not to be identified with the phallus anyway. But the veil is necessary; it is exposure that destroys the signification of the phallus, and its significance. That is the threat that undermines the Pardoner's masculine authority, the threat that deconstructs performative masculinity. The Pardoner fails to fulfill the ritual role of the reconstituted Osiris as understood by Goux: "the exhibition of the phallus, which has become the object of a cult in temples and which is carried in procession during certain festivals."[48] If the Pardoner hoped to transform himself into an ithyphallic, Osiris-like object of worship by means of the simulation of the phallus during the ritual procession to Canterbury, the Host's threatened procession parodies the ancient festivals by reducing the symbolic phallus to the mere missing physical organs. Insofar as the Pardoner possesses the phallus, then, it is not the traditional, spectacular phallus of the ancient myth, but what Goux calls the "post-traditional" phallus of modernity, invisible and known only indirectly: "a reserved, idiotic identity which is recognized only obliquely, by a hermeneutics of images produced by the unconscious and by the structural reconstitution which postulates or extrapolates its site more than it can designate any evidence of its being."[49] This phallus is "no longer an archetype of the One but rather an operand for indefinite substitutions."[50]

On the other hand, the Pardoner is as threatening as he is threatened; this is the power of the simulacrum. What Baudrillard says of Richard Nixon might equally be said of the Pardoner: he "arrived at the goal of which all power dreams: to be taken seriously enough, to constitute a mortal enough danger to the group to be one day relieved of his duties, denounced, and liquidated."[51] Why does the Pardoner, whose access to true authority seems so limited, nevertheless possess this kind of power? It is the power of simulation in Baudrillard's sense. Simulation and the simulacrum are even more powerful than transgression because transgression leaves the law in place. "Simulation is infinitely more dangerous because it always leaves open to supposition that, above and beyond its object, law and order themselves might be nothing but simulation."[52] The Pardoner calls into question nothing less than the law and the order of gender; and his gender simulation calls even more than that into question. The unveiling of the Pardoner, the revelation of his status as simulacrum, is necessary to the continued concealment of simulation on a grander scale. If the Pardoner resembles Baudrillard's Nixon, he also resembles Baudrillard's Disneyland, which "is presented as imaginary in order to make us believe that the rest is real, whereas all of Los Angeles and the America that surrounds it are no longer real, but belong to the hyperreal order and to the order of simulation."[53] References to Nixon and Disneyland may well seem out of place in a book on Chaucer and medieval mentalities, and Baudrillard is very specifically a theorist of the postmodern, locating the reign of the simulacrum in late capitalist culture[54]; his concept of the "real" that no longer exists seems to be rooted in conservative nostalgia for a precapitalist golden age. As we have seen, however, we may perhaps find in the Pardoner an early capitalist warning of Baudrillard's late-capitalist nightmare: like Baudrillard's "floating capital," he has no "real referent of production,"[55] and we may recall here that he generates wealth without providing any real service. (It should also be noted that Baudrillard locates a postmodern consciousness of the simulacrum in historical iconoclastic movements, suggesting that the postmodern consciousness is not limited to the late twentieth century.[56])

To return to the Host: he must reveal the unreal, simulated, imaginary status of the Pardoner's phallic authority (like Disneyland's America) in order to maintain the illusion of a more important reality, or, better, the illusion of the real itself, guaranteed by the existence of God. The second veil must be shown to be false in order to reassure the pilgrims, and the reader, that the first veil, the vernicle, is a *vera icon,* is true. But perhaps we should refuse this reassurance.

The Pardoner Performed

Lacanian psychoanalytic theory draws explicitly on the "ancient mysteries" of the veil, and places itself in the same tradition as medieval rhetorical theory. Both refer to the figure of the veil as simultaneously concealing and revealing, or deferring (and in this process creating desire for), an authority gendered masculine. Both can therefore be criticized as phallogocentric, and the best recent readings of the Pardoner acknowledge Chaucer's perhaps inevitable, but still conflicted, implication in this phallogocentric economy. Carolyn Dinshaw, for instance, insists that the Pardoner as a eunuch, necessarily outside the boundaries of such binary oppositions as male/female, points the way toward a medieval poetics of pure presence: "it would be a poetics founded on the body of Christ who is God, in whom there is no lack, no division, no separation, no difference."[57]

Dinshaw's vision is of a Logos that includes the feminine as the Pardoner's body does, of a Logos that is not phallogocentric. Although she correctly claims throughout her chapter on the Pardoner that his anatomical status remains a mystery,[58] her argument thus depends centrally on the idea of the Pardoner as a eunuch. Yet, as the process of veiling and unveiling shows, this cannot be assumed: the veil allows the Pardoner to gesture toward a masculine identity regardless of what may lie beneath it, and even the Host's verbal unveiling implies that something may be there to be cut off—even as it reminds us that this something may also not be there. Masculinity is indeed assumed in this process, though only as a re-iterated performance fraught with anxiety: recall that, for Baudrillard, the simulacrum is, in its peculiar way, not unreal. Chaucer's investment in the phallogocentric economy may therefore be less gender-inclusive than Dinshaw believes.

Nevertheless, regardless of this reproduction of masculine authority in Chaucer's discourse, we are also free to draw on other discourses in speculating about further possible meanings for the Pardoner's veils. In some ways, for example, that final unveiling seems comparable to the story of Salome and the stripping off of her veils as Garber analyzes it:[59] both unveilings are also associated with a symbolic castration (the beheading of John the Baptist and the Host's threat); with a silencing (of the prophetic voice and of the Pardoner); and with a kiss (Salome's kiss of the severed head, which is destined to become a relic; the Pardoner's invitation to the Host to kiss his relics; and the kiss of peace between Host and Pardoner arranged by the Knight [VI, 960–68]).[60] For Garber, reading Salome through Lacan's figure of the veiled phallus, hers is a story of "the paradox of gender identification, the disruptive element that intervenes, transvestism as a space of possibility structuring and confounding culture. . . . The cultural Imaginary of the Salome story is the veiled phallus and the masquerade."[61]

Judith Butler provides one further theoretical approach that may help elucidate Chaucer's representation of the Pardoner's gendered (or overgendered) subjectivity. Chaucer's language about the Pardoner, like the recent theorists of gender I have been discussing throughout this book, poses the possibility of an unstable, multiple, incoherent "contested subject." The

Pardoner's multiplicity of possible sexes, genders, and erotic practices may come to seem mutually exclusive, literally inconceivable, a non-sense, to use Kristeva's formula: how can we imagine a subject represented variously as masculine, feminine, and neuter in gender, as male and female in sex, engaged in same-sex and other-sex erotic practices, castrated and a eunuch from birth? Butler's idea that gender identities may be seen as performative may be useful here:

> [A]cts, gestures, and desire produce the effect of an internal core or substance, but produce this on the surface of the body, through the play of signifying absences that suggest, but never reveal, the organizing principle of identity as a cause. Such acts, gestures, enactments, generally construed, are performative in the sense that the essence or identity that they otherwise purport to express are fabrications manufactured and sustained through corporeal signs and other discursive means. That the gendered body is performative suggests that it has no ontological status apart from the various acts which constitute its reality.[62]

It is this performative aspect of gender identity that the language used to describe the Pardoner seems to expose: rather than suggesting a coherent identity, it presents an impossibly incoherent or non-sensical one. In its very incoherence, its conceptual impossibility, this language refuses the idea of an essential identity that "makes sense." The Pardoner's fractured, contested subjectivity, oscillating among various sexes, genders, and erotic practices, suggests that these identities are all being tried out, or tried on—performed—one after another. Theorists like Butler might call this kind of performance "camp," "drag," "masquerade" (in the psychoanalytical sense explored by Joan Rivière and her successors[63]).

This is not to suggest that identity is normally performed as a conscious choice; Butler has argued against readings of her work that suggest that there could be a "performer" prior to the performance: "First, what is meant by understanding gender as an impersonation? Does this mean that one puts on a mask or persona, that there is a 'one' who precedes that 'putting on,' who is something other than its gender from the start? Or does this miming, this impersonation precede and form the 'one,' operating as its formative precondition rather than its dispensable artifice?"[64] The Pardoner is undoubtedly a performer, but he is not represented as consciously performing his multiple gender identities; we might say instead that the clash of discourses I have been investigating all along *performs the Pardoner* in these various modalities of sex, gender, and erotic practice. The Pardoner is a site in which these preexisting discourses are sedimented, and Chaucer's language performs him differently as different discourses emerge. The *General Prologue* performs the Pardoner as sodomite in the "stif burdoun" passage; The *Wife of Bath's Prologue* performs him as actively "heterosexual" in his erotic practices, and as different from women; the *General Prologue*'s description performs him as similar to women, as hermaphroditic, or castrated, or a born eunuch; "I trowe he were a geldyng or a mare" performs him as masculine, then neuter, then feminine in gender; etc. These identities cannot be thought together except as successive performances in the linguistic construction of a contested subject.

Butler's primary example of gender performativity is drag. Given the similarities in their stories, might the Pardoner, like Salome, be seen as participating not only in the performative construction of masculinity, but unconsciously in its transvestic deconstruction as well? For the Pardoner's veils both specifically represent women's garments: the veils of Veronica and of Our Lady. As Bice Benvenuto and Roger Kennedy point out, "the transvestite identifies with the phallus as hidden under the mother's clothes—he identifies with a woman who has a hidden phallus."[65] From this point of view, Our Lady emerges as the phallic mother, the mother whose imagined body provides a transgressive gender identification for the male child. The veiled phallus in this case is even more clearly a construction, a performance or masquerade, and the Pardoner's veils a kind of drag.

Both veils. For the vernicle, too, represents a man's face in a woman's veil, a male head cut off from its body (which may remind us that the Crucifixion is another symbolic castration, and that some vernicles showed the face of a suffering Christ). The simulacrum ultimately poses a challenge to the divine itself. Once again, Baudrillard is worth quoting at some length:

> . . . what becomes of the divinity when it reveals itself in icons, when it is multiplied in simulacra? Does it simply remain the supreme power that is incarnated in images as a visible theology? Or does it volatilize itself in the simulacra that, alone, deploy their power and pomp of fascination—the visible machinery of icons substituted for the pure and intelligible Idea of God? This is precisely what was feared by Iconoclasts, whose millennial quarrel is still with us today. This is precisely because they predicted this omnipotence of simulacra, the faculty simulacra have of effacing God from the conscience of man, and the destructive, annihilating truth that they allow to appear—that deep down God never existed, that only the simulacrum ever existed, even that God himself was never anything but his own simulacrum.[66]

Baudrillard here transforms the historical iconoclastic position into a postmodern one and opposes it to that of the iconophiles analyzed by Baudinet; our reading of the Pardoner should encourage a Baudrillardian, postmodern iconoclastic position as well. Rather than reassuringly maintaining the sacred illusion that an icon embodies the real, the revelation of the simulated or imaginary status of the Pardoner's phallic authority represented by the second veil may, read from this perspective, subvert even the supposed guarantee of meaning represented by the vernicle. Gender construction has vast implications beyond itself. The perpetual construction of the Pardoner's masculinity reveals the constructed nature of the real—the parental icon, both maternal and paternal—itself. "It is not a coincidence but a profound necessity that makes the phallus depend on fabrication (bringing the cult, culture, into the order of representation, of the simulated recovery of that which is no longer present, presentable, but lost. . . .)"[67]

That the vernicle is the face of Christ in a woman's garment is thus all the more disturbing: Jesus in drag suggests that the Logos itself, like the phallus, is, after all, only a masquerade.

CHAPTER 5

A SPEAKING AND SINGING SUBJECT

Leeve mooder, leet me in! (VI, 731)

The Material Pardoner: Semiotics and Grammar

When we first meet the Pardoner, at the beginning of his *General Prologue* portrait, he is singing: "Ful loude he soong 'Com hider, love, to me!' / This Somonour bar to hym a stif burdoun . . ." (I, 672–73). At the end of the portrait, he's still singing, though the circumstances are quite different: "Wel koude he rede a lessoun or a storie, / But alderbest he song an offertorie; / For wel he wiste, whan that song was songe, / He moste preche and wel affile his tonge / To wynne silver, as he ful wel koude; / Therefore he song the murierly and loude" (I, 709–14). The Pardoner's voice, "as smal as hath a goot" (I, 688), dominates his portrait, less because of what it's saying than because of its sheer sound, its musicality, volume, and, oddly, inhumanness—he sings well, loudly, and merrily, though his voice sounds like a goat's. The Pardoner depends for his living on the impressive, and apparently intimidating, tones of his vocal instrument; as he tells the other pilgrims in the course of his own prologue, when fleecing a congregation of unsuspecting villagers, "I peyne me to han an hauteyn speche, / And rynge it out as round as gooth a belle, / For I kan al by rote that I telle" (VI, 330–32); "Myne handes and my tonge goon so yerne / That it is joye to se my bisynesse" (VI, 398–99); "For whan I dar noon oother weyes debate, / Thanne wol I stynge hym with my tonge smerte" (VI, 412–13).

And yet, as in his duet with the Summoner, the Pardoner's voice is not merely a business asset: it also sings of love. Before we hear of its financial usefulness, we hear it providing the Pardoner's connection to the erotic—perhaps his primary connection to the erotic, if the rest of his portrait is to be read as describing a eunuch of some sort.[1] His own emphasis on the tongue, with its penetrative, "stinging" quality, suggests a vocal/phallic link or substitution: it is the Summoner who "bar to hym a stif burdoun," or bass accompaniment (also with accompanying erotic innuendo), but the Pardoner himself calls the tune. The Pardoner's voice, then—not what he says, but the voice itself—would seem to initiate two different possibilities of exchange, the erotic and the economic. "Exchange" may be the wrong term, however, for relations that appear to go only one way: both sexually and financially, the Pardoner, with his simulated relics and possibly simulated genitals, takes in without giving back—except vocally.

For Julia Kristeva, certain purely vocal aspects of language—as distinct from the meanings of words—enact the survival of the prelinguistic mother-child relationship within the paternal Symbolic. The "semiotic" or "heterogeneous," as she calls it, both exists within the Symbolic order of language (especially, but not exclusively, in poetic language) and regularly threatens to subvert its signification, along with the paternal, post-Oedipal ego itself, though without ever being able to do so. She associates this "heterogeneousness" with "the first echolalias of infants" and with the non-symbolic "musical" and "nonsense" aspects of any language.[2]

Music and nonsense, as well as "carnivalesque discourse"[3] and "*sentential rhythms and obscene words*,"[4] are here presented as effects of the prelinguistic, and hence as subversive of such aspects of language as meaning or signification—though also dependent upon them. As the reference to infancy suggests, the "heterogeneous" may also be associated with the mother-child continuum before it is disrupted by the Lacanian Law of the Father: "Language as symbolic function constitutes itself at the cost of repressing instinctual drive and continuous relation to the mother. On the contrary, the unsettled and questionable subject of poetic language (for whom the word is never uniquely sign) maintains itself at the cost of reactivating this repressed, instinctual maternal element."[5] For Kristeva, then, the "semiotic" aspect of language—poetic, musical, nonsensical—represents a universal phenomenon: the return of the repressed, instinctive relation to the mother, within the very (paternal) Symbolic order that represses it. The singing Pardoner has much in common with "the unsettled and questionable subject of poetic language" invoked here by Kristeva: his language both invokes the maternal, semiotic aspect of speech and ultimately represses it in his assumption of paternal authority.

This vocal identification with the mother is also, Kristeva emphasizes, to be understood, at least within Christian cultures and especially those emphasizing the cult of the Virgin, as an identification with the body and as a return to primary narcissism:

Let us call "maternal" the ambivalent principle that is bound to the species, on the one hand, and on the other stems from an identity catastrophe that causes the Name to topple over into the unnamable that one imagines as femininity, nonlanguage, or body. . . . At the same time, the most intense revelation of God, which occurs in mysticism, is given only to a person who assumes himself as "maternal." Freedom with respect to the maternal territory then becomes the pedestal upon which love of God is erected. As a consequence, mystics . . . throw a bizarre light on the psychotic sore of modernity: it appears as the incapability of contemporary codes to tame the maternal, that is, primary narcissism.[6]

To this untamed primary narcissism Kriseva opposes the paternal symbolic tendency: "In an interpretive undertaking for which there is no domain heterogeneous to meaning, all material diversities, as multiple attributes, revert to a real (transcendental) object."[7] We have already observed such an interpretive undertaking in Alan of Lille's *Complaint of Nature,* with its insistence on reducing the material diversities of gender and erotic practice to a transcendental, "natural" unity; several of Chaucer's works allow for the alternate possibility (and it is no more than a possibility) of a maternal "heterogeneousness" that continues to trouble the very transcendental unity that contains it.

Kristeva's dazzlingly dense formulations produce a complex constellation of binaries: on the one hand, the forces of masculinity, paternal identity, mind, symbolic language, the name, and subjectivity; on the other, the forces that tend to subvert them: femininity, the mother-child continuum, body, prelinguistic vocalism, mystical union, and narcissism.

We have already observed a number of these characteristics in Chaucer's depiction of the Pardoner. His effeminacy and narcissism have been widely observed (the Pardoner is "womanish but not a woman" according to Dinshaw, and Leicester discusses him in terms of primary narcissism);[8] his voice, as just discussed, is notable for the same prelinguistic effects Kristeva describes; and his complex identification with Mother Mary has already been outlined. Mystical union with God may seem an unlikely characteristic for the Pardoner, but we may find a hint of it—or perhaps its obverse—in the juxtaposition of his face with that of Christ on the vernicle: the Pardoner at least tries to insert himself into the iconic chain of signifiers that leads to the Mother of God and to Christ himself.[9] A constellation of subversive effects similar to that proposed by Kristeva can also be constructed with reference to medieval thought, including, but by no means limited to, Chaucer's poetry.

Let us begin, as Chaucer begins the Pardoner's portrait in the *General Prologue,* with the voice considered in itself, apart from what it may be saying. While this was not its primary concern, medieval linguistic theory includes, from very early on, considerations of the voice itself. For the late antique grammarians, as for Kristeva, language has at least two aspects: the acoustic, which is commonly associated with materiality, irrationality, and the bodily senses; and the intelligible, associated with rationality, cognition, and mental experience. Martin Irvine shows that "the definitions in the *artes [grammaticae]* first treat speech as a material cause of a sensory event leading to the cognition of meaning"[10]; however, it should additionally be observed that these theorists also make room for an order of speech that remains purely sensory and does not lead to cognition. For Donatus in *De voce*, "omnis vox aut articulata est aut confusa. articulata est quae litteris conprehendi potest, confusa quae scribi non potest" ["{e}very spoken sound is either articulated or confused. Articulated is what can be comprehended in letters; confused is what cannot be written].[11] This speech that cannot be represented in letters is what Kristeva develops into her theory of the heterogeneous or the semiotic: it is, to use her terminology, nonsense.

Irvine is primarily interested in the relationship of writing to oral speech rather than of sense to nonsense; nevertheless, his arguments also demonstrate that grammarians following Donatus, such as Diomedes and Priscian, elaborated this theory of "confused" speech. Diomedes specifies the irrationality of this aspect of language, and includes music as a possible addition to the ranks of "confused utterance":

> confusa est inrationalis vel inscriptilis, simplici vocis sono animalium effecta, quae scribi non potest, ut est equi hinnitus, tauri mugitus. quidam etiam modulatam vocem addiderunt tibiae vel organi, quae, quamquam scribi non potest, habet tamen modulatam aliquam distinctionem.

> [Confused utterance is irrational and not scriptible, produced from simple utterance in the sound of animals {which cannot be written}, like the neighing of horses and the bellowing of bulls. Some also add the measured voice of flutes or musical instruments which, although it cannot be written, has, nevertheless, modulation in distinct units.][12]

Priscian explicitly removes this order of language from mental experience, and, again like Kristeva, points out that it may signify, though not in the same way as scriptible words:

> inarticulata est contraria, quae a nullo affectu proficiscitur mentis. . . . quaedam, quae non possunt scribi, intelleguntur tamen, ut sibili hominum et gemitus: hae enim voces, quamvis sensum aliquem significent proferentis eas, scribi tamen non possunt. . . . aliae vero sunt inarticulatae et illiteratae, quae nec scribi possunt nec intellegi, ut crepitus, mugitus et similia.

> [Non-articulated spoken utterance is the opposite {of articulated}, that which originates in no mental experience. . . . Some sounds which cannot

be written are still understood, like human hissing and groaning. These are spoken utterances—they signify some kind of meaning by those producing them—but they cannot be written. . . . And others are inarticulated and not resolvable into letters, not capable of being written or understood, like rattling and moaning and sounds like these.][13]

The presymbolic, purely acoustic properties of the voice thus function, for these early grammarians, in a manner noticeably similar to Kristeva's semiotic: they are material ("struck air" is the formula most often employed[14]— a formula we shall see reappearing in Chaucer); they are of the body rather than the mind; they signify only pre- or nonsymbolically; and they include (but are not limited to) both musicality and nonsense.

As Irvine insists, the grammarians' primary model of language is based on writing rather than acoustics, and their focus is on scriptible speech. Stephen Nichols has pointed out that St. Augustine, too, favors writing, and harbors a certain hostility to the sensory, bodily aspects of language. The physical aspects of voice are related to "the body in real human time against an ecclesiastical tradition that set eternity against human time, spirituality against sexuality"; thus for Augustine in the *Confessions,* "performance could play out a confrontation between mind and body, obedience and rebellion, *vox* and *Verbum.*"[15] Paul Zumthor makes a similar point in more general terms:

Toute voix émane d'un corps, et celui-ci . . . demeure visible et palpable dans le temps où elle est audible. C'est pourquoi, peut-être, une valeur centrale lui reste attachée, durant ces siècles, dans l'imaginaire, la pratique et l'éthique communes. Les attitudes négatives, les condamnations proférées en milieu ecclésiatique en témoignent à leur manière. Jongleurs et prostituées sont englobés dans la même réprobation cléricale vouée à qui fait commerce de son corps. La tradition ascétique, prônant le jeûne, la chasteté et le silence, concernait les trois manifestations majeures de la corporéité: dans les moeurs, autant qu'on en peut juger, régnèrent continûment une grand liberté sexuelle, une passion de la parole et (en désir tout au moins!) la goinfrerie.

[All voices proceed from a body, and this body . . . remains visible and palpable as long as it is audible. This is, perhaps, why a central value remains attached to it over the centuries, in the popular imaginary, practice, and ethics. The negative attitudes, the condemnations proffered in the ecclesiastical milieu, bear witness to this in their own fashion. Jongleurs and prostitutes are included in the same clerical reprobation devoted to those who use their bodies in commerce. The ascetic tradition, in extolling abstinence, chastity, and silence, addressed the three major manifestations of corporeality: in morals, as far as one can tell, a great sexual liberty, a passion for speech and (at least in desire!) gluttony.][16]

Those who make their living by the voice are condemned along with those who sell their bodies sexually; voice is thus linked to female sexuality and to gluttony as a manifestation of the body in a state of sin.

For Augustine, the physical dimension of voice must be transcended if the higher mental faculties of memory, contemplation, etc., are to proceed: "nam et voce atque ore cessante, peragimus cogitando carmina et versus, et quemque sermonem . . ." [For when the voice and tongue give over, yet then in our meditations go we over poems, and verses, and any other discourse . . .].[17] Mental speech or cogitation here can take the place of the physical voice fully, without any sort of loss; and the bodily voice is not merely unnecessary, but—unless and until it is transcended by mental speech—actually functions as a distraction from the Word of God:

nam qui haec negant, latrent quantum volunt et obstrepant sibi: persuadere conabor, ut quiescant, et viam praebeant ad se verbo tuo. . . . tu loquere in corde meo veraciter; solus enim sic loqueris; et dimittam eos foris sufflantes in pulverem et excitantes terram in oculos suos, et intrem in cubile meum et cantem tibi amatoria. . . .

[For as for those praters that deny all, let them bark and bawl unto themselves as much as they please; my endeavour shall be to persuade them to quiet, and to give way for thy word to enter them. . . . Speak thou truly in my heart; for only thou so speakest: and may I let them alone blowing upon the dust without doors, and raising it up into their own eyes: and may I enter into my chamber, and sing there a love-song unto thee. . . .][18]

In this passage, the bodily voice in itself is entirely reduced to mere "barking," that is, to the sounds that animals make and that are classified among "confused," "irrational," or "inarticulated" utterances by the grammarians. It is only in silent, internal contemplation that God can be truly praised, and his Word can be comprehended only through mental operations: the bodily voice is used properly only when it is transcended, or, as Nichols puts it, "performance as a step toward spiritual knowledge can only begin when the *vox corporis* (voice of the body) falls silent."[19] Otherwise, the bodily, physical dimension of voice is explicitly set against the divine: voice that physically produces breath (the grammarians' "struck air") only obscures the Word of God. Knowledge—cognition—of this Word is the goal for Augustine, and the bodily voice cannot contribute to this knowledge because it is "*precognitive*: the work of the mind begins at the moment the voice falls silent, allowing the body to recede."[20]

The conception of the physical voice as linked to body (and opposed to mind), and hence linked also to irrationality and to rebellion against legitimate authority, both temporal and spiritual, is thus to be found in the mainstream of earlier medieval philosophy and theology, and it survives into Chaucer's own period and beyond. Similar views of bodily utterance can be found throughout fourteenth-century English culture. Conservative contemporary accounts of the Peasants' Revolt of 1381, for example, regularly invoke the same categories of utterance (as adumbrated by the grammarians) that Augustine does, using them to classify the rebels as irrational and animalistic by linking these supposed characteristics to the peasants' perceived modes of vocalization. Thomas Walsingham in his *Historia Anglicana* consciously or unconsciously evokes the categories of "inarticulated speech" in his description of the peasants' abduction of Archbishop Sudbury from the chapel of the Tower of London:

> . . . sed pejores dæmonibus, qui Christi Sacramenta verentur et fugiunt, nihilpendentes Salvatoris præsentiam, trahunt per brachia, per caputium, per diversa loca ad eorum sectæ satellites, extra portas ad Montem Turris. Quo cum pervenisset, factus est clamor horrendissimus, non similis clamoribus quos edere solent homines, sed qui ultra omnem æstimationem superaret omnes clamores humanos, et maxime posset assimulari ululatibus infernalium incolarum. . . . Non tamen resonabant verba inter horrificos strepitus, sed replebantur guttura multisonis mugitibus, vel quod est verius, vocibus pavonum diabolicis.

> [Worse than those demons who fear Christ's sacraments and flee from them, they disregarded the presence of the Saviour and dragged the archbishop along the passages by his arms and hood to their fellows outside the gates on Tower Hill. When he arrived there, a most horrible shouting broke out, not like the clamour usually produced by men, but of a sort which enormously exceeded all human noise and which could only be compared to the inhabitants of hell. . . . Words could not be heard among their horrible shrieks but rather their throats sounded with the bleating of sheep, or, to be more accurate, with the devilish voices of peacocks.][21]

As for the grammarians and Augustine, the voice in itself is irrational and animalistic, but here it is also lawless and even sacrilegious. As Jesse M. Gellrich puts it, Walsingham "hyperbolizes peasant 'voice' as an unforgettable example of their hatred toward the law";[22] but in this passage (again as for Augustine) it is not only civil law but religious authority as well that is unjustly sabotaged by the untranscended bodily voice. It is difficult not to find an echo of such passages in Chaucer's famous reference to the Revolt in *The Nun's Priest's Tale*: "They yolleden as feendes doon in helle; / The dokes cryden as men wolde hem quelle; / The gees for feere flowen over the trees; / Out of the hyve cam the swarm of bees. / So hidous was the noyse—a, benedicitee!—/ Certes, he Jakke Strawe and his meynee /

Ne made nevere shoutes half so shrille / Whan that they wolden any Flemyng kille, / As thilke day was maad upon the fox" (VII, 3389–97).
Chaucer, too, comically links the irrational utterances of animals with
human lawlessness and the defiance of authority, even with rebellion
against God: "And therwithal they skriked and they howped. / It semed as
that hevene sholde falle" (VII, 3400–01).

Gellrich also notes[23] that Walsingham additionally calls the rebels
"doomed ribalds and whores of the devil,"[24] drawing the same link between prostitution and the bodily voice noted by Zumthor. As Nichols
demonstrates,[25] the body, rebellion, sin, and female sexuality (as well as irrationality and the nonhuman) are all linked to the voice in its purely
physical aspect.

Voice is thus connected with the feminine, and not only by its association with prostitution. In the twelfth century, Bernardus Silvestris, in his
commentary on the *Aeneid,* had used gender as a trope for the Augustinian transcendence of bodily utterance by mental language:

> Increpat Mercurius Eneam oratione alicuius censoris. Discedit a Didone et
> desuescit a libidine. Dido deserta emoritur et in cineres excocta demigrat.
> Desueta enim libido defficit et fervore virilitatis consumpta in favillam, id
> est in solas cogitationes, transit.

> [With a speech of certain censure, Mercury chides Aeneas, who leaves Dido
> and puts passion aside. Having been abandoned, Dido dies, and, burned to
> ashes, she passes away. For abandoned passion ceases and, consumed by the
> heat of manliness, goes to ashes, that is to solitary thoughts.][26]

Nichols says of this passage that Dido's death represents the turn away from
the body that is necessary to thought.[27] But Bernardus also explicitly links
thought to manliness, and the precognitive body to the feminine Dido.
This link between women, voice, and physicality in the Middle Ages has
been studied in particular by R. Howard Bloch, who suggests that in the
medieval antifeminist tradition, woman "is aligned . . . with the senses, the
body, and the material, portrayed as pure appetite (economic, gastronomic,
sexual), and such a portrayal cannot be disassociated from the desire to
speak." He also shows that medieval writers like Jean de Meun connect
woman specifically with carnivalesque "riot," a term that also refers to the
tradition of nonsense poetry.[28] This connection between voice and a
specifically female physicality and sexuality, already familiar from Kristeva,
is graphically illustrated for the medieval period in the fabliaux on talking
vaginas discussed by E. Jane Burns.[29]

Gellrich also finds a link between the "animalistic" peasant voice and
the feminine in the fourteenth century, citing Henry Knighton's confla-

tion of the peasant voice with the use of vernacular translation for the benefit of women: "Wyclif 'was to make vulgar for illiterates what was open to the wise and for women to read for knowledge what was only to be for the good of the understanding of clerks and literates; and thus he cast evangelical pearls before swine.' Moreover, Knighton continues, what was dear to clerks was tossed to the 'laughter of the commons' ('jocositas communis'). . . ."[30] In the references to swine and to peasant laughter we find again the familiar constellation of animality and nonscriptible, bodily utterance, but here also linked to women and to the peasant class.

Chaucer's own familiarity with the grammatical tradition and its views on acoustics is demonstrated in such texts as the eagle's speeches in Book II of *The House of Fame:* "Soun is noght but eyr ybroken; / And every speche that ys spoken, / Lowd or pryvee, foul or fair, / In his substaunce ys but air; / For as flaumbe ys but lyghted smoke, / Ryght soo soun ys air ybroke. . . ." (*HF,* 765–70) The concept of "struck air," familiar from the work of the grammarians, reappears here as "eyr ybroken," rooting the discussion of sound and speech that follows firmly in the material. Indeed, any distinction between speech and sound seems quite difficult to maintain in *The House of Fame.* Throughout much of this poem, symbolic language is quickly—and cynically—assimilated to the category of mere acoustics: what is emphasized about "every speche that ys spoken," regardless of its meaning, is that it "in his substaunce ys but air." Perhaps appropriately for a poem in which truth and falsehood, fame and rumor, are so difficult to distinguish, even the more basic categories of "speech" and "sound" are repeatedly described as having more similarities than differences. The eagle's description of the House of Fame itself declares

> That every soun mot to hyt pace;
> Or what so cometh from any tonge,
> Be hyt *rouned, red, or songe,*
> Or spoke in suerte or in drede,
> Certeyn, hyt moste thider nede. (*HF,* 720–24; emphasis added)

> . . . every *speche, or noyse, or soun,*
> Thurgh hys multiplicacioun,
> Thogh hyt were piped of a mous,
> Mot nede come to Fames Hous. (*HF,* 783–86; emphasis added; see also
>   819, 824, 832, etc.)

The verbal distinction between speech and mere sound is carefully maintained throughout, but both, it appears, have the same origin and the same characteristics—and those characteristics are the ones we have come to associate with material sound rather than symbolic language.

All sound, even speech, can be represented by the example of music. Speaking of the ways in which air is broken, the eagle says that

> But this may be in many wyse,
> Of which I wil the twoo devyse,
> As soun that cometh of pipe or harpe.
> For whan a pipe is blowen sharpe
> The air ys twyst with violence
> And rent—loo, thys ys my sentence.
> Eke whan men harpe-strynges smyte,
> Whether hyt be moche or lyte,
> Loo, with the strok the ayr tobreketh;
> And ryght so breketh it when men speketh.
> Thus wost thou wel what thing is speche (*HF* 771–81).

Music—for Diomedes a possible category of nonscriptible, irrational sound—becomes here, at the acoustic level, the model even for scriptible speech ("ryght so breketh it when men speketh"). And a very material violence is the origin of all sounds, speech included: the air is twisted, rent, and broken. Music does not appear here in the idealized, metaphorical, Augustinian form in which it transcends the physical; instead, it is a violent and inharmonious material or physical production. So is human language, for which this violent music provides (in the eagle's view, at least) a fully adequate representation.

Like the grammarians' "confused utterance" also, all sound in *The House of Fame* is comparable to the irrational utterances of animals and other natural sounds: the squeaking of a mouse has the same end as human speech. It is not only the eagle who draws such comparisons. He classifies the human speeches in the *House of Fame* as an irrational "grete swogh," (*HF*, 1031), and the dreamer is inclined to agree: they are "'lyk betynge of the see,' / Quod y, 'ayen the roches holowe, / Whan tempest doth the shippes swalowe, / And lat a man stonde, out of doute, / A myle thens, and here hyt route; / Or elles lyk the last humblynge / After the clappe of a thundringe . . .'" (*HF*, 1034–40). Here again human speech with its variety of symbolic meanings ("Bothe of feir speche and chidynges, / And of fals and soth compouned" [*HF*, 1028–29]) is assimilated to the pure, irrational, "confused" sounds of the natural world, this time by the narrator/dreamer. Similarly, in Book III he characterizes the language of the great company as the sound of a beehive: "I herde a noyse aprochen blyve, / That ferde as been don in an hive / Ayen her tyme of out-fleynge; / Ryght such a maner murmurynge, / For al the world, hyt semed me" (*HF*, 1521–25). The image may remind us of the beehive in *The Nun's*

Priest's Tale, and its critique of the irrational voice, or of Knighton's description of the animalistic mob.

If sound originates in a violent materiality in *The House of Fame,* it ends in the feminine. Fame itself is feminine, as the dreamer emphasizes, and is linked with music and with the body.

> A femynyne creature,
> That never formed by Nature
> Nas such another thing yseye . . .
> And soth to tellen, also she
> Had also fele upstondyng eres
> And tonges, as on bestes heres;
> And on hir fet woxen saugh Y
> Partriches wynges redely . . .
> And Lord, the hevenyssh melodye
> Of songes ful of armonye
> I herde aboute her trone ysonge,
> That al the paleys-walles ronge. (*HF,* 1365–67, 1388–92, 1395–98)

The description of this "feminine creature," like the dreamer's description of the sounds he hears in the *House of Fame,* brings together the familiar constellation of what the grammarians called "inarticulated" sound effects: the tongues and ears, which we might expect to be associated with symbolic language, instead are described in terms of animality ("bestes heres"). Lady Fame's music sounds heavenly, but it has a material effect similar to that of all sound in the eagle's speech: it strikes the palace walls, causing them to ring. All these effects come together in a specifically feminine creature. It is, perhaps, no wonder that the poem must stop without any conclusion at the appearance of the famous "man of gret auctorite": masculine authority disrupts the disordered, feminine sound-world of *The House of Fame,* as for Kristeva the maternal semiotic is ultimately contained by the paternal symbolic. The various degrees to which Chaucer's texts imagine this containment as desirable will now be explored further.

The House of Fame's cynical/satirical view of speech as mere disorganized sound cannot be taken at face value: neither the eagle nor the dreamer is a particularly authoritative or trustworthy source, and the "man of gret auctorite" never gets his chance to set things straight. A more serious consideration of the links between song, body, and the feminine, and one that makes these links even clearer, is the one Chaucer takes up in *The Prioress's Prologue* and *Tale,* as well as in her *General Prologue* portrait; the Prioress is also the *Canterbury Tales* pilgrim connected most suggestively with the Pardoner.

Singing Bodies: The Prioress

Like the Pardoner, the Prioress is introduced as a singer: "Ful weel she soong the service dyvyne, / Entuned in hir nose ful semely" (I, 122–23). Also like the Pardoner, the Prioress is more concerned with the bodily, acoustic properties of her voice than with what she is singing: she sings "wel" and "semely," and with an explicit physicality ("[e]ntuned in hir nose") that may seem at odds with the spirituality or the liturgical signif- icance of what she sings. It is not at all clear that the Prioress understands what she is singing in the "service dyvyne": fourteenth-century English nuns were not necessarily literate in Latin,[31] and though the narrator re- marks on this nun's provincial French (I, 124–26), he makes no mention of even such a limited accomplishment in Latin on her part. Pure sound is what counts here.

The Prioress herself values oral performances in which meaning is sec- ondary to the bodily utterance: "But as a child of twelf month oold, or lesse, / That kan unnethes any word expresse, / Right so fare I, and ther- fore I yow preye, / Gydeth my song that I shal of yow seye" (VII, 484–87). The Prioress identifies herself as a singer, as the narrator does, and her song is the kind of performance classified by the grammarians as inarticulated: she compares herself to a prelinguistic infant whose sounds are not words (compare the similar distinction drawn by Kristeva between "lexemes" and "the first echolalias of infants"[32]). Only the influence of Mother Mary, who as Muse is even more important to the Prioress than to the Pardoner, can guide these sounds into a coherent story.

The image of the singing infant recurs in *The Prioress's Tale,* suggesting that the Prioress identifies herself not with her tale's grieving, adult mother but with the mother-praising child.[33] Like the Prioress in her own self-de- scription, the heroic child sings in Latin without comprehending it. "He *Alma redemptoris* herde synge, / As children lerned hire antiphoner; / And as he dorste, he drough hym ner and ner, / And herkned ay the wordes and the noote, / Til he the firste vers koude al by rote. / Noght wiste he what this Latyn was to seye, / For he so yong and tendre was of age" (VII, 518–24). As Corey J. Marvin notes, Chaucer modifies his sources in mak- ing his hero only seven years old, thus placing him in his first term at school, that is, before the beginning of instruction in grammar.[34] The child is thus attracted by the material sound of the song despite his illiteracy in Latin, and he learns it by rote rather than through comprehension. Latin in this context, despite its medieval status as the language of masculine, pa- ternal authority (law, the Church, etc.), is subversively reduced to the prelinguistic nonsense sounds of the mother-child continuum; we also learn that it is the child's mother who has already taught him to perform the *Ave Maria* (VII, 507–09). The father tongue, reduced to pure sound, is thus feminized; rather than interrupting the mother-child continuum, paternal language reinforces it by becoming maternal in its nonsensical, acoustic materiality.[35]

The child does eventually learn that the *Alma redemptoris* is a hymn in praise of Mary, but Chaucer, and the Prioress, emphasize his continued lack of mental comprehension. After learning the first verse by rote, he inquires about its significance: "His felawe, which that elder was than he, / Answerde hym thus: 'This song, I have herd seye, / Was maked of our blisful Lady free, / Hir to salue, and eek hire for to preye / To been oure help and socour whan we deye. / I kan namoore expounde in this mateere. / I lerne song; I kan but smal grammeere'" (VII, 530–36). This pupil explicitly delineates the binary opposition of "song" and "grammeere" that we have already encountered in the grammarians' (especially Diomedes') distinction between scriptible speech ("grammeere," the grammarians' concern) and inarticulated utterance, including music ("song"). The children are occupied with musical utterance, not with the meaning of the Latin words they sing: note that even this older pupil knows what the song is about not because he understands it, but only because he has heard it said ("herd seye") by unspecified others that it is a hymn to the Virgin. Symbolic meaning recedes into rumor (as in *The House of Fame*); only the embodied, voiced song remains present. This reading contradicts Marvin's view that asking about the meaning of the song signals the child's entry into the Symbolic: the song does draw him "to the very threshold of the symbolic,"[36] but it leaves him at that threshold, which he refuses to cross. Similarly, Marvin's contention that the Jews' conspiracy represents the child's entry into language ("His murder projects him into a world of symbols, language, and selfhood"[37]) seems mistaken: the Jews' symbolic language is precisely what the child refuses in favor of the unbroken mother-child continuum.

The hero of the story, tellingly, draws the connection between music and motherhood for himself; though he does not understand the words *Alma redemptoris mater*, and though his equally ignorant companion has not mentioned that it refers to Mary specifically as mother, he himself conceives of Mary primarily in terms of motherhood: "'And is this song maked in reverence / Of Cristes mooder?' seyde this innocent. / 'Now, certes, I wol do my diligence / To konne it al er Cristemasse be went. / Though that I for my prymer shal be shent / And shal be beten thries in an houre, / I wol it konne Oure Lady for to honoure!'" (VII, 537–43). Song is directly linked to motherhood and to the Nativity—not because he understands the words of the song, which he explicitly does not, but because the child himself makes the connection. The bodily voice is also linked, as in Augustine, Walsingham, etc., to a rebellion against paternal authority, specifically the authority of Latin grammar, represented by the primer: not only is the heroic child ignorant of Latin's symbolic meanings, he actively resists learning them. The binary opposition of song/grammar is decisively resolved in favor of song by eliminating grammar altogether. The primer also represents a physical threat—beating: before being martyred to the Jews, the child is, at least in his mind, a martyr to Latin grammar. Like another female-centered pilgrim[38] previously encountered in *The Canterbury Tales,* the Wife of Bath, he is (in his imagination) "beten for a book" (III, 712). The opposition between scriptible speech (associated with paternal grammatical law—the Symbolic order—and punishment) and bodily song (associated with the uninterrupted mother-child continuum and resistance to paternal authority) delimits the child's entire experience. Along similar lines, both Judith Ferster and Corey Marvin have associated the child's death at the hands of the Jews with the Symbolic law of the father. Marvin writes that "[t]he Jews aim specifically at cutting off the symbolics of the hymn because they object to its sentence, which conflicts with their law's *reverence,*"[39] while Ferster points out that "[t]he Jews who mutilate and kill him are all men, and are associated with the serpent, who nests in the Jews' heart and swells up phallically (VII.559–60) to incite them to (symbolically) rape and murder him. . . . The boy rebels against, and is punished by, the male law in order to stay with the mother."[40]

   That his performance of the song is a physical rather than a mental process is emphasized in the following stanza as well: "His felawe taughte hym homward prively, / Fro day to day, til he koude it by rote, / And thanne he song it wel and boldely, / Fro word to word, acordynge with the note. / Twies a day it passed thurgh his throte, / To scoleward and homward whan he wente; / On Cristes mooder set was his entente" (VII, 544–50). Once again the rote-learning aspect of this performance is emphasized— he sings not according to the sense of the individual words, but according to their notes alone. Like the Prioress herself, the child associates song with a specific body part, in his case the throat rather than the nose, and this physical act of worship is directed at Mary in her role as mother.

   Through the Prioress, Chaucer, like Kristeva, appears to be engaged in a project of reevaluating the physical voice. The Prioress opposes St. Augustine's view that physical voice must be transcended in spiritual experience by the mental processes of contemplation, memory, etc.; for the Prioress, opposition to—even elimination of—mental processes seems to be a sign of a particularly powerful (because innocent) spirituality, as her *Prologue* would have it. This conception of worship as primarily physical rather than mental is demonstrated most powerfully in her climactic image of the miraculously singing corpse.

"My throte is kut unto my nekke boon,"
Seyde this child, "and as by wey of kynde
I sholde have dyed, ye, longe tyme agon.
But Jesu Crist, as ye in bookes fynde,
Wil that his glorie laste and be in mynde,
And for the worship of his Mooder deere
Yet may I synge *O Alma* loude and cleere.

"This welle of mercy, Cristes mooder sweete,
I loved alwey, as after my konnynge;
And whan that I my lyf sholde forlete,
To me she cam, and bad me for to synge
This anthem verraily in my deyynge,
As ye han herd, and whan that I hadde songe,
Me thoughte she leyde a greyn upon my tonge.

"Wherfore I synge, and synge moot certeyn,
In honour of that blisful Mayden free
Til fro my tonge of taken is the greyn;
And after that thus seyde she to me:
'My litel child, now wol I fecche thee
Whan that the greyn is fro thy tonge ytake.
Be nat agast; I wol thee nat forsake.'" (VII, 649–69)

This body is not exactly dead, but it is not exactly alive either: its only sign of life is the voice. Interestingly, the dead child continues to draw a binary opposition between his relationship with Mary and his relationship with Jesus. Jesus, a masculine person of the authoritative paternal Trinity, is associated with grammar; he is available to the child only through the mediation of books, the concern of grammar ("Jesu Crist, as ye in bookes fynde . . .").[41] Mary, on the other hand, is characterized by a warm, maternal presence expressed through her comforting voice ("To me she cam, and bad me for to synge"; "'Be nat agast; I wol thee nat forsake'"). Grammar and song remain two different realms of language, and Mary, like the child and also like the Prioress, chooses the feminine realm of song. Feminine song also continues to be associated with body; note the graphic bodily details associated with the singing corpse: throat, neck bone, and especially tongue.

Mary obviously plays the central maternal role at the end of the story, but, despite Marvin's claim that the child "remains forever alienated from his mother,"[42] Mary does not entirely displace the child's literal, physical mother, who remains an important presence in the *Tale*. She is a widow, we are told twice at the beginning of the story (VII, 502, 509), emphasizing the mother-child continuum and absence of paternal law even more clearly. And it is she who has taught the child the worship of motherhood from the beginning: "Thus hath this wydwe hir litel sone ytaught / Oure blisful Lady, Cristes mooder deere, / To worshipe ay, and he forgat it naught, / For sely child wol alday soone leere" (VII, 509–12). The shift in focus from this physical mother to the spiritual Mother Mary takes place only when the widow invokes Mary's aid herself: "And evere on Cristes mooder meeke and kynde / She cride" (VII, 597–98). The widow thus provides the purely feminine religious context that makes Mary's maternal miracle so appropriate. Rather than displacing physical in favor of figurative motherhood, *The Prioress's Tale* incorporates both.

"[M]ooder Marie" (VII, 690), who puts in a final appearance as the last words of *The Prioress's Tale,* is thus presented as a maternal alternative to the paternal Trinity. And the child's innocent refusal of the law of the father in favor of a continuous, prelinguistic mother-child bond provides an alternative model of faith, one with which, in its emphasis on the physical rather than the mental and on illiterate song rather than grammar, the Prioress can identify herself. The "men of dignitee" (VII, 456) cited in her *Prologue*—St. Augustine would be one of them—have their own ways of worship; the Prioress prefers the other way offered by "children . . . on the brest soukynge" (VII, 457–58).

Ferster has argued that this tale remains undecidably poised between male and female predominance: "[t]he competition for predominance between male and female figures is embedded in the text. . . . There is a discreet but constant jostling about who is more important."[43] I would argue that the Prioress, if not Chaucer, decisively favors the feminine, even if she does inevitably also remain within the discourse of patriarchy. Recall that Kristeva's "heterogeneous" exists within the paternal, Symbolic discourse, not independently of it; the same can be said of the Prioress' valuation of the feminine.

Singing Bodies: The Pardoner

Such a positive valuation of the feminine voice and of the body is turned upside-down by the Pardoner. For the Prioress, the maternal semiotic provides a permanent alternative to the paternal symbolic order that contains it. The Pardoner, on the other hand, regularly invokes the semiotic, but just as regularly refuses its subversive potential in his assumption of masculine authority.

Like the Prioress and her child hero, the Pardoner rejects writing, grammar, and traditional masculine authority in favor of a detailed physicality, with a specific focus on the voice. For example, he too reverses the Augustinian insistence that the physical be transcended in pursuit of spiritual experience.

In the *City of God,* Augustine focuses specifically on the tongue and hands:

> Nonne ita sunt in eo loca sensuum et cetera membra disposita speciesque ipsa ac figura et statura totius corporis ita modificata, ut ad ministerium animae rationalis se indicet factum? . . . Porro mira mobilitas, quae linguae ac manibus adtributa est, ac loquendum et scribendum apta adque conueniens et ad opera artium plurimarum officiorumque conplenda, nonne satis ostendit, quali animae ut seruiret tale sit corpus adiunctum?

> [Are not the sense organs and the other parts of that body so arranged, and the form and shape and size of the whole body so designed as to show that it was created as the servant to the rational soul? . . . Then the marvelous mobility with which his tongue and hands are endowed is so appropriate, so adapted for speaking and writing and for the accomplishment of a multitude of arts and crafts. And is not this sufficient indication that a body of this kind was designed as an adjunct to the soul?][44]

The body is of value only insofar as it ministers to the soul, specifically to the soul's expression in the arts. Tongue and hands are of interest because they express mental or spiritual experience, that is, because of the symbolic signification that can be attached to them, not for their own physical or bodily sake. And, as Nichols observes, "[t]he harmony of the body subordinates *the vox corporis* to a superior paradigm, the divine numbers. . . . The role of the body will be to strive toward the univocal harmony of the human with the divine."[45] Augustine focuses on the body only to insist that it be transcended.

The Pardoner, too, emphasizes his own tongue and hands in a passage that almost seems a parody of Augustine's. His *Prologue* features a famous description of his preaching technique: "Thanne peyne I me to strecche forth the nekke, / And est and west upon the peple I bekke, / As dooth a dowve sittynge on a berne. / Myne handes and my tonge goon so yerne / That it is joye to se my bisynesse" (VI, 395–99). Hands and tongue here are ends in themselves, performative objects of vision and hearing, bodily attributes that the congregation is to appreciate for themselves rather than for their transcendent symbolic expression. His body in performance creates "joye," or, one might argue, a sort of *jouissance,* in his audience. The Pardoner seems unaware of the possibility of spiritual transcendence that we might be tempted to attach to his words: for him, the dove is simply a dove stretching forth its neck, an expression of his own bodily movements, not an image of the Holy Spirit. Derek Pearsall has gone so far as to claim that the Pardoner has no spirituality that could be expressed, declaring instead that he is an automaton and that "[h]e is, both theologically and in ordinary human terms that need no gloss, dead."[46] If such a reading can be accepted, the Pardoner must appear as a perverse version of the singing corpse encountered at the end of *The Prioress's Tale,* one whose physicality is not a form of genuine worship but is rather self-referential and solipsistic. This perversity is further emphasized by the assumption of phallic superiority in the stretching-neck image noted above as well as in the position of physical superiority in which the Pardoner imagines himself with regard to the congregation. These references to the body and to animals do not associate the Pardoner with the feminine semiotic, but, again perversely, with the assumption of paternal authority.

Also like the Prioress and her hero, the Pardoner favors rote learning rather than comprehension in his relationship with the father tongue, Latin. As the Prioress does in her tale, the Pardoner in his *Prologue* explicitly associates the physicality of his voice with rote learning: "'Lordynges', quod he, 'in chirches whan I preche, / I peyne me to han an hauteyn speche, / And rynge it out as round as gooth a belle, / For I kan al by rote that I telle . . .'" (VI, 329–32). Symbolic meaning is again subordinated to physical sound or bodily sensation. The assembled congregation is imagined as processing the Pardoner's Latin phrases with their bodies rather than their minds or spirits; the words appeal to their physical senses: "And in Latyn I speke a wordes fewe, / To saffron with my predicacioun, / And for to stire hem to devocioun" (VI, 344–46). "To saffron" or "to spice" implies a sensory experience (of the tongue). Religious devotion ("devocioun") in this context thus becomes a bodily rather than intellectual or spiritual response; Augustine's ideal transcendence of the physical has not been achieved.

Quite the reverse. As we may recall from the *General Prologue,* little if any distinction is drawn between the Pardoner's "merry and loud" liturgical song, the offertory, and his erotic duet with the Summoner, any more than *The House of Fame* distinguishes among types of speech. If song is to be imagined as a refusal of symbolic meaning in favor of material utterance, as I have been arguing that Chaucer sometimes presents it, no such distinction could be made. Indeed, the pun on the Summoner's musical and erotic "stif burdoun," with its hint of anal penetration, brings the Pardoner's song to an even more fundamentally bodily level than can be found anywhere in *The House of Fame* or *The Prioress's Tale.*

And yet this apparent subversion of Latinity in favor of the body obviously does not have the same effect it had in *The Prioress's Tale:* unlike the illiterate child's or the Prioress', the Pardoner's speech is "hauteyn," and his Latin phrases are used not for worship but for intimidation. Once again his assumption of masculine authority contains the feminine semiotic—which nevertheless continues to trouble it. The Pardoner's voice may feminize him, as do other aspects of his description, but his own constant resistance to feminization commits him to the very discourse of male authority that tends to exclude him.

As we might expect, *The Pardoner's Tale* itself completes the series of associations we have been examining by bringing its narrator, through several of the characters, into the orbit of the feminine and the prelinguistic maternal. Scholars regularly associate the Pardoner who tells the *Tale* with the figure of the Old Man within the *Tale,* and the power of this conflation is undeniable. Both are obsessed with their imperfect or incomplete bodies and body parts, the Pardoner's possible eunuchry corresponding to the Old Man's deterioration in age; as Carolyn Dinshaw argues, the Old Man is "an incarnation of the Pardoner's anguished knowledge of his fragmentariness. . . . The old man wails for some redemption from his defective and dying corpse."[47] Both are also concerned with the acquisition of wealth. For the Old Man, the solution to his problems might lie in a return to the mother-child continuum:

> Thus walke I, lyk a restelees kaityf,
> And on the ground, which is my moodres gate,
> I knokke with my staf, bothe erly and late,
> And seye, 'Leeve mooder, leet me in!
> Lo how I vanysshe, flessh, and blood, and skyn!
> Allas, whan shul my bones been at reste?
> Mooder, with yow wolde I chaunge my cheste
> That in my chambre longe tyme hath be,
> Ye, for an heyre clowt to wrappe me!'
> But yet to me she wol nat do that grace,
> For which ful pale and welked is my face (VI, 728–38).

The flesh, blood, bones, skin, and "welked" face show us a body fragmented like the Pardoner's. Like the Pardoner also, he imagines two kinds of exchange or interaction, linking the perverse quasi-erotic with the financial as the Pardoner's singing does in the *General Prologue:* he knocks on his mother's "gate" with his staff, hoping to gain entrance, and when this strategy fails, offers instead, in a curious passage rarely remarked, an exchange of his wealth—the valuables collected in his "cheste"—for a shroud of hair-cloth. The image of impotence (the staff that cannot penetrate the female opening) resonates strongly with the Pardoner's sexual oddity, whatever it may be. And so does the substitution of fetishized objects—the Old Man's chest, which holds his wealth, and the Pardoner's relics, which gain him wealth—for erotic or spiritual potency. The Old Man's desire for the presymbolic mother-child continuum may, then, seem to complete for us in the Pardoner the pattern we keep encountering elsewhere, from the early grammarians to Julia Kristeva (especially in her linkage of the semiotic to incest and to fetishism):[48] the constellation of song–body–mother that apparently defies the laws of grammar–mind–father. Like the Prioress and her child hero, the Pardoner and his stand-in, the Old Man, appear to subvert paternal authority, whether through the opposition of song to grammar, the equation of erotic and liturgical song, the emphasis on the physical sound effects of the father tongue rather than its symbolic meanings, the obsession with body parts and refusal to sublimate the body to the spirit, or the longing for a return to the mother-child continuum. But once again, the Pardoner and his *Tale* cannot be taken simply as another version of the Prioress and hers; whereas the Prioress proposes these feminine effects as a fruitful alternative to male religion, the Pardoner and his *Tale* oscillate between these two possibilities—as he also oscillates among various gender roles.

The Old Man, for example, does not fit the pattern outlined above quite so simply. He wants to have it both ways. He longs for a return to the maternal body, but he refuses to give up the authoritative masculine status conferred by his age and sex: "But, sires, to yow it is no curteisye / To speken to an old man vileynye, / But he trespasse in word or elles in dede. / In Hooly Writ ye may yourself wel rede: / 'Agayns an oold man, hoor upon his heed, / Ye sholde arise'; wherfore I yeve yow reed, / Ne dooth unto an oold man noon harm now, / Namoore than that ye wolde men did to yow / In age, if that ye so longe abyde" (VI, 739–47). The Old Man is not a singer but a grammarian after all. He relies on the authoritative written word that the hero of *The Prioress's Tale* refused to learn, specified here as "Hooly Writ" to be read (like the rejected, bookish model of Christ opposed to the human presence of Mary at the end of *The Prioress's Tale*). This use of the biblical text is insistently masculine, commanding respect not only for age but for maleness as well ("an oold man"). And the Old Man here presents himself as a figure of paternal authority, giving not only the friendly advice of lines 739–40, but also the imperative of line 745.

The Old Man's offer of a bribe to Mother Earth in exchange for her nurturing haircloth in which to wrap himself also adumbrates a value system at odds with the feminized one we have been examining. The meaning of money, as R. A. Shoaf has demonstrated, was a matter of overpowering curiosity in the late Middle Ages, and one late medieval way of understanding wealth—not surprisingly, given my argument so far—was through a comparison with vocal utterance. Shoaf quotes Boethius' influential discussion in his second commentary on Aristotle's *De Interpretatione*:

non enim (ut dictum est) nomen et verbum voces tantum sunt. sicut nummus quoque non solum aes inpressum quadam figura est, ut nummus voce-
tur, sed etiam ut alicuius rei sit pretium: eodem quoque modo verba et
nomina non solum voces sunt, sed positae ad quandam intellectuum signi-
ficationem. . . . sed si vox aliqua nihil designat, nullius nomen est; quare si
nullius est, ne nomen quidem esse dicetur. atque ideo huiusmodi vox id est
significativa non vox tantum, sed verbum vocatur aut nomen, quemadmo-
dum nummus non aes, sed proprio nomine nummus, quo ab alio aere dis-
crepet, nuncupatur.

[For, as it has been said, names and words are not sound merely. Thus just as
a coin is copper impressed with a certain figure not only in order that it
might be called a coin but also in order that it might be the price of some
specific thing, so, in the same way, words and names are not only sounds, but
are imposed to a certain signification of thoughts. . . . But if some sound
designates nothing, it is the name of nothing; wherefore, if it is the name of
nothing, neither is it said to be a name. And thus, in this way, a sound—that
is, a significant sound—is not sound only but is called a verb or a name, just
as a coin is not called copper, but is called, by its proper name, a coin, by
means of what distinguishes it from other copper.][49]

Note the carefully drawn distinction, familiar from the grammarians, between mere sound and symbolic language, and the parallel distinction between the material from which money is made and its symbolic function:
as a medium of symbolic exchange, wealth transcends its presymbolic materiality. And as Shoaf notes, "'Aes figura impressum' is not a coin until it
is legal tender, until it is further differentiated by being the price of something else";[50] thus the Old Man in using his wealth for monetary exchange
enters the same paternal symbolic system that, in language, values symbolic
meaning over material sound.

Instead of the presymbolic mother-child continuum, this imagined
monetary exchange automatically implies a separation between the two,
and demonstrates the Old Man's continued involvement in the paternal,
symbolic system of wealth. In the Old Man we seem to have an example
of the typical subject described by Kristeva: one fully implicated in the masculine symbolic, but troubled by traces of the semiotic or heterogeneous—
which disturb the symbolic without really subverting it. The maternal is
desired, but it is also figured as death, and as impossibility.

Ideally, the Pardoner in his ecclesiastical function as *quaestor* should value
the symbolic transmutation of money as well. The function of a pardoner
was to offer indulgences, drawn from the treasury of merit established by
Christ and the saints, to the truly penitent—as evidenced by monetary contributions. This Pardoner values and desires the material/maternal even as

he identifies himself with the ideal/patriarchal; he wants material "wolle, chese, and whete," but tranmutes it in his *Prologue* into symbolic "moneie" (VI, 448) rather than into spiritual "satisfaction"; he even explicitly chooses these material goods over "the apostles" (VI, 447), which from this perspective looks like a refusal of his proper ecclesiastical function.

The Pardoner's treatment of the three rioters is equally indecisive. They, too, are figures of the Pardoner himself, and are presented by him as subversive of masculine, paternal authority, as Alfred David has argued.[51] In fact, the Pardoner condemns them for the very kinds of subversiveness he practices himself; and yet, like him and like the Old Man, the rioters ultimately reinforce the symbolic system they seem at first to resist, though as in those cases too, the semiotic remains a troubling presence.

The rioters, like the Old Man, are looking for Death, and the Pardoner's verbal style, emphasizing bodily fragmentation and decay in his discussion of them, as in the Old Man's speech, hints at the presence of imminent death throughout the tale, as in his long opening condemnation of their bad habits. The pure physicality of their existence is constantly emphasized: the opening description refers to the belly and its products, dung, farts, and belches, and to the drunkard's disfigured face, foul breath, and, significantly, loose tongue; thus the Pardoner's own vices of gluttony and drunkenness are projected in his language about the rioters. But he lays the heaviest emphasis on the materiality of their language, beginning and ending this description with swearing, which in the *Tale* is described as a verbal form of physical fragmentation:

> Hir othes been so grete and so dampnable
> That it is grisly for to heere hem swere.
> Our blissed Lordes body they totere—
> Hem thoughte that Jewes rente hym noght ynough (VI, 472–75).

> "By Goddes precious herte," and "By his nayles,"
> And, "By the blood of Crist that is in Hayles,
> Sevene is my chaunce, and thyn is cynk and treye!"
> "By Goddes armes, if thou falsly pleye,
> This daggere shal thurghout thyn herte go!" (VI, 651–55).

Christ is here imagined not as the Word of God, certainly not the grammatical written Word he is for the Prioress, but as a human body that continues to suffer in human time (note the odd shifts between past and present tense in these lines). Equally important, the rioters' language, their oaths, are endowed with a physical materiality: they have the power to break not only air, as in *The House of Fame,* but to break bodies as well—

both God's and their human competitors'. One might compare the rioters' oaths with Julia Kristeva's "carnivalesque discourse" and "obscene
words": "around the object denoted by the obscene word, and that object
provides a scanty delineation, more than a simple context asserts itself—the
drama of a questioning process heterogeneous to the meaning that precedes and exceeds it."[52] The oath too both refers to the body of Christ and
questions it by invoking a new context. The rioters' entire existence might
be cited as an example of carnivalesque or "Menippean" discourse as Kristeva understands it:

> The cynicism of the carnivalesque scene, which destroys a god in order to
> impose its own dialogical laws, calls to mind Nietzsche's Dionysianism. The
> carnival first exteriorizes the structure of reflective literary productivity, then
> inevitably brings to light this structure's underlying unconscious: sexuality
> and death. Out of the dialogue that is established between them, the struc-
> tural dyads of carnival appear: high and low, birth and agony, food and ex-
> crement, praise and curses, laughter and tears . . . the carnivalesque structure
> is anti-Christian and anti-rationalist.[53]

The rioters' language literally destroys a god, substituting its own riotous-
ness. To that extent it is anti-Christian, and the clash between the Pardoner's own supposedly Christian language and that of the rioters
produces the typical carnivalesque oppositions, with particular emphasis in
this case on high and low, food and excrement, and praise and curses. We
may recall at this point that for Kristeva, the carnivalesque forms an equation with the semiotic and the maternal in their shared opposition to the
symbolic law of the father or Word of God.

The rioters' existence embraces the feminine as an aspect of the carnivalesque. Significantly, music plays its expected role here as well. Like the
Pardoner and the Prioress, the rioters are associated with music and the
feminine from the very beginning:

>   In Flaundres whilom was a compaignye
> Of yonge folk that haunteden folye,
> As riot, hasard, stywes, and tavernes,
> Where as with harpes, lutes, and gyternes,
> They daunce and pleyen at dees bothe day and nyght. . . .
> And right anon thanne comen tombesteres
> Fetys and smale, and yonge frutesteres,
> Syngeres with harpes, baudes, wafereres,
> Whiche been the verray develes officeres
> To kyndle and blowe the fyr of lecherye,
> That is annexed unto glotonye. (VI, 463–67, 477–82)

In a nexus of activities reminiscent of Zumthor's association of the embodied voice with music, prostitution, and gluttony, the feminine
("tombesteres," "frutesteres," "baudes") stands out in terms of the subversive vocal qualities associated with it; the feminine is an essential aspect of
the carnivalesque.

    The subtexts of the carnivalesque, or more precisely that which the car-
nivalesque brings to light, are sexuality and death, according to Kristeva.
We have already seen the Old Man's association of the two, in his figura-
tion of the grave as the desired mother he wishes to enter; the rioters too
are looking for death, or Death, and according to the Pardoner they have
already unwittingly found it in their pursuit of sexual and other bodily
pleasures: "But, certes, he that haunteth swich delices / Is deed, whil that
he lyveth in tho vices" (VI, 547–48).

    The subversive values of the feminine and the carnivalesque are quickly
abandoned, however, when the rioters are presented with wealth. In contrast to the Old Man, who was ready to enter a financial transaction and
give up his treasure chest in order to gain admittance to the maternal
grave, the rioters are tempted to give up the pursuit of death when they
accept a similar treasure chest as a supposed substitute. The rioters have
perceived death itself as masculine all along; for them, Death is a man, the
ultimate paternal law that seeks to abolish their carnivalesque existence.
Death first appears as the killer of another of their fellow rioters: "He was,
pardee, an old felawe of youres, / And sodeynly he was yslayn to-nyght, /
Fordronke, as he sat on his bench upright. / Ther cam a privee theef men
clepeth Deeth, / That in this contree al the peple sleeth, / And with his
spere he smoot his herte atwo, / And wente his wey withouten wordes
mo" (VI, 672–78). Death, as the Pardoner insisted, comes for those whose
carnivalesque existence questions or subverts divine authority. In abandoning the attempt to kill death, then, the rioters are entering the paternal Symbolic realm signified, as for the Old Man, by money. In short, the
rioters' acceptance of wealth serves the same function as the Old Man's attempt to bargain with it: in both cases the characters enter into the paternal symbolic economy, abandoning what has until then appeared to be the
assertion of the subversive maternal semiotic.

    Like the Pardoner, then, the rioters take in without giving back—they
kill one another rather than sharing the wealth. In that sense they are even
better figures of the Pardoner than the Old Man, who vainly tries to use
symbolic means to a semiotic end. The rioters even abandon the homosocial or homoerotic bonding that the Pardoner shares with the Summoner[54]: their original use of carnivalesque language to form homosocial
bonds degenerates into the language of a conspiracy to destroy those bonds
(VI, 808–58).

For both the Old Man and the rioters, the symbolic economy ultimately asserts itself, destroying the subversive maternal *jouissance* of their original quests. The quasi-feminine erotic impulse of the Pardoner's love song at the beginning of his *General Prologue* portrait, then, is transmuted into the purely masculine economic one we find in his later song—not only in the *General Prologue* itself, but repeatedly in the *Tale* as well. The Pardoner violates Shoaf's observation that "there is no taking in love without giving, no giving without taking. Love is (at least) an exchange. Hence the love poets' fascination with economics."[55] The Pardoner, despite his song and his interest in economics, is no love poet: in his language, the maternal, semiotic, vocal aspects of speech repeatedly assert themselves, but are invariably contained and repressed by the Pardoner's ironic assumption of masculine authority.

From this perspective, Anne Laskaya's position, that "the Pardoner, by his very presence, becomes an 'Other' Chaucer uses to reaffirm the male pilgrims' masculinity and his own culture's gender definitions,"[56] seems too simple: our analysis reveals both the way that the heterogeneous maternal element troubles masculine authority, and the manner in which even such an ambiguous, "other" character as the Pardoner can still, however anxiously and ironically, assume that authority.[57]

Finally, this discussion of the association of voice and song—for Kristeva, all poetic language—with the feminine and maternal raises the question of how Chaucer situates himself as poet/performer with regard to gender. This question too will be taken up in the following chapter, and again in the conclusion to this book.

CHAPTER 6

THE DISMEMBERMENT OF THE PARDONER

Oure blissed Lordes body they totere (VI, 474)

I would next like to investigate another component of the constellations that include gender and song (or the materiality of the voice more generally), one I touched on only briefly earlier: the fragmented or dismembered body, which is of considerable interest to both the Pardoner and the Prioress. An investigation of this concern might be initiated with Chaucer's various treatments of the Orpheus myth—the myth that links dismemberment to poetry and to the feminine—as it was understood in the Middle Ages, an exploration I will undertake in this chapter. (The relevance of the related myth of Dionysus has already been discussed in chapter 1.)

Medieval Orpheus: Song, Dismemberment, and Gender

The myth of Orpheus, we should remember, brings together, especially in medieval readings of the tenth and eleventh books of Ovid's *Metamorphoses,* the same nexus of concerns that we observed in the portraits and tales of the Prioress and the Pardoner. Like them, Orpheus is a singer, indeed the mythic forerunner of all singers and poets. He is also centrally involved in myths of gender and eroticism: Orpheus pursues his wife Eurydice, emblem of the female, into the underworld and tries to win her back by means of his song. Failing in this attempt because he could not resist turning back to gaze at her, Orpheus rejects the feminine as embodied in all women, and turns to an exclusively male-male eroticism. Finally, Orpheus is dismembered: he is, most tellingly, decapitated by his former audience, the Bacchants, who are infuriated at his rejection of women.

Ovid's is the most influential version of this myth for the Middle Ages in general, and for Chaucer in particular, whether in the form of the Latin *Metamorphoses* itself or of the numerous medieval commentaries on classical

authors. A few passages from Ovid's work and that of his medieval interpreters will help illustrate the particular emphasis on the relationships among
poetry, gender, and dismemberment that Chaucer would have found in the
story of Orpheus. First, Ovid himself.

Orpheus, primarily, is the poet/singer par excellence, and for Ovid his
songs are exclusively concerned with erotic pursuit. Perhaps surprisingly,
they are also associated with death. Orpheus' famous song does not appear
in Ovid's account until he follows Eurydice to the underworld, where he
sings to its gods in an attempt to win her back:

> supera deus hic bene notus in ora est:
> an sit et hic, dubito. sed et hic tamen auguror esse,
> famaque si veteris non est mentita rapinae,
> vos quoque iunxit Amor.
> . . . pro munere poscimus usum.
> quod si fata negant veniam pro coniuge, certum est
> nolle redire mihi: leto gaudete duorum!

[{Love} is a god well-known in the world above; whether he may be so
here too, I do not know, but I imagine he is familiar to you also and, if there
is any truth in the story of that rape of long ago, then you yourselves were
brought together by Love. . . . I ask as a gift from you only the enjoyment
of her; but if the fates refuse her a reprieve, I have made up my mind that I
do not wish to return either. You may exult in my death as well as in hers!][1]

No distinction is drawn between the rape of Proserpine and Orpheus' own
desire for the "enjoyment" *(usum)* of his wife. Once this odd parallel has
been drawn it leads almost inevitably to a reunion imagined as having to
take place in the underworld: if Pluto and Proserpine are the model of desire, no other outcome is imaginable. The pursuit of the feminine is death.

It should be recalled here that in Book Five, Proserpine, like Eurydice,
was abducted from a world of female companions (dominated, in Proserpine's case, by her mother) in order to enter a heterosexual union. The
comparison between the two marriages is uncomfortably clear: they are
based on male enjoyment of the female regardless of her own desires,
which in both cases are depicted as homosocial rather than heterosexual.
Proserpine's mother Ceres calls this abduction a crime; her father Jupiter
calls it love: "'sed si modo nomina rebus / addere vera placet, non hoc iniuria factum, / verum amor est.'" [' . . . if you will only call things by their
proper names, this deed was no crime, but an act of love'].[2] A passage to
conjure with! God the Father lays down the masculine law of language—
calling things by their proper names—which is also the law of gender: if
maternal speech labels rape a crime, it is improper naming; only the pater-

nal name (rape is an act of love) is proper, because it is God the Father who declares it so.

In invoking this earlier passage in Ovid's text, Orpheus thus aligns himself with paternal logic and with rape: what counts is his "enjoyment" of Eurydice. Orpheus' song here is not the semiotic, maternal music of *The Prioress's Tale;* it is the language of patriarchy, the masculine logic of God the Father, as well as the language of heterosexual desire as death. No wonder Pluto, king of the underworld, is convinced. "nec regia coniunx / sustinet oranti nec, qui regit ima, negare: / Eurydicenque vocant. umbras erat illa recentes / inter et incessit passu de vulnere tardo." [The king and queen of the underworld could not bear to refuse his pleas. They called Eurydice. She was among the ghosts who had but newly come, and walked slowly because of her injury].[3] Pointedly, however, Ovid makes no mention of Eurydice's response—other than supplying an explanation of why she doesn't hurry (a detail that nevertheless, by its very inclusion, emphasizes a certain lack of enthusiasm).

Orpheus famously fails the test of not looking back. His desiring gaze literally kills Eurydice again: "iamque iterum moriens non est de coniuge quidquam / questa suo—quid enim nisi se quereretur amatam?—/ supremumque, 'Vale,' quad iam vix auribus ille / acciperet, dixit revolutaque rursus eodem est." [Eurydice, dying now a second time, uttered no complaint against her husband. What was there to complain of, but that she had been loved? With a last farewell which scarcely reached his ears, she fell back again into the same place from which she had come].[4] If Orpheus sings the paternal language of God the Father, Eurydice's only utterance is a faint farewell, the sign of her own death. (And note that Ovid himself, unlike the translator Mary M. Innes, does not even refer to her by name in this passage.) Given Orpheus' alignment of his own love with that of Pluto, and his language with that of Jupiter, the only possible reunion for these two is in death, which is what Apollo has planned for them: "hic modo coniunctis spatiantur passibus ambo: / nunc praecedentem sequitur, nunc praevius anteit / Eurydicenque suam iam tutus respicit Orpheus." [There they stroll together, side by side: or sometimes Orpheus follows, while his wife goes before, sometimes he leads the way and looks back, as he can do safely now, at his Eurydice].[5]

Before granting Orpheus this eternal scopophilic "enjoyment" of Eurydice in their shared death, however, Ovid has more in store for him and his lyre. After his loving gaze sends her back to the underworld, Orpheus reacts by refusing erotic contact with any other woman; he does not, however, remain celibate:

. . . omnemque refugerat Orpheus
femineam Venerem, seu quod male cesserat illi,

sive fidem dederat: multas tamen ardor habebat
iungere se vati: multae doluere repulsae.
ille etiam Thracum populis fuit auctor amorem
in teneros transferre mares citraque iuventam
aetatis breve ver et primos carpere flores.

[Throughout this time Orpheus had shrunk from loving any woman, either
because of his unhappy experience, or because he had pledged himself not
to do so. In spite of this there were many who were fired with a desire to
marry the poet, many were indignant to find themselves repulsed. However,
Orpheus preferred to center his affections on boys of tender years, and to
enjoy the brief spring and early flowering of their youth; he was the first to
introduce this custom among the people of Thrace.][6]

The reason for Orpheus' rejection of women at this point is unclear: that
given in many versions of the myth (including Virgil's)—that he is in
mourning for Eurydice—is not stated here, though it might be inferred.
But it is in keeping with Ovid's general lack of interest in Eurydice that
this passage does not name her, focusing instead on the detail of Orpheus'
homoeroticism. This custom is imported to Thrace from elsewhere; it is a
dangerously alien practice (as Orpheus shortly finds out). But where Orpheus gets it from, apparently, is Mount Olympus: his songs at this point
focus on the love of gods for young men; as he puts it, he sings "puerosque
canamus / dilectos superis, inconcessisque puellas / ignibus attonitas
meruisse libidine poenam" [of boys whom the gods have loved, and of girls
who, seized with unlawful passion, have paid the penalty for their amorous
desires].[7] One might wonder how these two topics are related, but all the
stories Orpheus tells here celebrate the power of the gods in human
erotics; and it is male-male desire that is celebrated in particular. If the story
of Orpheus imagines heterosexual union as the patriarchal law imposed on
women, and as death, it finds in male-male desire what at first appears to
be a more productive aspect of that law. Heterosexual desire can be con-
summated only in the underworld, but homosexual desire is of the heav-
ens. Nevertheless, even the tales of same-sex desire partake of an
unmistakable patriarchal authority, like the story of Zeus' rape of
Ganymede: "nec mora, percusso mendacibus aëre pennis / abripit Iliaden,
qui nunc quoque pocula miscet / invitaque Iovi nectar Iunone ministrat"
[Then without delay, beating the air on borrowed pinions, he snatched
away the shepherd of Ilium, who even now mixes the winecups, and supplies Jove with nectar, to the annoyance of Juno].[8] "Love" here ("amor," l.
155), as in the cases of Pluto and of Orpheus, is entirely a question of the
stronger party's "enjoyment" of the weaker—not just male enjoyment of
female, but the equally patriarchal enjoyment of weaker by stronger (in a

close parallel to the classical citizen's rights over women, boys, foreigners, and slaves): only the eagle—the hunter, not the prey—can embody Jupiter. Ganymede winds up a servant, and Juno is annoyed. Heavenly immortality rather than death in the underworld may be the reward, but the process of getting there is quite similar: we learn no more of Ganymede's feelings than of Eurydice's.

The next song, of Hyacinthus, provides an even closer parallel to the story of Orpheus. Having accidentally killed the human boy in an athletic competition, Apollo mourns him in terms reminiscent of those in which Orpheus mourned Eurydice:

> . . . ego sum tibi funeris auctor.
> quae mea culpa tamen? nisi si lusisse vocari
> culpa potest, nisi culpa potest et amasse vocari!
> atque utinam merito vitam tecumve liceret
> reddere! . . .
> semper eris mecum memorique haerebis in ore.
> te lyra pulsa manu, te carmina nostra sonabunt.

> [I am responsible for killing you. Yet how was I at fault, unless taking part in a game can be called a fault, unless I can be blamed for loving you? I wish that I might give my life in exchange for yours, as you so well deserve, or die along with you! . . . Still you will always be with me, your name constantly upon my lips, never forgotten. When I strike the chords of my lyre, and when I sing, my songs and music will tell of you.][9]

As in the case of Eurydice, being loved soon turns to death, while the lover/killer lives on to mourn the beloved in the poetry of patriarchal authority. It should be added that these songs of Orpheus celebrating the gods' powerful interference in human erotic affairs are the famous ones that enchant the forest trees, wild creatures, etc.: if his earlier song spoke to the world of the dead, these songs speak to the living world of nature, thus serving to naturalize this discursive hegemony of God the Father.

In the case of Orpheus, at least, the feminine gets something of its own back at last: even if the language in which Ovid tells this portion of the story diminishes its threat to his discursive power, the eruption of the feminine into this discourse remains a troubling aspect of Orpheus' myth:

> Carmine dum tali silvas animosque ferarum
> Threicius vates et saxa sequentia ducit,
> ecce nurus Ciconum tectae lymphata ferinis
> pectora velleribus tumuli de vertice cernunt
> Orphea percussis sociantem carmina nrevis.

e quibus una leves iactato crine per auras
"En," ait "en, hic est nostri contemptor!" . . .
cunctaque tela forent cantu mollita, sed ingens
clamor et infracto Berecyntia tibia cornu
tympanaque et plausus et Bacchei ululatus
obstrepuere sono citharae. tum denique saxa
non exauditi rubuerunt sanguine vatis.

[By such songs as these the Thracian poet was drawing the woods and rocks to follow him, charming the creatures of the wild, when suddenly the Ciconian women caught sight of him. Looking down from the crest of a hill, these maddened creatures, with animal skins slung across their breasts, saw Orpheus as he was singing and accompanying himself on the lyre. One of them, tossing her hair till it streamed in the light breeze, cried out: "See! Look here! Here is the man who scorns us!" . . . All their weapons would have been rendered harmless by the charm of Orpheus' songs, but clamorous shouting, Phrygian flutes with curving horns, tambourines, the beating of breasts, and Bacchic howlings, drowned the music of the lyre. Then at last the stones grew crimson with the blood of the poet, whose voice they did not hear.][10]

Once again, this constellation of effects should be familiar: the feminine is here associated with the irrational and with a sound-world entirely different from that of Orpheus. Their musical instruments produce a music that can easily be assimilated to mere clamor, and drowns out the measured, rational—and patriarchal—music of Orpheus and his lyre. Sound here is material and physical, literally beaten out on the female body as on tambourines: the repressed maternal semiotic (in Kristeva's terms) returns with a vengeance, usurping Orpheus' male gaze ("See! Look here!").

It is maternal not only in contrast to the masculine paternalism of God the Father, whose praise the music of Orpheus sings, but more particularly in its similarity to the death of Pentheus, also at the hands of Bacchants, which is narrated earlier in the *Metamorphoses;* recall that Pentheus is dismembered, indeed decapitated, specifically by his mother Agave in Book Three. A similar fate—dismemberment and decapitation at the hands of women—awaits Orpheus. And if the Pardoner has been associated with Bacchus and his female followers by means of gender transgression, he is also associated with their victim by means of dismemberment.

tendentemque manus atque illo tempore primum
inrita dicentem nec quicquam voce moventem
sacrilegae perimunt, perque os, pro Iuppiter!, illud
auditum saxis intellectumque ferarum
sensibus in ventos anima exhalata recessit. . . .

membra iacent diversa locis, caput, Hebre, lyramque
excipis, et—mirum!—, medio dum labitur amne,
flebile nescio quid queritur lyra, flebile lingua
murmurat exanimis, respondent flebile ripae.

[He stretched out his hands toward his assailants, but now, for the first time,
his words had no effect, and he failed to move them in any way by his voice.
Dead to all reverence, they tore him apart and, through those lips to which
rocks had listened, which wild beasts had understood, his last breath slipped
away and vanished in the wind. . . . The poet's limbs were scattered in different places, but the waters of Hebrus received his head and lyre. Wonder-
ful to relate, as they floated down in midstream, the lyre uttered a plaintive
melody and the lifeless tongue made a piteous murmur, while the river
banks lamented in reply.][11]

Washed ashore at Lesbos, Orpheus is finally released into death by
Apollo. The women are punished by Bacchus, who surprisingly appears
here on Apollo's side, abandoning Thrace along with some of his "choro
meliore" [more seemly revellers].[12] The denaturalized women—opposed to rocks, wild beasts, and river banks—have no reverence for Orpheus' patriarchal song, and are duly punished by another aspect of God
the Father—Bacchus this time, in his oddly rational role as Apollo's ally
and avenger of Apollo's poet, Orpheus (recall Evanthius' and Donatus'
references to "Liber pater" [Father Bacchus]). Orpheus himself, however, can magically continue to sing his naturalized song: and those sympathetic rocks, beasts, and banks, endowed with the very symbolic
linguistic skills that the women give up in favor of their irrational
clamor, are more "human" than the human women; that is, they participate in the dominant or hegemonic discourse that the women seek to
disrupt because Orpheus scorned them.

    It is instructive to compare Ovid's version of the myth with Virgil's ear-
lier one in *Georgics* 4, which was also known in the Middle Ages. Although
one must agree with Emmet Robbins' assessment of the evidence that the
Orpheus myth was profoundly misogynous from its earliest origins,[13] Virgil's text may seem to a modern reader distinctly less so than Ovid's. In
Georgics 4, for example, rape is rape, not love: Eurydice is bitten by the
snake and dies while trying to escape from the erotic assault of a character
not present in Ovid, the shepherd Aristaeus. Virgil thus at least hints at a
point of view other than the violently patriarchal in Eurydice's rejection
of heterosexual eroticism, whereas Ovid, though he may displace the scene
of rape from Eurydice's story to Proserpine's, also identifies Orpheus' love
with that of Pluto, thereby aligning the poet with the rapist, and justifying
both in Jupiter's judgment.

Virgil also gives Eurydice her own voice, and what she has to say is not particularly sympathetic to Orpheus:

> illa 'quis et me' iniquit 'miseram et te perdidit, Orpheu,
> quis tantis furor? en iterum crudelia retro
> fata vocant, conditque natantia lumina somnus.
> iamque vale: feror ingenti circumdata nocte
> invalidasque tibi tendens, heu non tua, palmas.'

> ['What is this, what great madness,' she said, 'has destroyed both poor me and you, Orpheus? Now again the cruel fates summon me back, and sleep (of death) drowns my swimming eyes. Goodbye: I am carried off, surrounded by massive darkness, holding out powerless hands to you, alas not yours to have.']¹⁴

It is Orpheus' "furor" that Eurydice directly blames for her second death: her dying breath is not a faint farewell, but a complaint lodged against Orpheus himself. If Virgil allows Eurydice a voice, Ovid takes it away again, not only essentially silencing her, but glossing the one final word he does allow her as an acknowledgment of the power of Orpheus' love. When Eurydice speaks, the scene is necessarily less scopophilic than Ovid's: if for Virgil Eurydice can be the subject of her own language, Ovid turns her into a pure object of Orpheus' vision.

The conclusion of Virgil's version of the story also fails to prepare the reader for Ovid's more misogynous one. Virgil's Orpheus does not embrace pederasty, nor does he sing of the divine patriarchal "love" of boys and the erotic misdeeds of women; instead, he rejects other women because he is mourning Eurydice, and on that basis alone the Thracian women dismember him, in a scene more succinct and less sensationalistic than the one in Ovid. Virgil's Orpheus continues to sing of Eurydice as his dismembered head floats down the river ("Euridicen vox ipsa et frigida lingua, / a miseram Eurydicen! anima fugiente vocabat: / Eurydicen toto referebant flumine ripae" ['Eurydice' the voice and cold tongue called out, 'poor Eurydice' with its failing breath; and the banks along the river echoed back: 'Eurydice']);¹⁵ Ovid's utters only a generalized lament, which Anderson translates less sympathetically than Innes as "something or other tearful."¹⁶

As Anderson has suggested, "Ovid expects his audience to know Virgil's poem and to relish the changes that he the later poet has made."¹⁷ The greater misogyny of Ovid's version, then, is a deliberate choice, and one that has its effect on medieval readings not only of Ovid's own text, but of Virgil's version of the story as well: medieval commentators were well aware of both versions, as is demonstrated, for instance, by the constant ref-

erences to Virgil's in the "Vulgate" commentary on Ovid's;[18] but medieval
Christian allegorizations more often follow Ovid's than Virgil's interpretation of the story.

In Ovid's Orpheus we have the myth of symbolic, paternal discourse,
the rational poetry that praises, and participates in, the patriarchal ideology,
which is naturalized as the hegemonic discourse. It is also, however, the
myth of the return of the repressed to trouble, though not to defeat or destroy, the dominant. Like Julia Kristeva's maternal "heterogeneous," the repressed feminine exists within the paternal symbolic even as it tends to
undermine it. Ovid returns these power relations to their normal, that is,
ideologically untroubled, state. He can do so only through death, however:
the particular nexus of stories revolving around the figure of Orpheus
(those of Eurydice, Hyacinthus, Pentheus, Prosperpine, even Ganymede)
imagines desire as a power relation not to be fulfilled in life.

Medieval readings of the Orpheus myth also find in it issues of gender
and rationality. The most influential reading after Ovid (and one heavily
indebted to him) is that of Boethius in the *Consolation of Philosophy,* which
Chaucer translated into English as *Boece* some time before embarking on
The Canterbury Tales. The story of Orpheus appears in Book Three, metrum
Twelve, and is exclusively concerned with the quality of Orpheus' song
and with his trip to the underworld. The lesson to be drawn from his story,
in Chaucer's version, is as follows: "This fable apertenith to yow alle,
whosoevere desireth or seketh to lede his thought into the sovereyn day,
that is to seyn, to cleernesse of sovereyn good. For whoso that evere be so
overcomen that he ficche his eien into the put of helle, that is to seyn,
whoso sette his thoughtes in erthly thinges, al that evere he hath drawen
of the noble good celestial he lesith it, whanne he looketh the helles, that
is to seyn, into lowe thinges of the erthe" (ll. 60–69). The allegorical interpretation of the Orpheus story that Chaucer chose to translate follows
Ovid's misogynous version of the myth: Boethius, and his translator, here
accept the familiar patriarchal view of the feminine as low, physical, and
earthbound, and of the masculine as lofty and intellectual. Orpheus, not
Eurydice, in this tradition is capable of looking to the "cleernesse of
sovereyn good"; feminine Eurydice represents the "lowe thinges of the
erthe" that tempt masculine Orpheus from his proper spiritual goal.

Similar readings are not unusual in the medieval commentators on the
different versions of Orpheus' myth. Commentators on Boethius (including Remigius of Auxerre, Notker Labeo, Guillaume de Conches, and
Nicholas Trivet), as might be expected, tend to elaborate on his reading of
the story, associating Orpheus with wisdom and Eurydice with perverse desire for earthly things; one such commentator in Chaucer's own century,
Peter of Paris, even blames Eurydice for nagging Orpheus until he killed

her, making the most explicit case for reading Orpheus as his wife's killer but at the same time excusing him and blaming her.[19] But even commentators on other classical texts often follow this tradition. Bernardus Silvestris is clear and representative in this respect: even though his twelfth-century commentary is on Virgil's *Aeneid,* his first mention of Orpheus and Eurydice reflects Ovid's (and Boethius') misogynous view. After explaining that the mythological descent into the underworld has a fourfold meaning (natural, virtuous, sinful, and artificial), Bernardus applies his system to the story of Orpheus: Hell, as in Boethius, represents the things of this world, and Orpheus descends to the physical only in order to transcend it, finding in it, in his function as representative wise man, an opportunity to exercise his intellectual faculties through meditation on a higher, spiritual reality. Eurydice, on the other hand, representing the vicious rather than the wise, is unable to rise above the physical *temporalia.* Bernardus' separation of the two is even more clear-cut than that of Boethius: his masculine Orpheus is not even tempted by the feminine Eurydice.[20]

Bernardus' second mention of the Orpheus myth refers directly to Virgil's *Georgics* 4, which he summarizes, including the character of Aristaeus. Eurydice here initially appears more neutral: not immediately associated with vice, she merely represents natural concupiscence ("naturalis concupiscentia"), or appetite for the good ("boni appetitus"). Oddly enough, however, even this initial positive reading of Eurydice quickly gives way to another: Aristaeus' attempted rape is glossed as divine virtue ("virtus divina"), which attempts to unite itself with this appetite for the good. In fleeing from rape, Eurydice thus flees from virtue, and the serpent's bite infects her with the desire for temporal, rather than eternal, good ("delectatione temporalis boni"). Orpheus, representing wisdom and eloquence ("Per Orpheum sapientem et eloquentem accipimus"), wins her back from the underworld (i.e., wisdom retrieves desire from improper, earthly objects), but only if he does not look back to these tempting *temporalia.*[21] Virgil's relatively positive view of Eurydice in *Georgics* 4 is replaced with an allegory more reminiscent of Ovid's misogynous version in the *Metamorphoses:* once again Eurydice winds up a symbol of perverted desire for earthly things, while Orpheus is glossed as wisdom; and, as in Ovid, rape is glossed as a kind of virtue.

As one might expect, commentaries on the *Metamorphoses* itself follow a similar pattern: for Arnulf of Orléans in the twelfth century, the story is again moralized as one of virtue (Orpheus) and vice (Eurydice). This tradition is more explicitly misogynous than the Boethius commentaries:

mulieres i. muliebriter viventes et viciosos vilipendit, sed amorem suum ad mares i. viriliter agentes transtulit. Unde mulieres eum quia de suo non erant

consortio lapidantes occiderunt s. luxuriose. Mulieres siquidem proniores
sunt in libidinem et vicia quam viri.

[{H}e shunned women, that is, those acting in a womanlike manner, drunk-
ards and vicious men, but transferred his love to men, that is, to those acting in a manly way. Whence, the women, because he shunned them, killed
him by stoning him, that is, they killed him from lust. Women indeed are
more prone to lust and vice than men.][22]

John of Garland's thirteenth-century *Integumenta Ovidii* sums up succinctly: "Pratum, delicie; coniunx, caro; vipera, virus / vir, ratio; Stix est
terra; loquela, lira" [Field is Pleasure, Wife is Flesh, Viper is Poison, / Man
is Reason, Styx is Earth, Lyre is Speech].[23] Fourteenth-century accounts
by Giovanni del Virgilio and Pierre Bersuire and in the *Ovide moralisé* follow suit, the latter two identifying Eurydice with Eve and Orpheus with
Christ, who redeemed mankind from Eve's sin. Eurydice in this view is
Eve accepting the forbidden fruit, as well as the soul and human nature;
all must be redeemed by "orpheus Christus."[24] Mainstream medieval
commentators, in short, whether following Ovid directly or Boethius'
reading of Ovid, consistently accept and elaborate the patriarchal and
misogynous tendencies evident in Ovid's retelling of Virgil's story, ultimately in Chaucer's period identifying the feminine not only with
human desire but with sin, and the masculine not only with wisdom but
with redemption.

Interestingly, this reading of Orpheus is not the only one possible in the
Middle Ages: late antique and early medieval commentators such as Ful-
gentius and Martianus Capella, and their followers, posed an alternate interpretation in which Orpheus is identified simply with poetry or music
and eloquence. In this tradition, it is Orpheus who is ultimately identified
with the physical, material qualities of the voice, while Eurydice comes to
represent the mental or theoretical aspects of music, as in Remigius' commentary on Martianus, which gives quite a different view of the pair than
that found in the same author's Boethius commentary:

Euridice interpretatur profunda inventio. Ipsa ars musica in suis profundis-
simis rationibus Euridice dicitur, cuius quasi maritus Orpheus dicitur, id est
ΩΡΙΟΣ ΦΩΝΗ id est pulchra vox. Qui maritus si aliqua neglegentia artis
virtutem perdiderit velut in quendam infernum profundae disciplinae de-
scendit, de qua iterum artis, regulas iuxta quas musicae voces disponuntur
reducit. Sed dum voces corporeas et transitorias profundae artis inventioni
comparat, fugit iterum in profunditatem disciplinae ipsa inventio quoniam
in vocibus apparere non potest, ac per hoc tristis remanet Orpheus, vocem
musicam absque ratione retinens.

[Eurydice is called profound thought. She is said to be the very art of music in its most profound principles, whose husband is said to be Orpheus, that is orios phone or beautiful voice. The husband, if he loses his singing power through any neglect of his art, thus descends into the lower world of deep study, from which he returns again, the notes of music being arranged according to the rules of art. But when {Eurydice} compares the corporeal and transitory notes to the profound theor$_y$ of the art of music, she—that is, thought itself—flees again into her deep knowledge because she cannot appear in notes; and because of this Orpheus remains sad, having the mere sound of music without possessing the underlying principles.][25]

The existence of this tradition, in which feminine Eurydice takes on the attributes of incorporeal mental processes while masculine Orpheus represents the "corporeal and transitory notes" of "mere sound," is a surprising alternative in medieval thought to the usual association of woman with body and man with spirit. As John Block Friedman argues, this is a less influential tradition than the mainstream one derived from Ovid and Boethius.[26] Yet it does demonstrate that medieval thinkers and writers had an alternative to the more patriarchal versions of the myth available to them. Where, then, does Chaucer position himself with regard to the story of Orpheus?

Chaucer and Orpheus

References to this myth can be found throughout Chaucer's works, and suggest a familiarity with both traditions. In *The House of Fame,* for example, the reference to Orpheus seems clearly derived from Martianus Capella, whose description of the allegorical wedding of Philology and Mercury included entertainment provided by the mythical musicians Orpheus, Arion, and Amphion: "uerum sequens heroum praecluis enituit admiratione conuentus. nam Orpheus Amphion Arionque doctissimi aurata omnes testudine consonantes flexanimum pariter edidere concentum" [A company of heroes that followed after, attracted great wonder and surprise; for Orpheus, Amphion, and Arion, most skillful musicians, were harmoniously playing a moving melody on their golden lyres].[27] Elsewhere, Martianus Capella presents Orpheus singing in praise of marriage generally,[28] and the medieval commentaries on Martianus just discussed also tend to value Eurydice more highly than the mainstream ones.

Chaucer's text also aligns Orpheus with Arion, placing them in the *House of Fame:* "Ther herde I pleyen on an harpe, / That sowned bothe wel and sharpe, / Orpheus ful craftely, / And on his syde, faste by, / Sat the harper Orion . . ." (*HF,* 1200–05). Similarly, the entertainment at the wedding of Januarie and May in *The Merchant's Tale* is compared with that described by Martianus Capella, this time linking Orpheus with Amphion: "Biforn hem stoode instrumentz of swich soun / That Orpheus, ne of Thebes Amphioun, / Ne maden nevere swich a melodye" (IV, 1715–17). The Merchant immediately makes an explicit connection between the two weddings, and hence between his own and Martianus' texts: "Hoold thou thy pees, thou poete Marcian, / That writest us that ilke weddyng murie / Of hire Philologie and hym Mercurie, / And of the songes that the Muses songe! / To smal is bothe thy penne, and eek thy tonge, / For to descryven of this mariage" (IV, 1732–37). In both *The House of Fame* and *The Merchant's Tale,* then, Chaucer refers directly to Martianus Capella and thus implicitly to the alternate tradition for reading the myth of Orpheus.[29]

In both cases, however, the context renders such references highly ambiguous. Clearly the Merchant in particular does not really intend to praise marriage or women, and May hardly turns out to be comparable to either Martianus' Philology or the intellectual Eurydice we encounter in the Martianus commentaries. If Remigius associated Eurydice with mental and spiritual processes, the Merchant invokes that interpretation of the myth only ironically, in order to discredit its relatively sympathetic view of women. The reference to the god Hymen (ll. 1729–31) may refer instead to Ovid's gloomier view of marriage and more misogynous view of women in his version of the myth: recall that in the *Metamorphoses,* Hymen refuses to bless the marriage of Orpheus and Eurydice at the beginning of Book Ten.

The reference to Orpheus and Arion in *The House of Fame* can also be read ironically, especially in view of the cynical understanding of speech and sound investigated in the previous chapter. As noted there, language in this poem tends to be reduced to material sound, that is, to that which Orpheus represents without Eurydice in the commentaries on Martianus Capella. Eurydice herself, representative of the higher poetic faculties, does not appear in *The House of Fame.* And though he invokes Martianus Capella in these texts by pairing Orpheus with either Arion or Amphion, Chaucer could also have known Ovidian versions of the latter two poets' stories: Arion appears in Ovid's *Fasti* 2, ll. 79–118, while Amphion appears in the *Metamorphoses* 6, ll. 178–79. To invoke Martianus Capella and his medieval commentators *ironically,* in short, is to resituate the Orpheus myth in the misogynous Ovidian tradition.

Ovid is invoked more directly in other Chaucerian references to Orpheus. In *The Book of the Duchess,* the Black Knight explains to the Dreamer that he is inconsolable: "May noght make my sorwes slyde, / Nought al the remedyes of Ovyde, / Ne Orpheus, god of melodye, / Ne

Dedalus, with his playes slye . . ." (*BD*, 568–71). The Ovidian text cited explicitly here is the *Remedia amoris*, but the context of the Black Knight's story—his need to stop his unnatural grieving and return to the natural order of things—recalls the *Metamorphoses*, in which Orphean song is explicitly linked to the natural world. This reference is thus an approving citation of Ovid's reading of Orpheus. Similarly, Criseyde refers to Orpheus and Eurydice in Book IV of *Troilus and Criseyde*: "Myn herte and ek the woful goost therinne / Byquethe I with youre spirit to compleyne / Eternaly, for they shal nevere twynne; / For though in erthe ytwynned be we tweyne, / Yet in the feld of pite, out of peyne, / That highte Elisos, shal we ben yfeere, / As Orpheus and Erudice, his feere . . ." (*T&C*, IV, 785–91). Though this passage is another example of Chaucerian irony, the irony here is directed against Criseyde, who will not remain eternally faithful to Troilus. Orpheus' and Eurydice's eternal reunion in the underworld in Ovid's *Metamorphoses* 11 is here understood (by Criseyde if not by Chaucer) as a genuine ideal, but it is one that Criseyde will fail to attain.[30]

Chaucer's direct citations of the Orpheus myth would thus seem to place him in the mainstream, patriarchal Ovidian tradition, even when he invokes the alternative one. Bearing this in mind, let us turn to the more indirect uses of this myth in *The Canterbury Tales*.

In their constant concatenation of song, gender, and bodily fragmentation, both of the pilgrims considered in chapter 5 subtly invoke the myth of Orpheus, whose song, like those of the Pardoner and the Prioress' child hero, is inextricably linked to the singer's dismemberment. The Prioress provides the more overt comparison: her singing hero, like Orpheus, descends into the underworld of the Jewry (and, more literally, of the latrine into which his body is cast) in his pursuit of the feminine—not Eurydice but the Virgin Mary—and is subsequently dismembered by a frenzied religious cult because of his song (Orpheus is dismembered because of his homoerotic refusal to remarry, which is expressed in song). It should be recalled that the child, too, whose virginity is emphasized, represents a rejection of heterosexual desire; and one of Chaucer's favorite authors, Jean de Meun, presents chastity and male-male desire as two equivalent refusals of the procreative function in his own reference to Orpheus, when Genius condemns those who

> Ne ja n'i tendront droite rue,
> Ains vont bestornant la charrue,
> Et conferment les regles males
> Par excepcions anormales,
> Quant Orfeüs vuelent ensivre,
> Qui ne sot arer ne escrivre
> Ne forgier en la droite forge

(Pendus soit il par la gorge,
Qui tex regles lor controuva,
Vers Nature mal se prouva!)

[. . . will never keep to the straight track, but instead go overturning the
plow, who confirm their evil rules by abnormal exceptions when they want
to follow Orpheus (he did not know how to plow or write or forge in the
true forge—may he be hanged by the throat!—when he showed himself so
evil toward Nature by contriving such rules for them).][31]

As Charles Dahlberg points out, Jean de Meun here follows Alan of Lille's
Complaint of Nature, in which the music of Orpheus, far from being naturalized as in Ovid's version of the story, is used as an image of Alan's bête
noir, the "unnatural" erotic coupling of men with men, and is opposed to
the music of Nature herself: Natura says that "[s]olus homo, mee modulationis citharam aspernatus, sub delirantis Orphei lira delirat" [Man alone
turns with scorn from the modulated strains of my cithern and runs deranged to the note of mad Orpheus' lyre]. But whereas Alan "sees Orpheus
as unnatural because of his pederasty, Genius sees 'those who follow Orpheus' as including those who follow a life of chastity."[32]
    The Prioress presents her hero's chastity as heroic, whereas Jean de
Meun's Genius condemns the chaste to a punishment of dismemberment:

    O tout l'escommeniement
Qui touz les met a dampnement,
Puis que la se vuelent aerdre,
Ains qu'il muirent, puissent il perdre
Et l'aumoniere et les estales
Dont il ont signe d'estre males!
Perte lor viengne des pendans
A quoi l'aumoniere est pendans!
Les martiaus dedens atachiés
Puissent il avoir errachiés!
Li grefe lor soient tolu,
Quant escrire n'en ont volu
Dedens les precieuses tables
Qui lor estoient convenables!
Et des charrues et des sos,
S'il n'en arent a droit, les os
Puissent il avoir depeciés
Sans estre jamés redreciés!

[. . . may they, in addition to the excommunication that sends them all to
damnation, suffer, before their death, the loss of their purse and testicles, the

signs that they are male! May they lose the pendants on which the purse hangs! May they have the hammers that are attached within torn out! May their styluses be taken away from them when they have not wished to write within the precious tablets that were suitable for them! And if they don't plow straight with their plows and shares, may they have their bones broken without their ever being mended!]³³

This vision of dismemberment immediately follows the reference to Orpheus, suggesting that for Jean de Meun all those who refuse procreative sexual behavior, the chaste included, deserve Orpheus' fate. The Prioress' hero is also dismembered, but receives a heavenly reward more reminiscent of Orpheus' eventual reconstitution and reunion with Eurydice after death: both are reunited with the female figures they have been pursuing throughout their stories.

The Prioress' child hero, then, is a Christian improvement over the classical Orpheus, who is glossed in one medieval mythographic tradition as a figure for the gaze of wisdom "misdirected toward the dark underworld of *temporalia.* Those earthly delights have misled concupiscence [Eurydice] . . . away from the light of the *summum bonum.*"³⁴ The child's innocent visit to the underworld is instead precisely a quest for the *summum bonum* represented by Mary; his concupiscence is directed rightly. *The Prioress's Tale* thus also corrects the misogyny of Ovid's and most medieval commentators' versions of the Orpheus story, in a manner reminiscent of the alternative tradition proposed by Martianus Capella and his followers. Song, the feminine, and eternal life are conflated in a new form of spirituality rather than separated as in the mainstream Orpheus tradition.

The Pardoner in Parts

The Pardoner, on the other hand, is—as always—a more ambiguous figure in his relation to the Orpheus myth. He lives a life dominated by improper concupiscence (normally represented by Orpheus' desire for Eurydice), but his identification with the Old Man and the three rioters points to a rejection of the feminine, unlike either Orpheus' improper pursuit of it or the Prioress' (and the alternative commentary tradition's) positive transvaluation of it. The Pardoner's connection with Orpheus comes through the refusal of heterosexual procreativity, linked to his possible dismemberment and to his singing: we first meet him singing a love song, but accompanied by the Summoner's "stif burdoun," a song that thus allows us to imagine both male-male desire (though a desire for the feminine is implied elsewhere, as in the Pardoner's encounter with the Wife of Bath) and the Pardoner's possible fragmentation or lack. The terms, however, are now reversed: instead of being dismembered, like Orpheus, as a result of this re-fusal of heterosexual desire, the Pardoner's (possible) refusal is (apparently) the result of his (possible) prior dismemberment, or is at least associated with it. Ironically, the feminine, rejected in his tale and apparently in his erotic object-choice, comes back to haunt him in his very identity. Rather than a Christian improvement on the pagan myth like *The Prioress's Tale,* the Pardoner is a parody of it, or of its usual medieval commentaries, strip-ping away or at least interrogating its usual spiritual significance.

Dismemberment appears almost everywhere the Pardoner turns up in *The Canterbury Tales.* Many of the portraits in the *General Prologue* tend to analyze their subjects as their bodies' component parts, following a com-mon medieval mode of visual description. The portraits of only a few pil-grims, however, dismember them as thoroughly as the Pardoner's. Some phrases give an overall impression of a pilgrim's body without such analy-sis: the "sclendre colerik" Reeve (I, 587), the Prioress who is "nat under-growe" (I, 156), the thin Clerk (I, 288–89), etc. Often the descriptions focus on one or two telling bodily details: the Squire's curled hair (I, 81), the Yeoman's "not heed" and "broun visage" (I, 109), the Prioress' courtly features (I, 152–54), the Friar's "nekke whit" (I, 238), the Cook's "mormal" (I, 386), the Wife of Bath's teeth (I, 468), and so on. A surprising number of pilgrims receive no descriptions of their bodies at all in the *General Pro-logue:* the Knight, the Second Nun and Nun's Priest, the five guildsmen, the Shipman, the Parson, the Plowman, the Manciple.

The fullest analysis or descriptive fragmentation of any pilgrims' bodies is reserved for four of the five low-class men grouped together at the end of the *General Prologue* portraits: the Miller, Reeve, Summoner, and Par-doner. These are also the *General Prologue's* most unattractive physical de-scriptions by conventional fourteenth-century middle-class standards. The Miller's body is analyzed as big muscles and bones, a thick neck ("short-sholdred" [I, 549]), a broad, red beard, a nose further subdivided into the famous hairy wart and wide, black nostrils, a big mouth, and a "golden thumb" (I, 545–66). The Reeve, besides being slender and choleric, has close-shaven hair and whiskers and long, skinny legs (I, 587–92), while the Summoner's diseased face is analyzed as a red complexion, pimples (men-tioned three times, as "whelkes" and "knobbes" [I, 632–33] as well as being part of his "saucefleem" complexion [I, 625]), "scalled browes blake," and "piled berd" (I, 627). This kind of fragmented description seems to be as-sociated with certain anxieties, both social and physical: these are class-bound descriptions of potential violence and disease, emphasizing both social disruption and physical dissolution.

Of all the pilgrims, including these last-described members of the lower orders, the Pardoner is the one who most fully embodies this threat of physical dissolution and fragmentation. He is the only pilgrim who may literally not have all of his body parts: "I trowe he were a geldyng or a mare" (I, 691), however it may be interpreted, carries on its surface the possibility of castration. And his verbal description fragments this body even further, subdividing the Pardoner into yellow hair (which is further subdivided or fragmented into "ounces" and individual "colpons" [I, 675–79]), shoulders (I, 678), glaring eyes (I, 684), lap (I, 686), beardless chin (I, 689–90), and tongue (I, 712). We are not allowed an overall impression of the Pardoner's body as a whole, such as we have of the burly Miller or slender Reeve, but experience it in disconnected bits and pieces.

The fragmentation associated with the Pardoner does not stop at the description of his body; besides being both literally (perhaps) and verbally fragmented, he also carries body fragments with him, the "pigges bones" (I, 700) that he passes off as relics. Fragmentation is, in a sense, his defining attribute.

We hear more about both these bones and his own body in the *Prologue* to his tale. His body, for instance, requires the protection of the bishop's seal on his pardoner's license (VI, 337–38), and he verbally fragments himself, just as the *General Prologue*'s narrator does, emphasizing the apparently independent actions of his neck, hands, and tongue: "Thanne peyne I me to strecche forth the nekke, / And est and west upon the peple I bekke, / As dooth a dowve sittynge on a berne. / Myne handes and my tonge goon so yerne / That it is joye to se my bisynesse" (VI, 395–99). The hands and tongue, especially, seem to take on an existence of their own in this passage, and they return again in lines 413 ("Thanne wol I stynge hym with my tonge smerte") and 444 ("I wol nat do no labour with myne handes"). And, again like the narrator of the *General Prologue*, the Pardoner also emphasizes his attributes of fragmentation, the supposed relics whose bodily and fragmentary nature is emphasized in the repetition of the word "bone":

Thanne shewe I forth my longe cristal stones,
Ycrammed ful of cloutes and of bones—
Relikes been they, as wenen they echoon.
Thanne have I in latoun a sholder-boon
Which that was of an holy Jewes sheep.
'Goode men,' I seye, 'taak of my wordes keep;
If that this boon be wasshe in any welle,
If cow, or calf, or sheep, or oxe swelle
That any worm hath ete, or worm ystonge,
Taak water of that welle and wassh his tonge,
And it is hool anon . . . (VI, 347–57).

The tongue appears yet again in this passage, now the sick cattle's instead of the Pardoner's, along with a desire for wholeness that we may be tempted to impute to the fragmentary Pardoner himself as well as to the cattle's owners. The dominant image here, however, is of dismembered bones: as in the *General Prologue,* these false relics appear as the Pardoner's defining attribute, comparable to the dismembered breasts with which St. Agatha is pictured. His attribute is an image of fragmentation. Yet these bones make the sick animals "hool": wholeness is paradoxically to be achieved through fragmentation; or fragmentation is to give way to an idealized wholeness.

The image of the hand also appears shortly hereafter: "Heere is a miteyn eek, that ye may se. / He that his hand wol putte in this mitayn, / He shal have multipliyng of his grayn, / Whan he hath sowen, be it whete or otes, / So that he offre pens, or elles grotes" (VI, 372–76). Like the tongue in the previous passage, this hand is not the Pardoner's; it belongs to a hypothetical villager who will profit from another relic—once more, imagined fragmentation gives way to an ideal plenitude, and once more we may be tempted to displace this desire for completion onto the Pardoner himself, especially given the references to his own verbally dismembered hands and tongue that follow these passages so quickly.

As we might by now expect, fragmented body parts are also to be found throughout *The Pardoner's Tale* itself: virtually everyone in this story is subjected to verbal or physical fragmentation. Foremost among those who suffer dismemberment is Christ himself, who is repeatedly—obsessively—imagined as being literally torn apart by the three rioters' verbal act of swearing oaths on the parts of his body: "Hir othes been so grete and so dampnable / That it is grisly for to heere hem swere. / Oure blissed Lordes body they totere— / Hem thoughte that Jewes rente hym noght ynough—/ And ech of hem at otheres synne lough" (VI, 472–76); "And many a grisly ooth thanne han they sworn, / And Cristes blessed body they torente" (VI, 708–09). The theoretical basis for such statements is presented in the section of the opening sermon devoted to swearing, and specific examples are given both in the sermon and in other descriptions of the rioters' behavior. Gambling and swearing are related to each other, and both rely on the imagery of bodily fragmentation: "'By Goddes precious herte,' and 'By his nayles,' / And 'By the blood of Crist that is in Hayles, / Sevene is my chaunnce, and thyn is cynk and treye!' / 'By Goddes armes, if thou falsly pleye, / This daggere shal thurghout thyn herte go!' / This fruyt cometh of the bicched bones two, / Forsweryng, ire, falsnesse, homycide" (VI, 651–57). The dice themselves are bones like the Pardoner's relics, but whereas the fruit of the supposed relics is an imagined plenitude, the fruit of these bones is division—both the physical fragmentation threatened in line 655 and the verbal fragmentation of

Christ's body into its component parts of heart and blood. The "nayles" themselves seem in this context to refer at least as clearly to fingernails as to the nails of the Crucifixion, and the "arms" as much to Christ's bodily limbs as to the *arma Christi*.[35] This is the sense in which the rioters tear and rend the body of Christ: "Ye, Goddes armes!" (VI, 692); "I make avow to Goddes digne bones!" (VI, 695). Such linguistic fragmentation is apparently opposed to the type of literal, bodily fragmentation (leading to a hypothetical wholeness or plenitude) in which the Pardoner himself claims to participate in his use of "holy" relics.

Dismemberment in the Pardoner's sermon is not limited to his disquisitions on gambling and swearing; gluttony and drunkenness, too, are imagined in terms of bodily fragmentation. Gluttons, according to the Pardoner, also participate in a sinful pleasure involving dismemberment: "Out of the harde bones knokke they / The mary, for they caste noght awey / That may go thurgh the golet softe and swoote" (VI, 541–43). This is yet another variation on the image of bones, this time imagined as a source of sinfully pleasurable food. The gluttons' punishment at the Pardoner's hands is to be repeatedly dismembered in their turn, his language (and that of St. Paul) reducing them to the organs of digestion and their excretions; one after another, the throat, mouth, and belly each plays its role, the results being belches, farts, and shit:

> Allas, the shorte throte, the tendre mouth. (VI, 517)

> Of this matiere, O Paul, wel kanstow trete:
> "Mete unto wombe, and wombe eek unto mete,
> Shal God destroyen bothe," as Paulus seith. (VI, 521–23)

> . . . of his throte he maketh his pryvee. (VI, 527)

> " . . . wombe is hir god!"
> O wombe! O bely! O stynkyng cod,
> Fulfilled of dong and of corrupcioun!
> At either ende of thee foul is the soun. (VI, 533–36)

In the Pardoner's language nothing is left of the glutton except his organs and his excrement. A similar linguistic fate awaits the "dronke man" (VI, 551), who is reduced, in turn, to disfigured face, sour breath, snorting nose, and wayward tongue (VI, 551–57).

It should be clear by now just how obsessive the imagery of dismemberment—or the dismembered imagery—becomes whenever the Pardoner is speaking or being spoken of. Even in his brief exchange with the Wife of Bath, in the course of her *Prologue,* he seems unable to resist presenting himself as alienated from his own flesh: "I was aboute to wedde a wyf; allas! / What sholde I bye it on my flessh so deere?" (III, 166–67). The figure for this fragmentation and alienation in the *Pardoner's Tale* proper is the Old Man.

As we have seen previously,[36] the Old Man is horribly conscious of his own physical decay. This self-conscious alienation from the body is expressed in imagery of dismemberment that, like his other characteristics examined in chapter 5, links him to the Pardoner's own obsessions and to the Pardoner's own possibly dismembered body: "Lo how I vanysshe, flessh, and blood, and skyn! / Allas, whan shul my bones been at reste? . . . / For which ful pale and welked is my face" (VI, 732–33, 739). Once again the dismembered bones surface, now as a stark reminder of physical dissolution, and once again the Pardoner's language further dismembers the Old Man into his component body parts: flesh, blood, skin, and withered face. This is not an image of death—the Old Man cannot die—but of suffering in life. It seems as if every aspect of life the Pardoner cares to mention— every human activity from the most virtuous to the most sinful—comes to be represented, for him, in terms of bodily fragmentation and alienation: from preaching (in *The Pardoner's Prologue*) and marrying (in *The Wife of Bath's Prologue*), to religious worship (again in *The Pardoner's Prologue*), to eating and drinking, to swearing (in the sermon), to aging (in *The Pardoner's Tale* proper).

An analysis of this kind of imagery in terms of gender must, once again, include Lacan's early writings. The image of the dismembered body, the *corps morcelé,* appears in several key essays devoted to the passage from dependent infancy into the Symbolic order. Lacan argues that the human relation to reality is "altered by a certain dehiscence at the heart of the organism, a primordial Discord betrayed by the signs of uneasiness and motor unco-ordination of the neo-natal months. The objective notion of the anatomical incompleteness of the pyramidal system and likewise the presence of certain humoral residues of the maternal organism confirm the view I have formulated as the fact of a real *specific prematurity of birth* in man."[37] The sense of "anatomical incompleteness" returns in adult dreams and fantasies related to "disintegration in the individual. . . . in the form of disjointed limbs, or of those organs represented in exoscopy, growing wings and taking up arms for intestinal persecutions—the very same that the visionary Hieronymus Bosch has fixed, for all time, in their ascent from the fifteenth century to the imaginary zenith of modern man."[38]

Another early essay of Lacan's asserts that a fixation on this *corps morcelé* is related to an adult aggressivity that seems especially relevant to our reading of the Pardoner: "Among these *imagos* are some that represent the elective vectors of aggressive intentions, which they provide with an efficacity that might be called magical. These are the images of castration, mutilation, dismemberment, dislocation, evisceration, devouring, bursting open of the body. . . ." Lacan also refers to practices that deny "respect for the natural forms of the human body," including fashion and the themes of decapitation and disembowelment in children's play. He suggests that

> [w]e must turn to the works of Hieronymus Bosch for an atlas of all the aggressive images that torment mankind. The prevalence that psychoanalysis has discovered among them of images of a primitive autoscopy of the oral and cloacal organs has engendered the forms of demons. These are to be found even in the ogee of the *angustiae* of birth depicted in the gates of the abyss through which they thrust the damned. . . .
>
> These are all initial givens of a *Gestalt* proper to aggression in man: a *Gestalt* that is as much bound up with its symbolic character as with the cruel refinement of the weapons he makes. . . .[39]

Like Bosch's images, Chaucer's, in those passages devoted to the Pardoner, virtually provide a catalogue of these *imagos* of the *corps morcelé,* and not only, as we might expect, of the image of castration. The "magical" efficacy of images of dismemberment are clearly seen throughout his *General Prologue* portrait, his own *Prologue,* and his *Tale:* in each case supernatural powers are attributed to dismembered bones, be they the supposed relics of the two *Prologues* or the vow sworn to "Goddes digne bones" (VI, 695) with which one of the rioters swears his intention to find and kill Death. Similar supernatural attributes—or invocations of divine assistance—are attached to the other oaths sworn by the rioters, which the Pardoner identifies, as we have seen, as the literal rending of Christ's body—Lacan's images of "mutilation, dismemberment, dislocation, evisceration."

The Pardoner's language in his *Tale* can itself, with its constant linguistic division of bodies into their component parts, be recognized in Lacan's catalogue as well: like Lacan's playing children, the Pardoner's emphasis is on the organs of mouth and belly with their excretions. He performs the same disembowelment in language as they. (And as for decapitation, let us recall only the dismembered face of Christ on the Pardoner's vernicle, as discussed in chapter 4.) And in a reversal of Lacan's reading of Bosch, the Old Man of *The Pardoner's Tale,* in his desire for death, imagines it as another passage through the maternal gates. The Old Man, whose flesh and blood are "vanishing," may recall the dream of a transparent body also recorded by Lacan.[40]

Even Lacan's reading of fashion as an extension of the *corps morcelé* finds its correspondence in the Pardoner who, we may recall from *The General Prologue,* is a fourteenth-century fashion victim: "But hood, for jolitee, wered he noon, / For it was trussed up in his walet. / Hym thoughte he rood al of the newe jet; / Dischevelee, save his cappe, he rood al bare" (I, 680–83). It may not be too far-fetched to relate even the Pardoner's well-filed tongue (I, 712), with which he claims in his *Prologue* to sting his enemies (VI, 413), to Lacan's cruelly refined weapons, understood as another projection of bodily dismemberment, as well to his citation of the "social practice" of incision.

Lacan might find that the Pardoner's fixation on the *corps morcelé* is also given an image in his aggressivity, located in his "recriminations, reproaches, phantasmic fears, emotional reactions of anger, attempts at intimidation,"[41] all amply demonstrated in the Pardoner's relations with both the villagers he fleeces and the other pilgrims, who are not taken in: "So wrooth he was, no word ne wolde he seye" (VI, 957).

Lacan's language in these essays ignores—or represses—gender, but it is present nonetheless. The infantile experience of incompleteness occurs before the mirror-stage allows the anticipatory assumption of a totalizing body-image and eventually of "the armour of an alienating identity, which will mark with its rigid structure the subject's entire mental development."[42] That is to say, though Lacan does not say so, incompleteness and fragmentation are experienced before the disruption of the mother-child dyad by the Law of the Father. Fantasies of dismemberment, like the Pardoner's, represent once again the return of the maternal feminine, which, as we have seen, troubles the assumption of masculine identity. The maternal presence is hinted at in Lacan's references to the infant's "humoral residues of the maternal organism," and perhaps in his characterization of the disintegrating subject as hysterical. For Lacan, a healthy relation to reality demands that the individual move beyond the mother-child continuum into the paternal Symbolic.

On the other hand, Lacan also insists, in "The Subversion of the Subject," that the subject constructed in this movement is illusory. As Bice Benvenuto and Roger Kennedy read it, "One might be tempted to restore the 'total' or 'unified' reality of the subject by counting on the concrete reality of the body; but Lacan considered that even this can be contested, merely by reference to the body in psychotic states of disintegration; or the hysterical and hypochondriacal bodily symptoms, which follow no medical reality; or the body of the infant before it is unified in the mirror image."[43] The illusory unity of the subject is thus marked by lack, "the object which is ungraspable in the mirror, the 'remainder,' the lacking or lost object. The unified body image, which can be grasped in the mirror, is only the 'clothing' or 'phantom' . . . of the lost object."[44] This lack is also associated with castration, and thus "unchains desire, especially desire for what is lacking with regard to the mother, and then what the mother desires."[45] For Lacan, this lack too is represented by

fragmentation, its concrete manifestation *(objet a)* appearing as the eroge-
nous zones,

> the result of a cut *(coupure)* expressed in the anatomical mark *(trait)* of a
> margin or border—lips, 'the enclosure of the teeth,' the rim of the anus,
> the tip of the penis, the vagina, the slit formed by the eyelids. . . . [T]his
> mark of the cut is no less obviously present in the object described by an-
> alytic theory: the mamilla, faeces, the phallus (imaginary object), the uri-
> nary flow. (An unthinkable list, if one adds, as I do, the phoneme, the gaze,
> the voice—the nothing.) For is it not obvious that this feature, this par-
> tial feature, is applicable not because these objects are part of a total ob-
> ject, the body, but because they represent only partially the function that
> produces them?[46]

Once again we may find the feminine and maternal between the lines (and
only between the lines) of this essay: this catalogue of eroticized partial objects represents the mother's lack and desire, and may remind the reader
(though once again Lacan does not say so) of the comparable catalogue of
images of the *corps morcelé* discussed above. And the addition of the
phoneme and the voice (not to mention "the nothing") must remind us
of Julia Kristeva's maternal semiotic. The lost object would seem to be implicitly feminine, and associated with the infant's experience of fragmented
dependency in the presymbolic mother-child continuum.

Feminist scholars following Lacan have provided a cogent critique of
his model by making explicit what remains unsaid in his own essays. Such
commentaries have taken a more and more oppositional stance toward
Lacan's thought in recent years. Jacqueline Rose, in her introduction to a
selection of Lacanian essays originally compiled in 1975, adheres closely to
Lacan in suggesting that the paternal intervention and castration threat that
severs the mother-child dyad need not be identified with a "real" father:

> Castration means first of all this—that the child's desire for the mother does
> not refer *to* her but *beyond* her, to an object, the phallus, whose status is first
> imaginary (the object presumed to satisfy her desire) and then symbolic
> (recognition that desire cannot be satisfied). . . . Thus when Lacan calls for a
> return to the place of the father he is crucially distinguishing himself from
> any sociological conception of the role. The father is a function and refers
> to a law, the place outside the imaginary dyad and against which it breaks.
> To make of him a referent is to fall into an ideological trap. . . . [47]

In that case, why refer to "him" as "father" and in terms of a "phallus?"
Subsequent feminist thinkers have pointed out this slippage in Lacan's
thought between the father and phallus as functions and as referents.[48]

In the 1980s, Jane Gallop, following Laplanche and Pontalis, pointed out that the *corps morcelé* and its discomforts, which apparently precede the illusory assumption of unity in the mirror-stage, can also be read as being produced retrospectively by it: "The mirror stage would *seem to come after* 'the body in bits and pieces' and organize them into a unified image. But actually, *that* violently unorganized *image only comes after* the mirror stage so as to *represent what came before*. What appears to precede the mirror stage is simply a projection or reflection."[49] The disorganized, fragmented body cannot be experienced as such except from the illusory perspective of organization and unity. Gallop uses this insight specifically to criticize Lacan's (and his followers') assumption that the infant's experience of fragmentation is one of insufficiency, anxiety, and anguish that is to be relieved only by the anticipation and ultimate assumption of an identity:[50] "But let us carefully examine the chronology implicit here. The infant is thrown forward from 'insufficiency' to 'anticipation.' However, that 'insufficiency' can be understood only from the perspective of the 'anticipation.' The image of the body in bits and pieces is fabricated retroactively from the mirror stage."[51] If this is so, we might further ask (taking Gallop's argument in a different direction) whether the *corps morcelé* in its connection with the mother could represent a positive lost experience that the alienated subject might desire, and indeed the dissolution of self and body into the maternal is just what the Pardoner's Old Man longs for. The slippage of the Pardoner's anxiously assumed masculine authority toward the feminine and maternal is a troublesome threat, but it is troublesome only insofar as it is also desired.

In the 1990s, feminist philosophers like Jane Flax took up an even more clearly oppositional stance with regard to Lacan. While Flax does not discuss the *corps morcelé* directly, her observations can be applied to Lacan's negative understanding of it.

> Inasmuch as women are associated with the presymbolic, they appear as the repressed within Lacan's theory. Yet like all repressed material they continue to affect the dynamics of the whole self, for to be repressed is *not* to be absent. The repressed is omnipresent as an unconscious force within the psyche and therefore in culture itself. This repressed material cannot be made conscious by Lacan's theory because he relegates it to the presymbolic and therefore to the unspeakable and unknowable. The presymbolic nevertheless haunts both symbolic systems and the subject.[52]

Thus Flax reconceives the presymbolic mother-child continuum as an image of relational plenitude rather than anxiety, anguish, and insufficiency: "Freud's drive theory and Lacan's rereading of it reflect in part an unconscious motive: to deny and repress aspects of infantile experience that are relational (e.g., the child's dependence upon and connectedness with her or his earliest caregiver, who is almost always a woman). Hence in utilizing the concepts of Freud and Lacan, we must pay attention to what they conceal as well as reveal, especially the unacknowledged influences of anxieties about gender on their supposedly gender-neutral concepts."[53] What is needed, then, is a discourse or interpretive strategy of difference rather than a discourse of sameness—or of unity. Such a discourse would value multiplicity and would itself be multiple, fragmentary:

> Masculine discourse is constituted by a binary logic (logocentrism) in which "a law organizes what is thinkable by oppositions." Logocentrism is inextricably connected to phallocentrism. . . . No true difference can exist within (masculine) discourse. The other is always reduced to being the other of the same, its inferior, reflection, "excess," hence still defined by and an extension of it. . . . Hence the insertion of *female* specificity into these discourses would explode the claim of sexual indifference and instead particularize these discourses as masculine. Female particularity would disrupt these unitary and solid discourses. *The same would fragment into multiplicity.*[54]

Fragmentation is here explicitly valued as the return of the repressed female.

Like the Maenads attacking Orpheus for his neglect of the feminine, dismembering his unitary phallic body in a vengeful return of the repressed, these critiques of Lacan dismember his discourse and, in the act of dismemberment, return to that of the neglected feminine and maternal. That which is devalued in both Ovid and Lacan may be revalued in a critique that proceeds from and deconstructs the misogynous text itself. Medieval as well as postmodern commentaries allow this revaluation of the fragmentary and the discontinuous.

Both ways of understanding bodily fragmentation—that which regards it with horror and that which embraces it—would have been familiar to late medieval readers, as several recent accounts by Caroline Walker Bynum have eloquently demonstrated: "Resurrection was asserted by theologians and believed by ordinary Christians both because bodily fragmentation was not really a threat and because it was!"[55] Bynum argues on the one hand that bodily fragmentation was, for example, a sign of damnation as represented in the visual arts: "[S]alvation is wholeness, damnation is decay and partition. . . . [T]he damned are represented in a state of fragmentation that is a symbolic expression of their sins. Heaven is associated with wholeness, Hell with partition; redemption is regurgitation and reassemblage."[56] Similarly, religious, legal, and medical discourse all imagined an association of fragmentation with sin and crime. Since decay and decomposition were associated with sin, saints and other holy persons were sometimes thought to resist the partition of their corpses, reassembling their own relics and protecting their bodies from interference.[57] Legally, torturers were forbidden to sever the body, and only the most abhorrent crimes were to be punished by bodily mutilation and dismemberment. Leprosy could be regarded as an expression of sinfulness because it caused the body's spontaneous fragmentation.[58]

On the other hand, bodily fragmentation was practiced more enthusiastically in the late Middle Ages than ever before. The dissection of corpses for various medical purposes had been introduced by the early fourteenth century; at the same time, the German practice of dismembering and distributing the corpses of rulers and aristocrats for political purposes (the *mos teutonicus*) was becoming more widely accepted.[59] Most significant for the Pardoner is the widespread traffic in relics, the fragmented and preserved body parts of the saints.

These two readings of fragmentation are not simply symmetrical alternatives: as Bynum demonstrates, the enthusiastic pursuit of bodily partition beginning in the twelfth century should not be understood as a rejection of the ideal of wholeness, but as another way of pursuing it as an ultimate goal in the body's resurrection. (Recall the Pardoner's fantasized passage from the relics' fragmentation to an imagined plenitude.) Modern feminist thinkers revalorize the Maenads' work, finding in fragmentation the return of the repressed feminine. In the later Middle Ages, however, beginning in the twelfth century, fragmentation might also be understood as an assertion of patriarchal power. The *mos teutonicus* mentioned earlier is a good example: "By 1200, especially north of the Alps, the bodies of prominent ecclesiastics or nobles were often eviscerated, boned, or boiled after death, and the resulting parts were buried in several places near several saints." [60] In other words, fragmentation could be a patriarchal privilege: this particular form of dismemberment was reserved exclusively for secular and ecclesiastical leaders. Far from only revalorizing the feminine, fragmentation in its medieval context could just as well reassert patriarchal wholeness. Bynum finds in this practice only one example of a more general enthusiasm for bodily partition and distribution "made possible by the confidence in ultimate victory over it. By the twelfth century, bodies were divided in order to bestow their power more widely, to associate them with disparate human communities; they were divided because they were crucial to, and therefore distributed, self."[61] Medieval fragmentation, then, can represent not a Lacanian dissolution of self, but the confidence that self will remain; regardless of the condition of our bodies on earth, they will be reassembled and perfected in Heaven—by God the Father. Both the horror of fragmentation and its enthusiastic pursuit, then, can be assimilated to the same patriarchal unity, earthly or heavenly.

In Heaven, in fact, the body's earthly defects will be repaired. By Chaucer's period, even by the thirteenth century, according to Bynum, "most thinkers held that each person possessed a *caro radicalis* (a core of flesh) formed both from the matter passed on by parent or parents to child and from the matter that comes from food. It was this *caro radicalis* that God reassembled after the Last Judgment. . . . If matter is somehow missing, the power of God must make up the deficit by miracle."[62] If the Pardoner is a castrated eunuch on earth, his original flesh will be supplied in Heaven. One might ask, though, whether this divinely supplied matter includes flesh that ideally should be part of one's physical makeup even if it was never part of the actual body in question: if the Pardoner is to be understood as a *eunuchus ex nativitate,* for instance, will his missing organs still appear at the Resurrection? Aquinas, John of Paris, and Durandus of St. Pourçain would seem to think so: God will use whatever is needed to make "a perfect human body."[63]

Earthly fragmentation, then, can be read, and by the fourteenth century was likely to be read, consciously at least, as expressing not the return of the repressed feminine but rather a confidence that it will ultimately be overcome: the monolithically patriarchal unity will be reasserted in Heaven, and earthly dismemberment is merely a preparation for it, even a privilege. The Pardoner's discourse is undoubtedly unitary and expressive of the church's masculine authority; his obsessive catalogues of body fragments are filled with disgust, with the anguish and sense of insufficiency that Lacan associates with the presymbolic and that we might expect of the subject whose masculine identity is so anxiously and repeatedly assumed and reassumed, and for whom feminization is an ever-present threat. In that sense the Pardoner is striving toward the unified, phallic body promised to be resurrected in Heaven. The linkage of his dismembered body to the supposed saints' relics of his *Prologue* and to the body of Christ in his *Tale* make this desire for wholeness especially clear: after the Last Judgment these are the selves who will be resurrected in perfect bodily form.

The Pardoner, however, is no saint. Although his attempts at bodily authenticity and completion in the *Prologue* ("That shewe I first, my body to warente" [VI, 338]), like his identification with the "relics," imply a longing for the perfectly masculine resurrection body, one that in Heaven would not require the anxious veiling explored earlier, the Pardoner is unlikely to achieve that unified and phallic physical being. As Bynum also points out, in the late medieval imagination, "[w]hether or not fragmentation or diminution is characterized as significant (or even in fact as occurring) depends not on what happens to the body physically but on the moral standing of the person to whom the bodily events pertain."[64] The

Pardoner's moral standing seems unlikely to get him to Heaven, though in his *Prologue* he does make some claims for the moral efficacy of his preaching: "Thus kan I preche agayn that same vice / Which that I use, and that is avarice. / But though myself be gilty in that synne, / Yet kan I maken oother folk to twynne / From avarice and soore to repente. / But that is nat my principal entente; / I preche nothyng but for coveitise" (VI, 427–33); "For though myself be a ful vicious man, / A moral tale yet I yow telle kan, / Which I am wont to preche for to wynne" (VI, 459–61). The claim to morality here resembles his claim to masculinity: neither can really be justified in their aspirations to states of perfection that the Pardoner fails to achieve even as he paradoxically lays claim to them. This idealized and ultimately rejected morality, masculine "virtue," is directly related to the equally idealized, masculine, phallic resurrection body, which is thus similarly beyond the Pardoner's reach; and the fragmented body is also the feminized body in an age that could conceive of the female as an imperfect or defective male.[65] His moral status condemns him to an eternity of fragmentation like the damned souls depicted in the visual representations of Hell and the Last Judgment examined by Bynum,[66] an eternity of longing for perfection (in both senses)—an eternity that has, for the Pardoner, already commenced. If fragmentation is a return of the repressed feminine, that return is marked by disgust and rejection, and thus serves as a reinforcement of the patriarchal values so prized by the Pardoner. From this perspective the Pardoner resembles not the fragmented hero of *The Prioress's Tale,* whose resurrection is foretold by the Virgin Mary, but the villainous Jews, who are the ultimate victims of legal dismemberment: "Therfore with wilde hors he dide hem drawe, / And after that he heng hem by the lawe" (VII, 633–34), a connection reinforced by the similarities between the Pardoner's stand-in, the Old Man, and the Wandering Jew.[67]

Nevertheless, it cannot be denied that the discourse of fragmentation is also, paradoxically, a discourse of desire, most nakedly in the Old Man's longing for a final dissolution and return to Mother Earth, but also in its association of fragmentation with the divine and the magical: the Pardoner's various bones are an attempt (one that he claims not to believe but which he nevertheless constantly reasserts) to redeem (his own?) bodily fragmentation, to find in it the source of maternal plenitude Flax discovers instead of—or in addition to—the anxiety of the illusory subjectivity emphasized by Lacan. It should not be forgotten that the Pardoner's anxious assertions of masculinity are also marked by a desire for union with the feminine, for instance in his *Prologue:* "I wol noon of the apostles countrefete; / I wol have moneie, wolle, chese, and whete, / Al were it yeven of the povereste page, / Or of the povereste wydwe in a village, / Al sholde

hir children sterve for famyne" (VI, 447–51). The desire for "moneie" here
quickly becomes the desire for more homely goods ("wolle") and for the
physical nurture represented by "chese, and whete," whether they come
from a boy or a woman, and the interchangeability of boys and women
may remind us once again of Orpheus: the "page" and the "wydwe" are
equally feminized as sources of nourishment for the needy Pardoner. His
insatiable, infantile desires here place him in the position of the hypothetical widow's children: he will take their place and be nourished by their
mother while they starve. This passage is a strange and disturbing amalgam
of, on the one hand, an asserted masculine privilege, dominating the page
and widow with typical phallic authority and, on the other, an all-con-
suming need for this representative, nurturing mother. The Pardoner's fragmented self seems to need both; the assertion of phallic, masculine
wholeness depends upon this desire for the feminine.

   The lines immediately following may also remind us of the Orpheus
myth: "Nay, I wol drynke licour of the vyne / And have a joly wenche in
every toun" (VI, 452–53). The constellation of these multiple wenches and
the wine he drinks with them might recall the Maenads, the Dionysiac
revelers who effect the dismemberment of Orpheus, but the Pardoner's
participation in their revels suggests that unlike the mythic singer, this
singing Pardoner desires the frightening, disorderly feminine. Once again,
unexpectedly, the assertion of masculine control is shown to be dependent
upon the very feminine that it also represses.

   The Old Man of *The Pardoner's Tale* makes these hidden relationships
clear. I argued earlier that the Old Man, though troubled by a desire for
the maternal, is ultimately another means by which the Pardoner reasserts
patriarchal authority. Here I would like to emphasize the troubling maternal itself, the feminine that is desired even as it is repudiated. The Old Man,
as we have seen, tries to fulfill this desire in the wrong way, through a patriarchal economic exchange: "Mooder, with yow wolde I chaunge my
cheste / That in my chambre longe tyme hath be, / Ye, for an heyre clowt
to wrappe me!" [VI, 734–36]). But despite his faulty approach to the feminine, this sentiment itself also bespeaks his desire to have done with the
symbolic world of money and to enfold himself in the maternal body: literally in a body, a shroud made of hair to be provided by the mother. The
feminine folds of the haircloth replace, in the Old Man's imagination, the
money–chest of paternal inheritance and economic exchange.

   And it is the Old Man who furnishes most directly the essential connection between bodily fragmentation and the desire for the feminine. His
return to Mother Earth is imagined as physical dissolution: "And on the
ground, which is my moodres gate, / I knokke with my staf, bothe erly and
late, / And seye 'Leeve mooder, leet me in! / Lo how I vanysshe, flessh, and

blood, and skyn! / Allas, whan shul my bones been at reste? . . . '" (VI, 729–33) The body that returns to the womb is the fragmented, disorganized body, the body before it assumes its illusory phallic unity. The Old Man thus represents an alternative to the idealized masculine resurrection body to be united with God the Father in Heaven: his desire is, instead, for a maternal resting place for his bones, for a feminine dissolution of the body itself into Mother Earth rather than the masculine perfection of the body by the Heavenly Father. The Old Man as stand-in for the Pardoner suggests, perhaps, the Virgilian rather than the Ovidian myth of Orpheus: here the Pardoner, dismembered singer, sings in his dismembered state of his longing for the feminine.

The union of masculine and feminine in a single body, or the dissolution of masculine into feminine, would hardly have been regarded as desirable by most medieval thinkers: the phallic resurrection body is the *desideratum*. As Alan of Lille demonstrates, gender ambiguity is a source of tremendous anxiety in the erotic just as it is in the grammatical realm.

Alan's specific complaint against Orpheus is not simply his introduction of male-male desire, but the conjunction of sodomy with the crossing of cultural and grammatical gender boundaries:

Solus homo, mee modulationis citharam aspernatus, sub delirantis Orphei lira delirat. Humanum namque genus, a sua generositate degenerans, in constructione generum barbarizans,Venereas regulas inuertendo nimis irregulari utitur metaplasmo. Sic homo, Venere tiresiatus anomala, directam predicationem per compositionem inordinate conuertit.

[Man alone turns with scorn from the modulated strains of my cithern and runs deranged to the notes of mad Orpheus' lyre. For the human race, fallen from its high estate, adopts a highly irregular (grammatical) change when it inverts the rules of Venus by introducing barbarisms in its arrangement of genders. Thus man, his sex changed by a ruleless Venus, in defiance of due order, by his arrangement changes what is a straightforward attribute of his.][68]

Alan, here once again, conflates erotic practice, gender (including, but not limited to, grammatical gender), and even anatomical sex: the sodomites are "tiresiatus," referring to the sex changes undergone by the seer Tiresias (and thus rightly translated by Sheridan as "sex changed"). Similar conflations of sex, gender, and erotic practice are not uncommon in high medieval discussions of sodomy, for example in Peter Damian's *Liber Gomorrhianus:* "Quis de clerico facit pellicem, de masculo mulierem?" [Who will make a mistress of a cleric, or a woman of a man?].[69] The continued influence of this tradition in the fourteenth century, and specifically among the authors Chaucer is known to have read, has been documented by McAlpine and more recently by Keiser.[70]

The Pardoner's association with the feminine in his voice and body might, therefore, raise the possibility of unauthorized erotic practices as well. The Pardoner's imaginary union of male and female, masculine and feminine, in one body—the longing for a state in which the sexes and genders are not differentiated—would have hinted at sodomy to a fourteenth-century audience. And the problem of his eroticism would have been intensified by his association with the Orpheus myth. If, as I have been arguing, Chaucer refers primarily to the mainstream medieval Orpheus tradition, derived from Ovid, rather than the alternate, Virgilian tradition, then we should explore the role that male-male eroticism plays in this connection as well.

Ovid's Orpheus, we may recall, assimilates male-male desire to the hegemonic discourse of patriarchy. His Ganymede and Narcissus are, like Eurydice, feminized victims of divine, authoritative masculine desire. The love of God the Father is primarily a relation of power that brings servitude and death to the beloved, who then becomes the subject of an ordered, patriarchal poetry whose function, for Ovid, is to naturalize this power relation. Masculine and feminine, then, are united not in the powerful male lover, whose desire feminizes its object regardless of anatomical sex, but only in the powerless, feminized objects themselves, such as Narcissus and Ganymede. For Orpheus (and, as we have seen, for the mainstream tradition of medieval Orpheus commentaries in which Chaucer places himself), this desire for the male is imagined specifically as a rejection of the female and of feminine characteristics. Women—the Bacchants—get something of their own back in the dismemberment of Orpheus, but Ovid punishes them and restores Orpheus to a position of scopophilic power over Eurydice in the underworld.

In this context, the Pardoner's apparent combination of sodomy and dismemberment suggests that he is marked by the fragmentary, disordered feminine.[71] Like Orpheus, he appeals to the divine—the Christian Logos represented by the vernicle—for restoration to wholeness and phallic authority. Unlike Orpheus, however, the Pardoner does not receive the divine guarantee of wholeness that he seeks. Instead, his gender confusions leave him in the position of powerlessness, a position that becomes explicit when he is exposed and humiliated by the Host. Such a position is foreshadowed in the receptive sodomitical role he plays with the Summoner: the episode with the Host re-imagines their sodomitical relationship as humiliation.

In the Pardoner's case, then, the link with sodomy is as troubling as his other gender confusions. It does figure the Orphic rejection of the "inferior" feminine characteristics that we find in the commentaries: we should recall here that only one of the Pardoner's songs is a love song; the other is an offertory, which, while he does use it primarily for its acoustic effects, nevertheless signals his participation in the masculine worlds of the church and economic exchange. But this connection to phallic masculinity is at best tenuous. The link with sodomy also implies that his anxiously repeated attempts to reject the feminine merely disguise a deeper longing for it. This feminization is marked on his very body and in the possibility of his erotic relations with the Summoner.

To return to the question that opened this chapter: What does any of this have to do with Chaucer's poetry? Like Orpheus and the Pardoner, Chaucer too is a poet/singer, creator, as he writes in the *Retraction,* of "many a song and many a leccherous lay" (X, 1086). He is also a feminized, and even a sodomitical, figure, according to Jane Chance's discussion of *The House Of Fame:* "Like the figure of Ganymede, the ravished figure of 'Marcia' suggests, on one level, the possibility of Chaucer's homosexuality, on another, his psychological identification with and insistence on female or feminized texts and textuality, and on yet another, his understanding of the passive feminized role of the contemporary vernacular poet who must bear the weight of Latin tradition."[72] The textual fragmentation and feminization of Chaucer's literary corpus, and the Pardoner's role in these processes, will be the subject of my concluding chapter, where I will also show that it is this troubling gender ambiguity that is taken up and exploited by subsequent authors who make use of Chaucer's figure of the Pardoner.

CONCLUSIONS

THE PARDONER IN AND OUT
OF *THE CANTERBURY TALES*

How lyketh you, by John, the Pardoner? (Spurious link)

In

We may regard the Pardoner and the Prioress as two different, if not opposed, possibilities for the feminine and maternal in language, but, because Chaucer left *The Canterbury Tales* in a fragmentary and apparently unfinished state, the question of where these two pilgrims' tales stand in relation to each other in the text has never been answered satisfactorily. It is a question of considerable importance, since the order in which we read the tales would necessarily affect our interpretation of *The Canterbury Tales* as a whole.[1] How, specifically, are we to understand the very different perspectives on gender and language offered by the Pardoner and the Prioress? Did Chaucer identify himself more with one position or the other? If he did, which of the two represents Chaucer's own thoughts? The unfinished, fragmentary nature of *The Canterbury Tales* itself complicates even further any attempt to specify Chaucer's own already ambiguous views on gender.

The interesting question of Chaucer's intentions, then, is not one that can be constructively resolved, but some speculation on the status of Chaucer's own poetic language with regard to these two opposed visions of gender and poetry is irresistible. Chaucer's own poetic corpus is as fragmentary as the bodies of the Pardoner and of the Prioress' hero—and of Orpheus. The *membra disiecta* of *The Canterbury Tales* itself are also a *corps morcelé,* composed in bits and pieces over the course of a lifetime, and, because they are poetry that belongs to a fragmented *corpus,* hint at connections with all three of these singers. Critics have regularly proposed that

Chaucer identifies himself with the Pardoner as the Pardoner identifies himself with his own literary creations (the three rioters, the Old Man),[2] but I would also claim that the fragmentary nature of the poetic *Tales* itself is reflected in the fragmentary singing bodies I have been examining in the last few chapters. *The Canterbury Tales* questions univocal paternal (or patriarchal) authority in its very fragmentation, a fragmentation that opens a space for the Kristevan semiotic or heterogeneous, which is to say for the feminine—a space that, however, may be closed down as soon as it is opened. Is this feminization to be taken seriously, as in *The Prioress's Tale,* or is it ironic, as in the *Pardoner's*?

That *The Canterbury Tales* has a fragmentary structure is hardly a new observation: the unfinished text was left in a state of disarray at Chaucer's death, and was tidied up (in different ways) by those who followed. The two manuscripts usually considered closest to the author's intentions, Hengwrt and Ellesmere, disagree in their arrangement of the surviving fragments, each fragment, consisting of one or more tales and the links among them, set off from the others by the absence of such links. One of the most venerable critical traditions is to try and arrange the fragments in the order Chaucer supposedly intended. A second and equally important tradition, however, has argued that Chaucer had no final intentions in this matter, and that there is thus no correct order for the fragments.[3] Even the individual fragments themselves, one might argue, were still in a state of flux at the author's death: as is well known, for instance, the epilogue to *The Man of Law's Tale* (II, 1163–90) implies that another tale was to follow it in the same fragment, which results, in certain manuscripts, in some shifting of tales from other fragments.[4] This kind of indecision is not unusual for Chaucer: many of his works were abandoned in fragmentary form, including *The House of Fame, Anelida and Arcite, The Legend of Good Women,* and several of the individual *Canterbury Tales* themselves. Interestingly, the first tale told by the Chaucerian persona himself, *The Tale of Sir Thopas,* is one (like *The Monk's Tale*) whose fragmentary status is clearly intentional: famously, the Host interrupts the pilgrim Chaucer's "rym dogerel" (VII, 925) in the middle of a line (VII, 918), forcing him to leave his tale unfinished. *The Monk's Tale,* though interrupted by the Knight as *Sir Thopas* is by the Host, is nevertheless, in another sense, finished: it consists of a series of "tragedies" all of which, including the last, "Cresus," are complete; while the Monk might have added to the series endlessly, in terms of structure it is as finished as it could ever be, even in its interrupted form, as the concluding *Explicit Tragedia* demonstrates—there is no "*explicit*" at the end of *Sir Thopas.* We might argue, then, that in this case Chaucer deliberately identifies himself with the fragmentary: his own tale is the one, of all *The Canterbury Tales,* that is left unfinished by design.

Under the circumstances, one might well imagine that *The Canterbury Tales* itself could have remained fragmentary even if Chaucer had lived longer.

We might place the fragmentary *Tales* not only in the context of Chaucer's other fragmentary works, but also in the larger context of medieval textual fragmentation. Consider the importance of a number of unfinished medieval texts: Chrétien's *Chevalier de la charrette* (completed, the text tells us, by Godefroy de Leigni) and *Conte du Graal* as well the *Conte's* unfinished continuations; Guillaume de Lorris' *Roman de la rose* (completed and expanded by Jean de Meun); and Gottfried von Strassburg's *Tristan,* to name a few beyond *The Canterbury Tales* itself. Consider also the apparently finished major texts treated as if they were fragments by being continued, either by the same or another author: the *Lancelot-Grail* (or *Vulgate*) Cycle; and, contemporary with Chaucer, Langland's *Piers Plowman.*

In such a situation it seems sensible to pursue A. J. Minnis' call for "an aesthetic of the unfinished," or, better, an aesthetic of the fragment, which would, as Minnis puts it, "celebrate" alternative possibilities, especially for the arrangement of *The Canterbury Tales'* fragments, rather than reducing them to unity.[5] Jerome Mandel has provided the most exhaustive analysis of the *Tales* as "essentially fragmentary," arguing for the unity of each fragment, and thus, implicitly for the most part, for a view of Chaucer's text as inherently open-ended and unfinishable.[6] Mandel's main concern is with the unity of the links, not the fragmentary nature of *The Canterbury Tales;*[7] this section of my conclusion will approach the *Tales* in terms of its fragmentariness and of the implications of poetic fragmentation for gender (and vice versa).

The "dismemberment of Orpheus" has famously been linked to poetic fragmentation by Ihab Hassan in his book of that title—a book that does not concern itself with medieval literature, but was, rather, among the first to attempt a definition of literary postmodernism. Nevertheless, if the postmodern has its roots in earlier periods, Hassan's observations may strike us as further evidence of this possibility. For example, Hassan's "postface" (written for the second edition of his book in 1982) lists a number of "postmodernist" characteristics that we have encountered as problems in *The Canterbury Tales,* especially as regards the Pardoner: "Antiform (disjunctive, open)" as opposed to "Form (conjunctive, closed)"; "Play" as opposed to "Purpose"; "Process/Performance/Happening" as opposed to "Art Object/Finished Work"; "Decreation/Deconstruction" as opposed to "Creation/Totalization"; "Dispersal" as opposed to "Centering"; "Text/Intertext" as opposed to "Genre/Boundary"; "Rhetoric" as opposed to "Semantics"; "Combination" as opposed to "Selection"; "Polymorphous/Androgynous" as opposed to "Genital/Phallic"; and "Difference-Differance/Trace" as opposed to "Origin/Cause," among others.[8]

Note how many of Hassan's "postmodern" categories are concerned with fragmentation and with an aesthetic of the unfinished: a disjunctive or open "antiform," play, process, dispersal, difference (or differance), etc., as well as an opposition to the finished, the totalized, the bounded, the semantically meaningful: just the characteristics we have observed in association with that unfinished subject-in-process, the Pardoner. These characteristics can also, like the Pardoner, be linked to a problematic of gender, as in Hassan's category of the polymorphous or androgynous, especially as it is opposed to the phallic and genital. In the Pardoner's case, however, these categories, particularly as they relate to the ambiguous categories of gender, are problems to be negotiated, not values to be embraced, as in Hassan's postmodernism.

But Hassan here is discussing literary texts, not characters, and from that point of view the Pardoner may be seen as emblematic of Chaucer's text itself. That is to say, *The Canterbury Tales* may also be regarded as a negotiation between the whole and the fragment, the finished and the unfinished—for that matter, between the phallus and "this sex which is not one" (or perhaps "these sexes").[9] David Greetham has recently described the possibility of a gendered approach to medieval textuality in general. This approach would take *écriture féminine* as a model to help us understand the unfinished, multiple nature of manuscript *mouvance* or variance, rather than attempting, using a unitary, phallic model, to reduce this variance to a single, authoritative text. Drawing on the work of Kristeva, Irigaray, Wittig, and Cixous, Greetham concludes his paper with a series of unanswered questions:

> . . . [W]e might take Irigaray's challenge in both *This Sex Which Is Not One* and *Speculum of the Other Woman* to confront both sameness and difference, repression and authority, hierarchy and delegation, in a textual environment in which these concepts have often been taken as unexamined *donnas* of editorial practice: for example, is there a textual space to accommodate Irigaray's claim that the genital formation of woman (the two lips of the vulva as opposed to the one-eyed monster of the phallus) creates a "mystery that woman represents in a culture claiming to count everything, to number everything by units" . . . so that "*She is neither one nor two*"? What are the implications of this feminist a-numerical thesis to the editing of such textual dualities as the opposed witnesses of *The Owl and the Nightingale* or the F and G versions of the Prologue to *The Legend of Good Women,* or even for "one-eyed" witnesses like the *Beowulf* manuscript or the works of the *Pearl* poet?[10]

Not only the unitary, phallic "one," but also the very notions of numbering, authority, arrangement, and hierarchy, which form the unexamined theoretical basis of "modern" print textuality ("modern" here signifying, for Greetham, a temporary historical moment between the premodern and the postmodern), are called into question by *écriture féminine*—and in a way that claims a particular applicability to (premodern) medieval manuscript textuality (and to Chaucer).[11] Citing Cixous, specifically on the topic of writing, he goes on to speculate about the relevance of her "anti-linear, discursive, multiply orgasmic writings" to the "heterogeneity" of medieval manuscript compilations.[12] The feminine (or *féminine*), orgasmic overflow of fluids "coming to writing" opposes multiplicity, the heterogeneous, and disorder to the unitary principles of order and hierarchy that modern, print-oriented editors seek to impose on medieval miscellanies. The answer to Greetham's unanswered questions would seem to be that the heterogeneous and feminine ("heterogeneous" thus, perhaps, specifically in Kristeva's sense) may be more characteristic of medieval (or premodern) manuscript textuality than the masculine order that traditional "modern," print-oriented scholarship can recognize.

As Greetham argues, Irigaray ultimately valorizes the fragmentary, though she initially regards feminine nonphallic multiplicity as possibly the result of the denial of feminine sexuality: "Must this multiplicity of female desire and female language be understood as shards, scattered remnants of a violated sexuality? A sexuality denied? The question has no simple answer. The rejection, the exclusion of a female imaginary certainly puts woman in the position of experiencing herself only fragmentarily, in the little-structured margins of a dominant ideology, as waste, or excess. . . ."[13] While Irigaray's critics accuse her of biological essentialism,[14] passages like this one speculate that the feminine as fragmentary may also be a cultural construction, a response to patriarchal oppression. Her view here does seem transhistorical, but only because patriarchy has been a transhistorical phenomenon; this reading of the feminine with the fragmentary may well be, in that case (and perhaps Irigaray would argue that it is), as relevant to the Middle Ages as to the twentieth century.

Nevertheless, Irigaray also asks "if the female imaginary were to deploy itself, if it could bring itself into play otherwise than as scraps, uncollected debris, would it represent itself, even so, in the form of *one* universe? Would it even be volume instead of surface? No."[15] The "female imaginary" would necessarily resist the universalizing tendency of the masculine, because for Irigaray, female sexuality, "always at least double, goes even further: it is *plural*."[16] Thus "[w]oman's desire would not be expected to speak the same language as man's; woman's desire has doubtless been submerged by the logic that has dominated the West since the time of the Greeks."[17] Her language is therefore fragmented and uncontainable by masculine logic. "Hers are contradictory words, somewhat mad from the standpoint of reason, inaudible for whoever listens to them with ready-made grids, with a fully elaborated code in hand."[18] From this perspective, Minnis' fragmentary aesthetic would necessarily also be an aesthetic of the feminine.

Cixous' famous 1975 essay "The Laugh of the Medusa" links *écriture féminine* to the fragmentary by way of the female body, invoking, in a fashion that may remind us of the Pardoner's concern with dismemberment, "[m]y eyes, my tongue, my ears, my nose, my skin, my mouth, my body-for-(the)-other" and declaring that

> [i]f there is a "propriety of woman," it is paradoxically her capacity to de-propriate unselfishly, body without end, without appendage, without principle "parts." If she is a whole, it's a whole composed of parts that are wholes, not simple partial objects but a moving, limitlessly changing ensemble, a cosmos tirelessly traversed by Eros, an immense astral space not organized around any one sun that's any more of a star than the others.[19]

Cixous never abandons this early interest in the relationship of parts to wholes: her 1993 essay "The School of Roots" describes the *écriture féminine* of Clarice Lispector as "[a] tangling, of arms, legs, kinds, and species as well as spheres, perspectives, and experiences"; Cixous' own writing has been described as "festive fragments elaborated from scenes heralding points of the female body."[20] Parts that are wholes, a moving, limitlessly changing ensemble: the female body as imagined here by Cixous resembles the *mouvance* of a medieval manuscript text, whose varying versions may also multiply endlessly. It may not be too fanciful to find here a reflection of such fragmentary texts as *The Canterbury Tales,* literally composed of parts that are wholes and that can be, and have been, arranged and rearranged in accordance with differing principles of order and hierarchy. One must ask, then, if such a text can be said to obey any given principle of order: Derek Pearsall's proposal for a "loose-leaf" edition of *The Canterbury Tales,* in which the fragments could be placed in any order the reader chose, responds to this impulse against unitary hierarchical principles: "This is how, ideally, it should be presented, partly as a bound book (the first and last fragments are fixed) and partly as a set of fragments in a folder, with the fragmentary information as to their nature and placement fully displayed."[21] Such a text would correspond to Cixous' understanding of feminine writing (which, despite its links with the female body, is not limited to biological women)[22] as "sweeping away syntax":[23] "No, I-woman am going to blow up the Law: an explosion henceforth possible and ineluctable; let it be done, right now, *in* language. . . . It's not to be feared that language conceals an invincible adversary, because it's the language of men and their grammar. We mustn't leave them a single place that's any more theirs alone than we are."[24] "Men and their grammar" should be familiar to us from Alan of Lille's fulminations against sodomy as ungrammatical. But it is not only the possibly sodomitical Pardoner who violates Alan's grammatical propriety; perhaps more tellingly, *The Canterbury Tales* itself, in its very fragmentation, violates the unitary syntactical structure of narrative, opening up multiple possibilities of arrangement and hence of interpretation.

As regards the Pardoner, his fragmentary subjectivity and obsession with dismemberment (and his possibly dismembered body) find their textual reflection in the *membra disiecta* of *The Canterbury Tales* itself. In fact, *The Pardoner's Tale* belongs to the fragment of *The Canterbury Tales* that most clearly demonstrates the text's fragmentary nature, the so-called floating fragment.[25] Most of the fragments (aside from Fragment I, the obvious beginning, and Fragments IX and X, usually considered a single unit and the more or less obvious ending) can be found in a variety of placements in different manuscripts, but Fragment VI, in addition, includes no internal evidence to relate it to any other fragment or to assist in placing it in any given position on the Canterbury pilgrimage. The references to the Wife of Bath (Fragment III) by the Clerk (Fragment IV), for example, imply that IV follows III, and in a number of manuscripts, including Ellesmere, the Host's speeches at the end of Fragment IV and the beginning of Fragment V are presented as continuous, perhaps making IV and V another unit. References to time and to geography also allow at least some speculation as to where Fragments II, VII, and VIII fit.[26]

Fragment VI, however, includes no such indications. Although editors, beginning with fifteenth-century editors in the decade following Chaucer's death, have tried to fix its position with regard to the other tales, the very multiplicity of attempts to do so serves primarily to underscore the fragment's unattached status. The Pardoner, in short, cannot be stabilized textually any more than he can be fixed in terms of gender: he floats unanchored through the text of *The Canterbury Tales*. To return to the question with which this chapter began, then: How does this variation in the placement of Fragment VI affect the relationship between the Prioress' and the Pardoner's visions of gender?

Depending on where in the text the two tales are found with respect to each other, *The Pardoner's Tale*—if, as the "Bradshaw Shift" would have it, it follows *The Prioress's Tale*—may function as a cynical parody of the Prioress' desire to assert a feminine/maternal (or semiotic) spiritual language. In this reading, Chaucer would use the Pardoner to reassert patriarchal values in opposition to the Prioress' attempt at asserting a feminine or maternal poetics. The feminine would be repressed in *The Canterbury*

Tales as it is repressed in the Pardoner's own anxious gender-identity formation. Or it would be exposed, like the Pardoner himself in his encounter with the Host at the end of his Tale, as merely a lack, an inferior position within the hegemony of medieval—Chaucerian—patriarchy.

If, on the other hand, as in the Ellesmere order, *The Pardoner's Tale* precedes *The Prioress's Tale,* the latter may function as an idealized corrective to the Pardoner's cynicism. In this reading, the Pardoner's hidden, nostalgic longing for the feminine, repressed in his own performance, would ultimately be manifested and revalorized in the Prioress' feminine poetic language. The Pardoner would thus be exposed, not so much as lacking masculinity, but rather as insufficiently feminine in his attempts to repress the maternal and to assert phallic authority. This failure of the feminine would, then, be rectified (if not for the Pardoner, then for *The Canterbury Tales* as a whole) by the introduction of the Prioress and her feminized—and valorized—hero, as well as the Virgin Mary, representing a comforting return of the repressed.

The fragmentary status of Chaucer's text makes the choice between these two positions, and thus the question of Chaucer's own intentions, undecidable—like so many other questions regarding Chaucer's own position with regard to so many other issues addressed in *The Canterbury Tales.* And yet the very undecidability of Chaucer's intentions, reflected in the indecisive fragmentation of his text, may itself—if Greetham is correct in invoking *écriture féminine* as a model for medieval textuality—provide an alternative way of understanding the relationship of gender to Chaucer's poetics. In this regard it may be useful to recall that Chaucer identifies his persona within *The Canterbury Tales* with both the fragmentary *Sir Thopas* and the *Melibee,* with its female wisdom figure, Dame Prudence; that is to say, the pilgrim Chaucer is himself both masculine and feminized.

Susan Bordo, like other gender theorists, has recently suggested that masculinity itself needs to be reconceived, and her observations seem particularly relevant to the Pardoner and to *The Canterbury Tales* in general. As a corrective to Irigaray's declaration that the female is "*ce sexe qui n'en est pas un*" (in opposition to the unitary, phallic masculine sex), Bordo argues that we may also imagine that the male sex—at least as represented by real, individual men—"*n'en est pas un*" either, especially if we use the penis rather than the phallus as our synecdoche for masculinity:

> The phallus is haunted by the penis. And the penis most definitely is *not* one. It has no unified social identity (but is fragmented by ideologies of race and ethnicity). Rather than exhibiting constancy of form, it is perhaps the most visibly mutable of bodily parts; it evokes the temporal not the eternal. And far from maintaining a steady will and purpose, it is mercurial, tempera-

mental, unpredictable. . . . Far fresher insights can be gained by reading the
male body through the window of its vulnerabilities rather than the dense
armor of its power—from the "point of view" of the mutable, plural penis
rather than the majestic, unitary phallus. This is not to deny the formidable
social, historical, and cultural actualities of male dominance, but to reveal the
ways in which that dominance maintains not only the female body but the
male body as a place of shame, self-hatred, and concealment.[27]

The penis is male/masculine; however, it is not one but plural, "fragmented." We may recall that the Pardoner's continuous, anxious self-con-
struction as "masculine" could be described in similar terms: his
masculinity, signified by the masculine pronoun "he," is assumed as phallic,
but seems to be constantly on the verge of dissolving into the penile (in
Bordo's sense). We may recall that it is his testicles, not his penis, that seem
to be in question, but regardless of which organs the Pardoner is or is not
missing, the penis seems a more appropriate synecdoche for him than the
phallus. He himself is mutable, plural, temperamental, vulnerable, without
"a unified social identity" despite his ongoing attempts to construct one.
And "phallic dominance"—represented by the Host—maintains the Pardoner's body as "a place of shame, self-hatred, and concealment" (recall that
the threat of exposure is what ultimately silences the Pardoner).
   The title of Bordo's essay, "Reading the Male Body," imagines the body
as a kind of text, and the fragmentary text of *The Canterbury Tales* itself may
also benefit from the penile point of view. From this perspective, Chaucer's
book embodies in a more positive form the mutability, openness, and vulnerability manifested as shame in its figure of the Pardoner. An aesthetic of
the fragment—an acceptance or, in Minnis' term, even a "celebration" of
fragmentariness—allows us to value, in the poetic text, what the Host, and
the Pardoner himself, find shameful in a person. "Modern" (i.e., neither
premodern nor postmodern) editors who attempt to fix the order of *The
Canterbury Tales*' fragments continue to imitate those flawed characters,
anxiously seeking a phallic textual unity, which, like the Pardoner's phallic
masculinity, is never—and can never be—finally achieved. Bordo's essay
has the great virtue of substituting for an idealized, fantasized masculinity
the actual, fluctuating, fragmentary experiences of real bodies. It allows us
to perceive Chaucer's bodies of discourse, his poetic *corpus* or *membra
disiecta,* as real bodies too, in all their material disunity, and provides a basis
in gender theory for the open, plural medieval textuality—and for an undecidable text of *The Canterbury Tales*—described respectively by Greetham
and by Pearsall.
   The undecidability of such a text would not be limited to the order of
the fragments. Greetham, referring specifically to the Pardoner, also asks

whether postmodern editors of premodern texts might allow all variant readings an equal voice:

> We might consider whether some of the accusations made by Monique Wittig against the culture of the *Straight Mind* do not have *textual* ramifications: for example, what does the charge that the "straight mind" [that] promotes a "tendency toward universality . . . cannot conceive of a culture, a society where heterosexuality would not order not only all human relations [sic] but also its very production of concepts and all the processes which escape consciousness as well" *mean* for "unstraight" or "queer" textualities? Could one of the ramifications be whether the cultivation of *difference* as a marker ("good" and "bad" readings and witnesses, "authentic" and "untrustworthy" testimony, and so on) is just one of the more blatant textual exemplifications of the bipolar, bicameral, structuralist mentality that still produces so many of our editions of medieval texts.[28]

If "the straight mind" is a structuralist mentality of binary differences or oppositions—in textual terms, of good vs. bad readings—then it would seem that a queer textuality, one that opposes, in Wittig's terms, the heterosexual culture of difference in favor of a culture of sameness or "similitudes," would value all readings equally. The very concept of the difference between "good" and "bad" readings would be seen as analogous to—what is, according to Wittig—the politically motivated concept of the difference between "man" and "woman" (a difference Wittig seeks to abolish).[29]

In that case, a queer textuality might revalorize textual variants that are usually ignored or discarded. Where the Pardoner is concerned, these variants are of considerable interest for a queer reading. To look only at the first two lines of his *General Prologue* description, for example, the Pardoner is described—in most editions—as "gentil" (I, 669); but a variant reading, present in two manuscripts (Paris Anglais 39 [Ps] and Cambridge Gg.4.27 [Gg]) describes him not as "gentil" but as "ioly." "Ioly" or "joly" has a number of possible connotations in Chaucerian usage, including "merry" or "cheerful"—but also including both "lusty" or "amorous" and "pretty" or "attractive." Similarly, the following line says he is the friend and "compeer" (I, 670), or familiar, of the Summoner. One manuscript, though—Ps again—calls him, instead, the Summoner's "feere," a term Chaucer uses elsewhere to mean "companion"—or "mate," or "spouse." Thus, whereas the standard editions of Chaucer introduce the Pardoner as the Summoner's gentle companion, these variant readings, especially occurring together as in Ps, might be understood to introduce him as the Summoner's amorous mate or spouse. Furthermore, whereas most editions have the Pardoner singing, in his duet with the Summoner, "Com hider, love, to me" (I, 672), in three manuscripts (New College D 314

[Ne], Northumberland [Nl], and Trinity College Cambridge R.3.15 [Tc²]) he sings "com hider leue grom"—the term "groom" referring, in all its possible meanings, to a specifically male person. A queer textuality, then, valuing all readings equally, even if they occur in only one or two manuscripts, might find a greater intimacy between the Pardoner and the Summoner asserted at the outset of the Pardoner's description, and thus also find further support for the sodomitical reading of the "stif burdoun" line (I, 673).[30]

This pursuit of a queer text of *The Canterbury Tales* could be continued, as regards the Pardoner, beyond the *General Prologue* and into the Pardoner's *Prologue* and *Tale,* and perhaps even into his appearance in *The Wife of Bath's Prologue.* If queering the text means, as Greetham proposes, refusing the good-bad distinction and revaluing *all* variant readings (not only those that increase the number of references to same-sex desire), then the text of *The Canterbury Tales* as a whole might be queered by paying attention to all such neglected readings. These are tasks for other occasions, however. For now, it should suffice to point out that medieval, and specifically Chaucerian, textuality, like Hassan's postmodern textuality, is plural or multiple, like the real male and female bodies theorized by Bordo—and like the Pardoner. The author and the text cannot make the Pardoner speak univocally in their language; but in some sense, the text can be made to conform to the Pardoner's own disjunctive voices, voices that expose the plural, disjointed linguistic constructions that govern sex, gender, and sexual practices and that to some extent are still embedded in modern discourses on gender. As Wittig insists, language is material, it is of the body.[31] All discourse or textuality will therefore inevitably escape and even deconstruct the ideal fantasy of the phallus.

If one way to queer the text is to revalue variant readings that were probably not produced by the singular author Chaucer, but that were produced by readers or copyists within the discourse of Chaucerian textuality (perhaps, in the cases examined above, in response to their own understandings of the Pardoner), another way to queer the text would be to revalue all the later non-Chaucerian additions to that discourse. (This might also mean revaluing editions such as John Urry's usually scorned 1721 *Works of Geoffrey Chaucer,* which printed for the first time the spurious tales of *Gamelyn* and *Beryn*).[32] If the Pardoner floats unanchored through the text of *The Canterbury Tales,* it is also true that he cannot even be contained by *The Canterbury Tales* itself. He also floats entirely out of it and into later works by other authors. The remainder of this book will examine, in terms of gender, the Pardoner's literary afterlife, both in the fifteenth-century pseudo-Chaucerian additions to *The Canterbury Tales* and in later literature.

Out

The Pardoner does have a literary life after Chaucer, though often not in the cultural texts where one might expect to find him. Although Pasolini's famous (or infamous) film of *The Canterbury Tales* includes his version of *The Pardoner's Tale,* the Pardoner himself is nowhere to be found in it—perhaps surprisingly, given Pasolini's interest in alternatives to heterosexuality. Neither is the Pardoner to be found in such offerings as George Dyson's choral work *The Canterbury Pilgrims,* a musical setting of selections from Chaucer's *General Prologue* (perhaps less surprisingly, given Dyson's "Merrie Englande" nostalgia, which might have some difficulty accommodating the Pardoner's troubling gender ambiguity). Nevertheless, a number of literary texts, appropriately outside the mainstream, do respond to Chaucer's Pardoner.[33]

The earliest responses are to be found in the fifteenth-century additions to, and continuations of, *The Canterbury Tales.* In one way or another, all of those that mention the Pardoner seem to be attempts to "normalize" him. Most famously, he attempts a sexual encounter with a woman, Kit the tapster, in the *Canterbury Interlude* that precedes the spurious *Tale of Beryn* in Northumberland MS 455. But other post-Chaucerian additions are also of considerable interest.

A number of spurious passages, for example, are designed to link together various fragments of *The Canterbury Tales.* Several such links specifically connect Fragment VI, the "floating fragment" that contains *The Pardoner's Tale,* with other tales, thus attempting to fix the Pardoner more firmly in place in the text than Chaucer did; that is, to render both the Pardoner and *The Canterbury Tales* more univocal and authoritative than Chaucer left them. The British Library MS Lansdowne 851, dated to the 1410s, includes two such links, attaching Fragment VI to *The Canon's Yeoman's Tale* on the one hand and to *The Shipman's Tale* on the other, though neither one mentions the Pardoner.[34]

Fragment VI is attached to the same tales with different links in several other manuscripts, the earliest of which is dated to the 1420s.[35] That which links the Pardoner to the Shipman uses Chaucerian language but ignores the Pardoner's humiliation by the Host that concludes *The Pardoner's Tale:*

> "Now frendes," saide oure Hoost so deere,
> "How lyketh you, by John, the Pardoner?
> For he hath unbokeled wel the male;
> He hath us told right a thrifty tale
> As touching of mysgovernaunce.
> I pray to God, geve hym good chaunce.
> As ye have herde of thise riotoures thre,

Now gentil Maryner, hertly I pray thee,
Telle us a good tale and that right anone."[36]

This link attempts to normalize the Pardoner not only in terms of the
structure of *The Canterbury Tales,* but also in terms of the character's place
in the company of pilgrims: the Host here approves of his tale and prays
that he should have "good chaunce"; the vicious hostility that marked
their previous relations is here entirely glossed over. The use of the terminology of the "male" that is to be unbuckled, however, harks back, first,
to the Pardoner's own problematic "male" and his invitation to the Host,
at the end of his tale, to "[u]nbokele anon thy purs" (VI, 945), the invitation that so infuriates the Host with its possible erotic implications. It may
also, however, remind us of the Host's response to *The Knight's Tale* ("un-
bokeled is the male" [I, 3115]), where "male" is also rhymed with "tale."[37]
Intentionally or not, tale-telling is here associated with unauthorized
erotic activity—but in a way that assimilates the Pardoner to the Knight,
that representative of phallic authority.

More interestingly ambiguous is Lydgate's "Prologue" connecting his
Siege of Thebes to *The Canterbury Tales* (dated to the early 1420s), which
conflates the Pardoner with the Summoner in his brief description of the
former: "And ek also with his pylled nolle, / The Pardowner, beerdlees al
his chyn, / Glasy-eyed, and face of Cherubyn, / Tellyng a tale to angre with
the Frere. . . ."[38] As the editor of this text points out, it is the Pardoner
whom Chaucer describes as beardless and glassy-eyed (I, 684–690), but it
is the Summoner who has a "piled berd" and "cherubynnes face" (I,
624–27) "symptomatic of venereal leprosy" and who tells a tale to anger
the Friar (III, 1665–2294).[39] The conflation of the two figures is an interesting one: apparently Lydgate associated the Summoner's venereal disease
with the Pardoner's beardlessness. The sexual anomalies of both characters—in *The Canterbury Tales* proper, possible partners in sodomy—are here
brought together in the Pardoner. Though Lydgate does not reproduce the
Chaucerian implications about the Pardoner, he nevertheless remains a
troubling character in specifically sexual ways, though one who troubles
Lydgate's text only briefly and disappears immediately.

The most important of the post-Chaucerian additions, for our purposes, is the "Canterbury Interlude" itself, which has been connected to
the Canterbury jubilee of 1420.[40] This fabliau-like story follows up on the
Pardoner's own claims of heterosexual desire in *The Wife of Bath's Prologue*
(III, 166) and in *The Pardoner's Prologue* (VI, 453); in it, he lustfully pursues
Kit the tapster, and we have the narrator's words, not only the Pardoner's
own, for his erotic desire: "He wold be logged with hir—that was his hole
entencioun."[41] Again, the addition fails to make good on Chaucer's

sodomitical suggestions about the Pardoner (though he still associates with the Summoner), and the impulse is toward normalization in that sense.

However, at the heart of this "Interlude" lies a battle for possession of the phallus—a battle that the Pardoner loses. At the pilgrims' initial arrival in Canterbury, the Pardoner "toke his staff to the tapstere,"[42] and he never does get it back. The central scene concerns a fight for this staff between the Pardoner, who is trying to get into Kit's bedchamber in order to secure her favors in return for the money he has spent on her, and her "paramour." Kit is a transgressive female, whose unladylike behavior requires an apology from the narrator:

> Ye woot wele I ly nat, and where I do or no,
> I woll nat here termyn it, lest ladies stond in plase,
> Or els gentil women, for lesing of my grace
> Of daliaunce and of sportes and of goodly chere.
> Therefor, anenst hir estates I woll in no manere
> Deme ne determyn, but of lewd Kittes
> As tapsters and other such that hath wyly wittes
> To pik mennes purses and eke to bler hir eye;
> So wele they make seme soth when they falssest ly.[43]

The narrator, like the Pardoner, wishes to please ladies and therefore declares that only lower-class women like Kit can be accused of this transgressive behavior, though the discussion of his motive for doing so allows for the possibility that he believes all women to be similarly transgressive. Kit's transgression, it immediately appears—the behavior for which the narrator condemns her—is specifically gender transgression: she appropriates, by means of her lover, the Pardoner's phallic staff and uses it against him:

> Kit began to render out al thing as it was,
> The wowing of the Pardoner and his cost also,
> And howe he hoped for to lygg al nyght with hir also—
> But therof he shall be siker as of Goddes cope!—
> And sodenly kissed hir paramour and seyd, "We shul
>   sclope
> Togider hul by hul as we have many a nyghte,
> And yf he com and make noyse, I prey yew dub hym knyght."
>   "Yis, dame," quod hir paramour, "be thow nat
>   agast.
> This is his own staff, thow seyest; thereof he shal
>   atast."[44]

The circumstances plainly reveal what is really at stake here. The Pardoner has been both tricked out of his money and displaced sexually (and the linkage of the two demonstrates just how carefully the author of this interlude must have read Chaucer's text). The sign of this sexual displacement is specifically the Pardoner's staff, which has passed from the Pardoner himself to Kit and now to his replacement in her bed, the paramour. Not only has Kit appropriated the phallus and passed it to her lover, but the two here conspire to use it against its original possessor: his "own staff" becomes the tool of his sexual humiliation. The euphemistic reference to dubbing him knight may recall as well the Pardoner's earlier sexual humiliation at the hands of the Host, when order of a sort was restored by the Knight; but in this case the knight exists only in Kit's ironic language, and no one will restore the Pardoner's status.

The Pardoner's symbolic castration is completed in the ensuing fight for the phallic staff:

"In soth," quod he, "I woll nat from the dorr wend
Tyll I have my staff, thou bribour!"—"Then have the toder
          end!"
Quod he that was within, and leyd it on his bak,
Right in the same plase as chapmen bereth hir pak.
And so he did too mo, as he coude arede,
Graspyng after with the staff in length and eke in
          brede,
And fond hym otherwhile redlich inowghe
With the staffes ende highe oppon his browe.[45]

There is no contest, really: the paramour, following Kit's instructions, takes possession of the Pardoner's phallic staff and beats him with it. The Pardoner is reduced to using a ladle as a weapon, with a pan on his head for a helmet.[46] Nor does his humiliation end there: he winds up spending the night in a kennel, terrorized by the tavern dog. Like Chaucer's own Pardoner, the Pardoner in this interlude is threatened with further dismemberment (by the dog), signaling his symbolic castration: "The warrok was awaked and caught hym by the thy / And bote hym wonder spetously, defendyng wele his couch, / That the Pardoner myght nat nere hym nethere touch, / But held hym asquare by that other syde / As holsom was, at that tyme, for tereing of his hyde."[47] The Pardoner even bears the signs of this symbolic castration upon his own body, as the paramour tells the innkeeper: "[a]nd eke of his own staff he bereth a redy mark";[48] the Pardoner's own phallus is used as the very weapon that castrates him. Ironically, this dismemberment is precisely what the Pardoner wished upon Kit when he discovered her appropriation of the phallus: "'A! Thy fals body!' quod he. 'The devill of hell thee tere!'"[49]

This interlude, then, is of considerably greater interest in terms of gender roles and the possession of the phallus than merely as a demonstration

that late medieval readers understood the Pardoner as motivated by heterosexual desire. It stands at the beginning of the Pardoner's post-Chaucerian afterlife, a tradition in which the Pardoner consistently appears as the
marker of gender transgression.[50]

A sixteenth-century play by John Heywood, *The Four P.P.,* addresses the
issue of gender (among other topics) even more directly. This brief, and
very funny, interlude, dated possibly to the 1520s, depicts a satirical debate
among three "P"s—a Palmer, a Pardoner, and a Pothecary—as to who shall
have mastery over the others, a competition to be judged by the fourth "P,"
a Pedlar.[51] It has been noted since the nineteenth century that Heywood
is clearly indebted to Chaucer for the figure of the pardoner:[52] like
Chaucer's Pardoner, Heywood's shows off his spurious relics to the others
in an attempt, or a pretended attempt, to convince them of the benefits to
be obtained from him by acknowledging his spiritual superiority and by
making an appropriate payment. Also like Chaucer's Pardoner (in the
episode with the Host that concludes *The Pardoner's Tale*), Heywood's pardoner specifically invites the others to kiss his relics.

> And here be relics of such a kind,
> As in this world no man can find,
> Kneel down all three, and when ye leave kissing,
> Who list to offer shall have my blessing.
> Friends, here shall ye see even anon
> Of All-Hallows the blessed jaw-bone,
> Kiss it hardily with good devotion.[53]
>
> Nay, sirs, behold, here may ye see
> The great-toe of the Trinity:
> Who to this toe any money voweth,
> And once may roll it in his mouth,
> All his life after, I undertake,
> He shall never be vexed with the toothache.[54]
>
> Here is a relic that doth not miss
> To help the least as well as the most:
> This is a buttock-bone of Pentecost.[55]

Heywood's humor is broader and more clearly farcical than Chaucer's.
Even if this pardoner's relics were genuine, they would be ridiculous (he
treats feast-days as if they had bodies, and goes on to offer "a slipper / Of
one of the Seven Sleepers" and "an eye-tooth of the Great Turk.")[56] And
whereas Chaucer makes the Host draw the connection between his Pardoner's relics and unclean body parts ("Thou woldest make me kisse thyn

olde breech, / And swere it were a relyk of a seint, / Though it were with thy fundement depeint!" [VI, 948–50]), Heywood's pardoner himself quickly assimilates his own relics to the lower bodily strata, descending rapidly in the scale of impurity from jawbone to toe to buttock-bone. The Pothecary, like Harry Bailly, consistently makes the unclean physicality of these "relics" explicit, declaring of All-Hallows' jawbone, for example, "[y]e were as good kiss All-Hallows' arse"[57] and, of the buttock-bone of Pentecost, that "[t]his relic hath beshitten the roast."[58] But this pardoner himself also says that kissing his relics will provide physical rather than spiritual pleasure, referring to the "pleasure" and "savour" of the slipper.[59]

A generally merry tone prevails throughout *The Four PP:* this pardoner is no worse a humbug than the Pothecary or the Palmer, and he escapes the humiliation imposed on Chaucer's Pardoner. He also displays none of the poignant complexity or gender ambiguity that continue to fascinate readers of *The Canterbury Tales* and that have been the subject of this book. But Heywood's debt to Chaucer extends beyond a satirical exposure of the uncleanness that masquerades as spirituality.

The final relics to which Heywood's pardoner refers are relics of Eve: a box full of bees that stung her as she tasted the forbidden fruit, and the ale drunk at her wedding to Adam. These "relics" introduce the theme of gender, and specifically the theme of female transgression: "Here is a box full of humble bees, / That stang Eve as she sat on her knees, / Tasting the fruit to her forbidden."[60] The second half of the play is concerned with judging which of the three disreputable "P"s is the best liar, and all three compete with lies about dangerous women. The Pothecary, in his role as healer of the body, claims to have cured a woman of epilepsy by means of a suppository inserted in her "tewel" that she expelled with such violence that it destroyed a castle.[61] The Pardoner, in his role as healer of the soul, counters this tall tale of physical salvation with one of spiritual salvation: he claims to have traveled to purgatory and to hell in order to rescue the soul of a female friend, one Margery Coorson; as it turns out, the devils were happy to get rid of her, since women cause them so much more trouble than men. In return, the Pardoner claims, he had to promise to save as many women's souls as possible, so the devils should no longer have the trouble of dealing with them:

Now, by our honour, said Lucifer,
No devil in hell shall withold her;
And if thou wouldest have twenty mo,
Wert not for justice, they should go.
For all we devils within this den
Have more to do with two women,

> Than with all the charge we have beside;
> Wherefore, if thou our friend will be tried,
> Apply thy pardons to women so,
> That unto us there come no mo.
> To do my best I promised by oath;
> Which I have kept, for, as the faith goeth,
> At this day to heaven I do procure
> Ten women to one man, be sure.[62]

The Palmer eventually wins the lying contest by telling the ultimate lie: that he has never seen a woman "out of patience."[63]

In other words, this play is about the establishment of a patriarchal or phallic hierarchy among three (or four) men: the Pedlar determines that the Pardoner and the Pothecary must serve the Palmer. But this hierarchy is established by judging what the men say about women: women are excluded from the hierarchy, and from the play, but an obsession with female transgression, with women going out of bounds, is the very reason both the play and the hierarchy it creates exist. Women do not appear in this play because it represents the female as that which cannot be contained in proper language, just like the sodomite in the *Complaint of Nature* and *The Canterbury Tales*. In the world of this play, women transgress the concept of a unitary, true discourse: they can appear here only negatively, in self-declared lies.

Even the narrative lies of the Pothecary and the Pardoner suggest that women are transgressive, and cannot be defined or contained. The women in these stories are comically destructive of all male attempts at closure, judgment, and limitation. Margery Coorson cannot be contained in hell because she figuratively makes it too hot for the male devils; her place in hell is in the kitchen, where she creates excessive heat: "For many a spit here hath she turned, / And many a good spit hath she burned; / And many a spitful hot hath roasted, / Before the meat could be half roasted."[64] Margery is therefore set loose from hell, and left to wander the open spaces of this world: "And so we departed on Newmarket-heath. / And if that any man do mind her, / Who lists to seek her, there shall he find her."[65] Margery's spirit has no resting place, even in hell: she remains on earth, apparently in a dangerous, material, bodily form attractive to men, but nevertheless still a spirit, and one that roams the heath rather than remaining at rest. Margery, in short, transgresses all boundaries: those between this life and the afterlife and between body and spirit, as well as geographical boundaries. She even manages to escape the divine "justice" that the devil mentions.[66]

In the Pothecary's lie, too, women are depicted as destroying masculine strongholds, this time with their powerful "tewels." (The insistence on the power of the fart may, of course, be another sign of Heywood's indebtedness to Chaucer.) Woman's bodily health is here directly related to the destruction of phallic power represented by the castle: when his patient expels her suppository or "tampion," the walls of masculine containment come tumbling down:

> Now mark, for here beginneth the revel:
> This tampion flew ten long mile level,
> To a fair castle of lime and stone,
> For strength I know not such a one,
> Which stood upon an hill full high. . . .
> But when this tampion at this castle did light,
> It put the castle so fair to flight,
> That down they came each upon other,
> No stone left standing, by God's Mother! . . .
> So was this castle laid wide open,
> That every man might see the token.
> But in a good hour may these words be spoken
> After the tampion on the walls was wroken,
> And piece by piece in pieces broken.
> And she delivered with such violence
> Of all her inconvenience,
> I left her in good health and lust;
> And so she doth continue, I trust.[67]

The Pothecary's female patient appropriates phallic power to her own body, which is described as a cannon for firing the "tampion": "For when I had charged this ordnance, / Suddenly, as it had thundered, / Even at a clap loosed her bombard."[68] And this appropriation effectively destroys the symbols of phallic male power: the strong castle on a high hill is reduced to its constituent parts, and is laid open in a passive, feminized position. The literally explosive female body destroys unitary masculine authority: it is no wonder that this power cannot be contained in a unitary truth. And this destruction of masculine values is directly related to feminine well-being: this woman's body returns to robust health only when it expels the male-imposed "tampion" and destroys the castle.

Heywood's Pardoner and Pothecary thus both acknowledge female bodily power; but they do so in a comic mode that reduces women *only* to their bodies, to their unmanageability and uncontainability. The term "revel" at the beginning of the Pothecary's speech just quoted implies that what follows should be considered carnivalesque: in Bakhtin's sense, a moment of liberatory laughter in which high (the masculine castle on a hill) and low (the feminine "tewel" and its "tampion") change positions and in-

vert the power relations of class, gender, etc. Bakhtin's critics, however, have
often pointed out that carnival is not only liberating: these inversions are
themselves contained by the carnival's sanctioned position within official
culture, and, furthermore, an exchange of power positions does nothing to
subvert the power structure itself. Here the anatomically female has merely
taken over the traditional male role (phallic and penetrating in the cannon
imagery), while the castle is given the traditionally female (open and passive) role.[69] Heywood's characters thus both recognize the power of the
feminine and, as representatives of established authority, police it with
satire. And while these two stories are presented as lies, in the world of this
play they are closer to the truth of women than the opposite point of view
voiced by the Palmer, who specifically disagrees with the Pardoner:
"Whereby much marvel to me ensueth, / That women in hell such shrews
can be, / And here so gentle, as far as I see. . . . / Yet in all places where I
have been, / Of all the women that I have seen, / I never saw nor knew
in my conscience / Any one woman out of patience."[70] The Palmer, presented throughout as a naive and simple character in contrast to the cynical Pardoner and Pothecary, may intend this statement to be understood as
the truth about women, but the Pedlar judges it to be the greatest lie of
the three, and therefore places the Palmer at the top of the competitive
masculine hierarchy, judging that the other two must serve him.[71] In the
world of this play, the tall tales of women's dangerous power, which attempt to limit that power through satire, are less great lies than this apparent truth about female gentleness: by crowning it the greatest lie, the
Pedlar, and the play, tacitly approve the Pardoner's and Pothecary's anxiety
about women and their satirical attempts to contain what they have acknowledged to be uncontainable.

Ultimately the masculine hierarchy itself is disestablished: being suspi-
cious of such servants as the Pardoner and the Pothecary, the Palmer dis-
charges them.[72] According to this development, the masculine competition
and phallic authority have been irrelevant after all, and the whole plot has
been pointless. This ironic conclusion to the contest might seem to open
up the play itself to the possible rejection of hierarchical, traditionally phallic values, but that possibility does not last long; the play ends with a final
reassertion of unitary, patriarchal religion, uttered by the Palmer:

> Then to our reason God give us his grace,
> That we may follow with faith so firmly
> His commandments, that we may purchase
> His love, and so consequently
> To believe his church fast and faithfully;
> So that we may, according to his promise,

Be kept out of error in any wise.
And all that hath scaped us here by negligence,
We clearly revoke and forsake it;
To pass the time in this without offense,
Was the cause why the Maker did make it;
And so we humbly beseech you take it,
Beseeching Our Lord to prosper you all
In the faith of his Church Universal.[73]

The play is repeatedly reinscribed under the sign of patriarchal and hierarchical religion, apologizing for its own possible errors in terms reminiscent not only of other early modern plays, but of Chaucer's *Retraction* to
The Canterbury Tales as well. If female transgression is temporarily represented, in the Pardoner's and Pothecary's narratives, as having the potential
to destroy patriarchal attempts at containing it, both human and even divine, that potential is quickly closed off, both by the satirical tone of the
two narrators and here, even more forcefully, by the play itself, which
firmly endorses the containment of all "error" within the Universal
Church.

Like Chaucer's Pardoner, then, the Pardoner in *The Four P.P.,* along
with the other characters, has a troubled relationship with the feminine.
Although he does not have the same complex anxiety about embodying
the feminine that troubles Chaucer's Pardoner, Heywood's still finds in
women the Kristevan "heterogeneous," the potential for disruption of
masculine order and divine justice. And, like Chaucer's Pardoner, he also
finds that this disturbing potential must be repressed. Heywood's play
demonstrates that sixteenth-century readers of Chaucer responded to the
same gender issues that I have been exploring in this book, even if Heywood's Pardoner does not embody them with the same complexity or ambiguity as Chaucer's.

Three hundred years after Heywood, Sir Walter Scott inserted himself
into the tradition I have been examining, in his historical novel *The Abbot,*
a sequel to *The Monastery* that concerns Protestant/Catholic conflicts in
Scotland at the time of Mary, Queen of Scots. Disguise is a major plot element in this typically Romantic novel, and volume 2, chapter 7, rings
some particularly interesting changes on the theme. It includes a scene in
which a play similar to Heywood's *Four P.P.* is performed before a post-
Reformation English audience that includes several of the novel's main
characters. (The setting is, significantly, a carnival.) This play within the
novel demonstrates Scott's literary debts by including in its cast of characters a pardoner clearly based on Heywood's and, ultimately, Chaucer's: "a
quæstionary or pardoner, one of those itinerants who hawked about from

place to place reliques, real or pretended, with which he excited the devotion at once and the charity of the populace, and generally deceived
both the one and the other. The hypocrisy, impudence, and profligacy of
these clerical wanderers, had made them the subject of satire from the time
of Chaucer down to that of Heywood."[74] Unlike Heywood's ultimately
devout drama, the play within the novel satirizes "the superstitious practices of the Catholic religion."[75] This pardoner's audience of dupes within
the play thus consists of "devout Catholics" of unspecified social class to
whom he sells pig's bones (a detail apparently derived directly from
Chaucer rather than Heywood) and other false relics. But most of Scott's
description of his performance focuses on the issue of female sexual fi-
delity: he has a vial of water supposedly from the spring in which Susannah bathed, which magically reveals a wife's or maiden's illicit sexual
activity by making her sneeze. Scott gives this pardoner a pseudo-
Chaucerian speech: "Hath a wife made slip or slide, / Or a maiden step-
p'd aside; / Putteth this water under her nese, / Wold she nold she, she shall
snese."[76] The play's pardoner proceeds to test the vial on each female on
stage, all of whom sneeze, to general amusement.

Thus the pardoner here appears not as sexually ambiguous himself, as
in Chaucer, nor even satirically as a liberating figure for female energy, as
in Heywood, but as a "sex cop," to use Cixous' term,[77] comically investigating and exposing female sexual misbehavior—he is now a force of conventional morality, policing sexuality and binding it into its most
patriarchal form, male control of the unruly female body. And *all* female
bodies prove to be unruly, with the possible exception of Susannah's. The
pardoner recalls the scene of her exposure to male voyeurism ("Wher chast
Susanne in times long gon, / Was wont to wash her bodie and lim"),[78] and
her association with this water—that is to say, Susannah's chaste refusal of
sexuality—is what gives it its magical power to expose unchaste women:
in the explanation of the theatrical trick (quoted below), it is her chastity
that counts, not her resistance to male domination. The control of female
sexuality is thus emphasized throughout.

On the other hand, as in Heywood, here too these concerns with female energy are played for laughs: the joke is that only the "devout
Catholics" being satirized in this play could believe such foolishness—the
pardoner and his false magic are now associated with a subordinated religion (the novel's plot concerns in part the Protestant persecution of
Catholics during the imprisonment of Mary, Queen of Scots, and the Earl
of Murray's regency), and thus in the larger context of the carnival he is
made to seem as foolish as the women he dupes. Nevertheless, the novel's
characters still take him seriously to some extent: when the vial is offered
to one of the "real" characters in the audience, she too sneezes, and is so

offended that she strikes the actor (both because of the insult to her chastity and because she herself is Catholic). Eventually she is reassured that the theatrical device is only that: the author of the joke, a doctor, explains that "the chaste Susanna herself could not have snuffed that elixir without sternutation, being in truth a curious distillation of rectified *acetum*, or vinegar of the sun, prepared by mine own hands."[79] The pardoner's attempt to police female sexuality is explicitly exposed as only a theatrical trick, a performance—the patriarchy and its attempts at binding sexual expression are, for this moment at least, only performative. Scott's pardoner serves this narrative purpose: the exposure, at least for the moment, of the performative nature of patriarchal authority. Scott immediately proceeds to take full advantage of this exposure with a range of tantalizingly ambiguous gender relations.

It cannot be accidental that the rest of Scott's chapter is directly concerned with the performative nature of identity, and specifically of gender identity. Another member of the audience is the page Roland Græme, who identifies the veiled woman who struck the pardoner as his beloved Catherine Seyton (whom he believes he has previously, and troublingly, encountered in masculine attire). However, he quickly loses confidence in this identification when she fails to behave in the expected ladylike manner, cursing the veil when it slips and adjusting it clumsily. Roland is shocked at Catherine's apparent transgressions, and she responds with a critique of gender roles in terms of religion:

> " . . . the times which make females men, are least of all fitted for men to become women; yet you yourself are in danger of such a change."
> "I in danger of becoming effeminate!" said the page.
> "Yes, you, for all the boldness of your reply," said the damsel. ". . . If you are driven from the faith of your fathers from fear of a traitor, is that not womanish?—If you are cajoled by the cunning arguments of a trumpeter of heresy, or the praises of a Puritanic old woman, is that not womanish?—If you are bribed by the hope of spoil and preferment, is not that womanish? . . ."[80]

Roland says that if she were a man, he would respond to these insults physically; she replies:

> "Beware of such big words," answered the maiden; "you said but anon that I sometimes wear hose and doublet."
> "But remain still Catherine Seyton, wear what you list," said the page, endeavouring again to possess himself of her hand.
> "You indeed are pleased to call me so," replied the maiden, evading his intention, "but I have many other names besides."[81]

Note the exchange of gender roles here: the supposed Catherine deliberately takes on a masculine role and figuratively castrates Roland, or, more
accurately, claims that he has castrated himself in abandoning his religion.
The (supposedly) anatomical woman is a better man than the anatomical
man, who is "womanish." "Catherine"'s true identity remains a mystery in
this chapter; there follows a passage of dialogue in which she claims multiple identities—both feminine and masculine.

> "Oh some do call me Jack, sweet love.
>   And some do call me Gill;
>   But when I ride to Holyrood,
>   My name is Wilful Will."
> "Wilful Will!" exclaimed the page, impatiently; "say rather, Will o' the
> Wisp—Jack with the lantern, for never was such a deceitful or wandering
> meteor!"[82]

Roland unwillingly acknowledges her fluid identities and even adds another masculine name, Jack, to her repertory. Indeed, he reluctantly recog-
nizes the performative aspect of her identity when he asks her to be
serious. She refuses, preferring merriment: "'[Y]ou have the cruelty to ask
me to be serious during the only merry moments I have seen perhaps for
months?'"[83] Her fluidity of identity is thus specifically (and appropriately,
given the setting) carnivalesque: once again gender identity as a performative is emphasized.

Subsequent chapters continue the gender play regarding Catherine.
The mystery is eventually resolved with the revelation that the masculine
"Catherine" is actually her brother. Recalling that he initially appeared
veiled, and that his difficulty in handling this female garment was one of
the first clues about his true sex, this revelation rings yet another interesting change on the question of the veiled phallus. In any case, this revelation is delayed through much of the remainder of the novel. As Dale
Bauer notes, the carnival "cannot last. It is functional, a means of resisting
conventions and revising them, without destroying them completely."[84]
Scott thus eventually returns his characters to their "proper" gender roles;
but the figure of the pardoner, appearing only briefly in this chapter,
seems to allow for the possibility of considering gender itself as perfor-
matively fluid. He introduces a troubling, nonpatriarchal gender ambiguity into a long segment of the novel. The exposure of the pardoner's
patriarchal policing of gender boundaries as merely performative allows
for a sequence of chapters in which men can be women, women can be
men, and the hero can even (unwittingly) love another man if the man
bears a strong enough resemblance to his sister: "The carnival is the realm

of desire unmasked. . . . [T]he carnivalized discourse renders invalid any codes, conventions, or laws which govern or reduce the individual to an object of control."[85] Although Scott's pardoner does not himself embody the gender ambiguities explored here, as Chaucer's does, Scott nevertheless goes further than Heywood in exploring the implications of Chaucer's Pardoner for the rule of the phallus, and uses the figure of the Pardoner to initiate his explorations.

In 1994 an American author, Robert Glück, also deliberately inserted himself into the tradition of Chaucer's Pardoner, and directly into the late Middle Ages itself, in his novel *Margery Kempe*. Although the fragmented narrative draws parallels between the Christian mystic Margery Kempe's love for Jesus in the fifteenth century and a gay love affair (with a lover identified as "L.") of the narrator's in the late twentieth, and in spite of the novel's title, Glück declares at the center of his story that Margery Kempe is less relevant to his own experience as a Jew out of place among WASPs than is the Pardoner:

> Jesus and Mary act out my love. Is that a problem? Every star in every galaxy spurts in joyful public salute my orgasms with L. But I look for the Jew from Cleveland and he confuses me. A photo from 1988: L.'s sisters, their mates, L., and myself on a wooden bench in L.'s family's compound in the Adirondacks. I am jolted to see five sleek WASPs smiling into the camera and a visitor from an alternative universe—pallid, averted, big headed, un-American. I recognize my isolation, a mix of longing and hostility.
>
> Margery held a mistaken belief in the value of her experience. A tradition I *can* claim as my own links me to her—of farce and uncertainty, the broad comedy of terror, the fable a community of doubt tells itself: "The Pardoner's Tale," the *Talmud, The Ship of Fools,* Kafka's slapstick, Freud's case histories, the sarcasm of Marx, Brecht, Fassbinder—
>
> I'm in a wooden tub. Face slack, thoughtless, half submerged, neck severed, trunk and limbs hacked apart and soaking in rotting blood and gore. That seems appropriate, a feeling of accuracy and fulfillment overrides the horror of having been murdered in some derelict industrial subbasement. Poignancy in the disheveled air. The whole atmosphere lives with joyous expectation of a visit from L., who wears a black cape in the dream.[86]

This passage occurs at the mathematical center of Glück's novel. Given his concern with Margery Kempe as well as the reference to Chaucer in the passage just quoted, Glück is obviously working in a medieval tradition, and, as scholars have often noted, the mathematical center of a medieval romance is often a moment of special significance.[87] *The Pardoner's Tale,* then, is here given special prominence at the heart of Glück's own text—

and at the beginning of the literary tradition that Glück constructs in which to place himself.

This tradition is one of "uncertainty" and of "a community of doubt," characterized by the "isolation, a mixture of longing and hostility" experienced by a gay Jew surrounded by heterosexual WASPs. It includes many texts written by Jews, and, in the reference to the gay filmmaker Fassbinder, includes gay texts as well. The Pardoner as outsider—as, figuratively, Jew and as, for Glück, gay-identified—thus provides the basis for a literary tradition of the outsider, both hostile to, and longing to join, the mainstream: we may think here both of the Pardoner's attempts to assert authority over the other pilgrims and of the Host's rejection of the Pardoner at the end of *The Pardoner's Tale,* as well as of the Prioress' dismemberment of the Jews in her tale and of the similarities between the Pardoner's Old Man and the Wandering Jew.

Almost inevitably, then, given that the Pardoner initiates the literary tradition in which Glück is working, images of fragmentation pervade his novel, especially after the introduction of the Pardoner as his literary ancestor:

> All we know of the external world is our own shit, piss, tears, sweat, spit, snot, come, pus, babies, and sometimes blood. Margery said, "For your love I would be chopped up as stew meat for the pot." Her lips parted in sexual hunger. Flesh was not all flesh but partly appetite.
>
> Before she met Jesus, Margery had appeared refined to herself: she was a mayor's daughter. She had recognized in Jesus her own aristocracy. Little by little she adopted vulgar manners to conform to Jesus's view of her; her words retreated to where substances and bodies pass into the world, like this stew-meat image used by the young roofer who rejected her—like the dream of my carcass chopped up in a tub![88]

The images of fragmentation and dismemberment may call to mind Lacan's *corps morcelé,* but they also emphasize the more positive discourse of desire adopted by feminist thinkers: desire fragments the self, it destroys the phallic unity of the Lacanian Symbolic and allows a return of the repressed feminine (recall the comparable fragmentation in the 1420 "Canterbury Interlude"). I have proposed that the Old Man's desire for physical dissolution reveals a longing for the feminine and maternal on the Pardoner's part as well. Glück thus makes explicit what remains unspoken in *The Pardoner's Tale:* the Pardoner's obsession with fragmentation is re-imagined as not only horrifying, but satisfying, too: "a feeling of accuracy and fulfillment overrides the horror."

The necessity of dismantling the unified, phallogocentric Body of God the Father, as imagined by feminist thinkers like Flax, is played out in gendered terms in *Margery Kempe,* again through images of fragmentation and dismemberment:

> His voice, a clarinet; his eyes, blue geodes; the tilt of his head; the hair tumbling down his brow; his dazzled expression; his small translucent teeth; his pointed tongue; his straight back; the vein running down his inner thigh; the ankles and the arch. He is already breaking into parts. More than that: Margery's urge to strip Jesus, to complete him, to uncover, to make him respond and respond. There *is* no body that precedes his body yet it is overwhelmingly passive. Panicked, she looks for it in continual expectation of making love. She *separates* his knees, *opens* his crotch; her hand on his hip *rotates* his torso; she *shoves* his knees to his ears, his asshole contracts, the amazing flesh moves as the floor slides out from under her. She *tips* his head back, *exposes* his throat. Trying to explain him she dismantles a complex of refinements—ropy strands of sperm—there won't be any Jesus after Margery outdoes the cross.[89]

Glück's language "dismantles" or fragments the divine phallic body into its component parts, in a manner reminiscent of the Pardoner's obsessive catalog of body parts in the *Tale.* But again, Glück explicitly explores the implications of this dismantling for gendered positions, whereas for Chaucer they remain unconscious. Here it is not merely the unified body in general, but literally the Logos itself, the embodied Word of God (gendered—and sexed—male) that is dismembered, not only body, but soul or self: "'Your hips are too wide, you are knock-kneed. Your nipples are too small, you have pimples on your ass.' She drags farts out of him, his ignorant seagull expression as people look up and sniff and her insides roll with joy. She doesn't know how to diminish him. 'He's just a *boy,* but extremely *beautiful,*' she adds, puzzled. She could never deface that beauty but she pulls his soul apart like tissue."[90]

Body and soul are actively dismembered by a woman: the italicized verbs in the passage quoted previously insist on the activity of the feminine in fragmenting the perfect, but passive, divine body. The feminine demands some response from the passive masculine; and Glück, by constantly linking his narrator's love affair to Margery's relationship with Jesus, appropriates this feminine to gay sexuality, imagining himself as Margery and L., the wealthy WASP, as the divine body requiring fragmentation, thus making good on the Pardoner's sodomitical potential.

The novel concludes with the destabilization of gender positions:

> I leave Margery in a suspended moment as the inevitability of L. subsides along with my fear of dying. I dreamt that Margery wants to see me. Who would know to pass himself off as her? Only L., I surmise, because I asked

him not to contact me. Now *I* am the god of nonrelation. If he takes my
place as Margery, do I take his place as Jesus? At last my position is not so
fixed. I feel the anguish of rejecting him, but I'm not sure I do—a quandary
of wanting and not wanting.

A failed saint turns to autobiography. Love *amazes* me; I *exult* in my luck,
in our sex; L. *exasperates* me; I am *exasperating;* I am *abandoned.* I want to contain my rambling story in a few words.

exult, exasperate, abandon, amaze[91]

Identity itself is unmoored here, as the narrator takes on both active and
passive roles in the italicized verbs, as well as both masculine and feminine,
divine and human, desiring and not-desiring roles in the fragmentary narrative as it concludes. This literal unfixing of gender identities once again
makes explicit an aspect of Chaucer's Pardoner that remains implicit in
Chaucer's text: as in the "Canterbury Interlude," *The Four P.P.,* and *The
Abbot,* a reference to Chaucer's Pardoner introduces the destabilization of
gender.

In many ways the postmodern Glück seems to be the most appropriate
gloss on the Pardoner with which to conclude this book. His reference to
the Pardoner introduces these images of fragmentation and of destabilized
gender identities; he therefore returns us to the unstable Pardoner himself.

NOTES

Preface: The Pardoner in Discourse:
Theories, Histories, Methods

1. C. S. Lewis, *The Allegory of Love* (Oxford: Oxford University Press, 1938), p. 1.
2. Luce Irigaray, *Je, tu, nous: Toward a Culture of Difference,* trans. Alison Martin (New York: Routledge, 1993), p. 30.
3. Bill Readings and Bennett Schaber, "Introduction: The Question Mark in the Midst of Modernity," in *Postmodernism Across the Ages: Essays for a Postmodernity That Wasn't Born Yesterday,* eds. Bill Readings and Bennett Schaber (Syracuse: Syracuse University Press, 1993), p. 15.
4. See, for instance, Lacan's use of Hieronymous Bosch, St. Augustine, and Dante in "Aggressivity in Psychoanalysis," in his *Ecrits: A Selection,* trans. Alan Sheridan (New York: Norton, 1977), pp. 11, 20, 28, or of St. Thomas Aquinas in "The Subversion of the Subject and the Dialectic of Desire in the Freudian Unconscious," in *Ecrits,* p. 297, or of the medieval imagery of armor and tournaments that dominates "The Mirror Stage as Formative of the Function of the I as Revealed in Psychoanalytic Experience," in *Ecrits,* pp. 1–7 (discussed in Robert S. Sturges, "*La(ca)ncelot,*" *Arthurian Interpretations* 4.2 [Spring, 1990]: 12–23).
5. John Boswell, "Categories, Experience, and Sexuality," in *Forms of Desire: Sexual Orientation and the Social Constructionist Controversy,* ed. Edward Stein (1990, repr. Routledge: New York, 1992), pp. 133–134. This essay, and the collection as a whole, give a useful and balanced view of the entire debate to that point. See also Boswell's "Revolutions, Universals, and Sexual Categories," in *Hidden From History: Reclaiming the Gay and Lesbian Past,* eds. Martin Bauml Duberman, Martha Vicinus, and George Chauncey (New York: New American Library, 1989), pp. 17–36.
6. Boswell, "Categories," p. 137. The identification of the "gay subculture" is one of the main thrusts of Boswell's *Christianity, Social Tolerance, and Homosexuality: Gay People in Western Europe from the Beginning of the Christian Era to the Fourteenth Century* (Chicago: University of Chicago Press, 1980).
7. Samuel R. Delany, "Appendix: Closures and Openings," in his *Return to Nevèrÿon* (1987; repr. University Press of New England/Wesleyan University Press: Hanover, NH: 1994), p. 273. For committed anti-essentialists

who are nevertheless queer historians, see David Halperin, *Saint Foucault: Towards a Gay Hagiography* (Oxford: Oxford University Press, 1995), and two further essays in *Hidden From History:* Halperin's "Sex Before Sexuality: Pederasty, Politics, and Power in Classical Athens," pp. 37–53, and Robert Padgug, "Sexual Matters: Rethinking Sexuality in History," pp. 54–64. And cf. Carolyn Dinshaw's useful analysis of these issues in "A Kiss Is Just a Kiss: Heterosexuality and its Consolations in *Sir Gawain and the Green Knight,*" in *Critical Crossings,* eds. Judith Butler and Biddy Martin, special issue of *Diacritics* 24.2–3 (Summer-Fall, 1994): 206–207. Gay uses of the past, including historiography, have been analyzed, partly in terms of the essentialist/constructionist debate, by Scott Bravmann, *Queer Fictions of the Past: History, Culture, and Difference* (Cambridge, Eng.: Cambridge University Press, 1997).

8. Eve Kosofsky Sedgwick, *Epistemology of the Closet* (Berkeley: University of California Press, 1990), p. 83. Figure 2, p. 88, conveniently summarizes the extent to which the "minoritizing" and "universalizing" views can be identified with the "essentialist" and "constructionist" positions, and can be applied to gender identities as well as to sexualities.

9. Jonathan Dollimore, *Sexual Dissidence: Augustine to Wilde, Freud to Foucault* (Oxford: Clarendon Press, 1991), p. 26.

10. Dollimore, *Sexual Dissidence,* p. 26, citing Diana J. Fuss, *Essentially Speaking: Feminism, Nature, and Difference* (New York: Routledge, 1989), p. 104.

11. See the discussion of this issue in the conclusion to this book.

12. "To achieve a human, potentially divine, sexuality we must therefore reconsider the civil identity of each sex and rethink possible myths and religions in a way that respects the difference between the sexes." Luce Irigaray, *Thinking the Difference: For a Peaceful Revolution,* trans. Karin Montin (New York: Routledge, 1994), p. xviii.

13. For a useful survey of responses to Irigaray's work, see Naomi Schor, "Previous Engagements: The Receptions of Irigaray," in *Engaging with Irigaray: Feminist Philosophy and Modern European Thought,* eds. Carolyn Burke, Naomi Schor, and Margaret Whitford (New York: Columbia University Press, 1994), pp. 4–14.

14. Fuss, *Essentially Speaking,* p. 5. For a trenchant critique of Fuss' philosophical position, see Deborah G. Chay, "Reconstructing Essentialism," *Diacritics* 21.2–3 (1991): 135–47.

15. Fuss, *Essentially Speaking,* p. 20.

16. Controversial work on the biological aspects of homosexuality has been done, for example, by Dean Hamer and Peter Copeland, *The Science of Desire: The Search for the Gay Gene and the Biology of Behavior* (New York: Simon and Schuster, 1994) and by Simon LeVay, *The Sexual Brain* (Cambridge, MA: MIT Press, 1993); see also the essays collected in *Sexual Nature, Sexual Culture,* eds. Paul R. Abramson and Steven D. Pinkerton (Chicago: University of Chicago Press, 1995). Much of this work is surveyed by Francis Mark Mondimore, *A Natural History of Homosexuality*

(Baltimore: Johns Hopkins University Press, 1996), pp. 97–157. Mondimore, perhaps paradoxically, is careful not to take an essentialist position
when writing historically, as on pp. 1–95.

17. Rictor Norton, *The Myth of the Modern Homosexual: Queer History and the
Search for Cultural Unity* (London: Cassell, 1997), pp. 11–12.

18. Gregory Woods, *A History of Gay Literature: The Male Tradition* (New Haven,
CT: Yale University Press, 1998), pp. 51–52.

19. Judith Butler, *Bodies That Matter: On the Discursive Limits of "Sex"* (New
York: Routledge, 1993), p. 10. cf. Diana J. Fuss:

> The dream of either a common language or no language at all is
> just that—a dream, a fantasy that ultimately can do little to ac-
> knowledge and to legitimate the hitherto repressed differences
> between and within sexual identities. But one can, by using these
> contested words, use them up, exhaust them, transform them into
> the historical concepts they are and have always been. Change
> may well happen by working on the insides of our inherited sex-
> ual vocabularies and turning them inside out, giving them a new
> face.

This is from "Inside/Out," her introduction to *Inside/Out: Lesbian Theories,
Gay Theories,* ed. Diana J. Fuss (New York: Routledge, 1991), p. 7.

20. It will be obvious that my emphasis on discourse in gender construction
has been crucially influenced by the larger postmodern question of the
construction of subjectivity in general, but I judge that pursuing that issue
(outside of this note) would take me too far afield. Most directly relevant
to my concerns here are: Michel Foucault, *The History of Sexuality, Volume
I: An Introduction,* trans. Robert Hurley (1978, repr. Vintage: New York,
1980); John Champagne, *The Ethics of Marginality: A New Approach to Gay
Studies* (Minneapolis: University of Minnesota Press, 1995); and Judith
Butler, *The Psychic Life of Power: Theories in Subjection* (Stanford, CA: Stanford University Press, 1997).

21. Dollimore, *Sexual Dissidence,* p. 24. In the electronic discussion mentioned
above, James D. Cain briefly and usefully attempted such an examination
of these modes of transmission in the Middle Ages. Discussing the use of
Juvenal's satires by medieval and eighteenth-century authors to categorize
certain types of erotic behavior in their own periods, he suggested that
"[i]n both cases, citations of Juvenal to describe one's own contemporaries
seems to be working rhetorically to filter perceptions about the present
through texts from the past—and vice-versa. The conflation of past with
present and the presumption of the historical continuity of sexual deviance
across the centuries are made by the writers from these later periods themselves" rather than being evidence of a transhistorical homosexual identity.
(James D. Cain, "Re: Facts, Texts and Theories," electronic communication
posted to medgay-l@ksu.edu, June 9, 1999). It is precisely this type of sedimentation that I examine in part I of this book.

22. Glenn Burger, "Kissing the Pardoner," *PMLA* 107 (1992): 1151–52.

23. Burger, "Kissing," p. 1145. And cf. the work of Carolyn Dinshaw, *Chaucer's Sexual Poetics* (Madison: University of Wisconsin Press, 1989) and "Chaucer's Queer Touches / A Queer Touches Chaucer," *Exemplaria* 7 (1995): 75–92; and of Steven F. Kruger, "Claiming the Pardoner: Toward a Gay Reading of Chaucer's Pardoner's Tale," *Exemplaria* 6 (1994): 115–39. One might also compare this view of the Pardoner to Slavoj Žižek's definition of the "symptom": "a particular, 'pathological,' signifying formation, a binding of enjoyment, an inert stain resisting communication and interpretation, a stain which cannot be included in the circuit of discourse, of social bond network, but is at the same time a positive condition of it." Or, "a terrifying bodily mark which is merely a mute attestation bearing witness to a disgusting enjoyment, without representing anything or anyone." See *The Sublime Object of Ideology* (New York: Verso, 1989), pp. 75 and 76.
24. Fuss, *Essentially Speaking,* p. 2.
25. Dollimore, *Sexual Dissidence,* p. 87. And see the discussion of this term in chapter 1, below.
26. R. Howard Bloch, "Critical Communities and the Shape of the Medievalist's Desire: A Response to Judith Ferster and Louise Fradenburg," in *Reconceiving Chaucer: Literary Theory and Historical Interpretation,* ed. Thomas Hahn, special issue of *Exemplaria* 2.1 (Spring, 1990): 205–06.
27. Fuss, *Essentially Speaking,* p. 10.
28. Nancy J. Vickers, in "The Status of Evidence: A Roundtable," *PMLA* 111 (1996), p. 29.
29. Antoine Compagnon and Martha Banta, in "The Status of Evidence," pp. 30–31. Queer Theory has had to confront the problem of the unsaid as evidence most directly; in a sense, of course, one of its foundational works, Sedgwick's *Epistemology of the Closet,* is primarily about the problem of finding evidence of that which cannot be spoken, and much subsequent work in the field may be understood as an attempt to work out the difficulties of doing so. For a recent example, see the chapter entitled "The Evidence of Things Not Seen," in Norton, *Myth,* pp. 148–79.

**Introduction: The Pardoner,
the Preacher, and (Gender) Politics**

1. Thomas Walsingham, *Historia Anglicana,* ed. Henry Thomas Riley, 2 vols. (Rolls Series, 1863–1864), 1:459; trans. R. B. Dobson, in *The Peasants' Revolt of 1381,* ed. R. B. Dobson, 2nd ed. (London: Methuen, 1983), p. 172.
2. Alfred David, *The Strumpet Muse: Art and Morals in Chaucer's Poetry* (Bloomington: Indiana University Press, 1976), p. 92.
3. Steven Justice, *Writing and Rebellion: England in 1381,* The New Historicism: Studies in Cultural Poetics 27 (Berkeley: University of California Press, 1994), p. 225.
4. See Justice, *Writing and Rebellion,* pp. 225–31.

NOTES

173

5. Lee Patterson, *Chaucer and the Subject of History* (Madison: University of Wisconsin Press, 1991), p. 279.

6. Paul Strohm, *Social Chaucer* (Cambridge, MA: Harvard University Press, 1989), pp. 153–54, 152.

7. Susan Crane, "The Writing Lesson of 1381," in *Chaucer's England: Literature in Historical Context,* ed. Barbara Hanawalt, Medieval Studies at Minnesota 4 (Minneapolis: University of Minnesota Press, 1992), p. 215.

8. Strohm, *Social Chaucer,* p. 153. Strohm discusses the Pardoner in social terms, as a threat to the community of pilgrims, but not in terms of the Peasants' Revolt, pp. 155–57.

9. Walsingham, *Historia Anglicana,* 2:32; trans. Dobson, *Peasants' Revolt,* p. 374.

10. See Walsingham, *Historia Anglicana,* 2:32–33; trans. Dobson, *Peasants' Revolt,* pp. 374–75.

11. Quoted by Henry Knighton in *Knighton's Chronicle 1337–1396,* ed. G. H. Martin (Oxford: Clarendon Press, 1995), p. 224. The authorship of this and the other letters associated with the Revolt is discussed by Justice, *Writing and Rebellion,* pp. 13–23.

12. Walsingham, *Historia Anglicana,* 2:33; trans. Dobson, *Peasants' Revolt,* p. 375. Henry Knighton makes the same point: see *Knighton's Chronicle,* pp. 210–11.

13. *Anonimalle Chronicle, 1333 to 1381,* ed. V. H. Galbraith (Manchester: Manchester University Press, 1927), p. 137; trans. Dobson, *Peasants' Revolt,* p. 128.

14. See, for example, the sermon described by Jean Froissart, quoted in Dobson, *Peasants' Revolt,* p. 371.

15. Walsingham, *Historia Anglicana,* 2:32; trans. Dobson, *Peasants' Revolt,* 373–74. For another account of Ball's punishment, see Froissart's description quoted in Dobson, *Peasants' Revolt,* p. 198.

16. Walsingham, *Historia Anglicana,* 1:457, 459; trans. Dobson, *Peasants' Revolt,* pp. 169, 172. Compare the accounts of the peasants' unruly behavior in the *Anonimalle Chronicle,* pp. 140–50; trans. Dobson, *Peasants' Revolt,* pp. 154–68; and in *Knighton's Chronicle,* pp. 210–17.

17. John of Salisbury, *Policraticus,* 6.25, ed. and trans. Cary J. Nederman (Cambridge: Cambridge University Press, 1990), pp. 137–39; Marie de France, "The Fable of a Man, His Belly, and His Limbs," in Cary J. Nederman and Kate Langdon Forhan, eds., *Medieval Political Theory—A Reader: The Quest for the Body Politic, 1100–1400* (New York: Routledge, 1993), pp. 24–25; Christine de Pizan, "The Book of the Body Politic," in Nederman and Forhan, eds., *Medieval Political Theory,* pp. 230–47.

18. See, for example, the beheadings of the archbishop of Canterbury, of Sir Robert Hales (Treasurer of England), of Brother William Appleton (described as having influence over the Duke of Lancaster), of John Legge (the king's serjeant-at-arms), and of various others, as reported in the *Anonimalle Chronicle,* p. 145; trans. Dobson, *Peasants' Revolt,* p. 162. See also the *Eulogium Historiarum sive Temporis,* ed. F. S. Haydon, 3 vols. (Rolls Series,

1858–63), 3:353, trans. Dobson, *Peasants' Revolt,* p. 207, for the beheading of the archbishop and others; and the threat that all literate persons should be beheaded, reported in the *Anonimalle Chronicle,* p. 144, trans. Dobson, *Peasants' Revolt,* p. 160.

19. Jean Froissart, *Les Chroniques de Sire Jean Froissart,* 2.118, ed. J. A. C. Buchon, 3 vols. (Paris: Desrez, 1835), 2:166; *The Chronicles of Froissart,* trans. Lord Berners, ed. G. C. Macaulay (London: 1895), in Dobson, *Peasants' Revolt,* p. 315.

20. Walsingham, *Historia Anglicana,* 2:14, 19; trans. Dobson, *Peasants' Revolt,* pp. 307, 311.

21. Walsingham, *Historia Anglicana,* 2:20; trans. Dobson, *Peasants' Revolt,* p. 313.

22. Strohm, *Social Chaucer,* p. 153; Walsingham, *Historia Anglicana,* 2:16; trans. Dobson, *Peasants' Revolt,* p. 309.

23. See Carolyn Dinshaw, *Chaucer's Sexual Poetics* (Madison: University of Wisconsin Press, 1989), pp. 162–68.

24. Carolyn Dinshaw, "A Kiss Is Just a Kiss: Heterosexuality and its Consolations in *Sir Gawain and the Green Knight,*" in *Critical Crossings,* eds. Judith Butler and Biddy Martin, special issue of *Diacritics* 24.2–3 (Summer-Fall, 1994), cites Peter Damian, Aquinas, and the *Penitential of Cumean* as evidence that kisses between men might be perceived in the Middle Ages as potentially, and sinfully, erotic, as well as in terms of "conventional cultural practice," p. 210.

25. Caroline Walker Bynum, "Women Mystics and Eucharistic Devotion in the Thirteenth Century," in her *Fragmentation and Redemption: Essays on Gender and the Human Body in Medieval Religion* (New York: Urzone, 1992), pp. 146–47; Introduction to *Feminist Approaches to the Body in Medieval Literature,* ed. Linda Lomperis and Sarah Stanbury, New Cultural Studies (Philadelphia: University of Pennsylvania Press, 1993), p. ix.

26. London, British Library, MS Arundel 350, fol. 17v, cited by Crane, "Writing Lesson," p. 221, n. 51; trans. Crane, p. 215.

27. Crane, "Writing Lesson," p. 216.

28. *Anonimalle Chronicle,* p. 144; trans. Dobson, *Peasants' Revolt,* p. 160.

29. Crane, "Writing Lesson," p. 217, citing R. Howard Bloch, "Medieval Misogyny," *Representations* 20 (Fall, 1987): 1–24. Bloch's arguments are developed further in his book *Medieval Misogyny and the Invention of Western Romantic Love* (Chicago: University of Chicago Press, 1991); on "woman as riot," see especially pp. 17–22.

30. *Knighton's Chronicle,* pp. 212–13.

31. Jeffrey Richards, *Sex, Dissidence and Damnation: Minority Groups in the Middle Ages* (New York: Routledge, 1991), p. 143. See also, among others, Michael Goodich, *The Unmentionable Vice: Homosexuality in the Later Medieval Period* (Santa Barbara, CA [?]: Dorset Press, 1979), pp. 7–10, and John Boswell, *Christianity, Social Tolerance, and Homosexuality: Gay People in Western Europe from the Beginning of the Christian Era to the Fourteenth Century* (Chicago: University of Chicago Press, 1980), pp. 283–86.

32. Walsingham, *Historia Anglicana*, 2:32; trans. Dobson, *Peasants' Revolt*, p. 374. See also the passages on Wyclif and John Ball in the accounts by Walsingham, by Knighton, and in the *Fasciculi Zizaniorum* collected and translated in Dobson, *Peasants' Revolt*, pp. 373–78.

33. Froissart, *Chroniques*, 2.110, ed. Buchon, 2:155; trans. Lord Berners, in Dobson, *Peasants' Revolt*, p. 144. Peasant status is discussed as the unjust loss of an originary equality in, for example, Walsingham's account of John Ball's sermon, including the famous couplet "Whan Adam dalf, and Eve span, / Wo was thanne a gentilman?" See Dobson, *Peasants' Revolt*, pp. 374–75.

34. Walsingham, quoted and trans. Elizabeth B. Keiser, *Courtly Desire and Medieval Homophobia: The Legitimation of Sexual Pleasure in Cleanness and its Contexts* (New Haven: Yale University Press, 1997), p. 150. On effeminacy in this context, see pp. 150–51. On Richard II's court, see also Dinshaw, "A Kiss," pp. 222–23. Scholarship on the long historical association of effeminacy with male-male desire is surveyed by Kaja Silverman, *Male Subjectivity at the Margins* (New York: Routledge, 1992), pp. 347–73, as part of a chapter arguing that femininity is not merely a historical construct within male homosexuality, but that it psychically (essentially?) "inhabits male homosexuality in all kinds of interesting, enabling, and politically productive ways," p. 387.

35. For instance, by Alfred David, *The Strumpet Muse: Art and Morals in Chaucer's Poetry* (Bloomington: Indiana University Press, 1976), p. 6, and by Dinshaw, *Chaucer's Sexual Poetics*, p. 160.

Chapter 1: The Pardoner's Genders: Linguistic and Other

1. R. W. Connell, *Masculinities* (Berkeley: University of California Press, 1995), p. 71.

2. Judith Lorber, *Paradoxes of Gender* (New Haven, CT: Yale University Press, 1994), p. 1.

3. Lorber, *Paradoxes*, p. 21. Lorber here tacitly joins a number of scholars who have criticized Judith Butler's influential but perhaps over-optimistic reading of cross-dressing as gender subversion in her *Gender Trouble: Feminism and the Subversion of Identity* (New York: Routledge, 1990), especially pp. 128–49. Butler herself has explicitly critiqued *Gender Trouble* in a later book, *Bodies That Matter: On the Discursive Limits of "Sex"* (New York: Routledge, 1993), pp. ix-xii.

4. Donna J. Haraway, "'Gender' for a Marxist Dictionary: The Sexual Politics of a Word," in her *Simians, Cyborgs, and Women: The Reinvention of Nature* (New York: Routledge, 1991), p. 131; Gayle Rubin, "The Traffic in Women: Notes on the Political Economy of Sex," in *Toward an Anthropology of Women,* ed. Rayna R. Reiter (New York: Monthly Review, 1975), pp. 157–210.

5. Haraway, "'Gender,'" p. 148.
6. Donald R. Howard, *The Idea of the* Canterbury Tales (Berkeley: University of California Press, 1976), pp. 343–44.
7. Dinshaw, "Chaucer's Queer Touches / A Queer Touches Chaucer," *Exemplaria* 7 (1995), p. 89.
8. Connell, *Masculinities,* p. 3.
9. Monica McAlpine, "The Pardoner's Homosexuality and How It Matters," *PMLA* 95 (1980), p. 11. On the slippage in medieval discourse among sex, gender, and sexuality, see also Joan Cadden, *Meanings of Sex Difference in the Middle Ages: Medicine, Science, and Culture* (Cambridge, Eng.: Cambridge University Press, 1993), pp. 169–227.
10. Guillaume de Lorris and Jean de Meun, *Le Roman de la rose,* ll. 2169–74, ed. Daniel Poirion (Paris: Garnier Flammarion, 1974), pp. 94–95; *The Romance of the Rose,* trans. Charles Dahlberg (Princeton: Princeton University Press, 1971), pp. 60–61, quoted in Monica McAlpine, "The Pardoner's Homosexuality and How It Matters," *PMLA* 95 (1980), p. 11.
11. Although this fragment of *The Romaunt of the Rose* is not by Chaucer, it is included in *The Riverside Chaucer;* this quotation is at ll. 2284–88.
12. Michel Foucault, *The History of Sexuality, Volume I: An Introduction,* trans. Robert Hurley (1978, repr.Vintage: New York, 1980), p. 101.
13. Alan of Lille, *Anticlaudianus,* 9.265–69, ed. R. Bossuat (Paris:Vrin, 1955), p. 193; *Anticlaudianus or the Good and Perfect Man,* trans. James. J. Sheridan (Toronto: Pontifical Institute of Mediaeval Studies, 1973), p. 211.
14. *Anticlaudianus,* trans. Sheridan, p. 211, n. 8. Sheridan attributes these errors to "haste and lack of revision"; see also nn. 6–7.The topic of masculine anxiety has produced its own theoretical literature in recent years; pioneering in this regard is Kaja Silverman, *Male Subjectivity at the Margins* (New York: Routledge, 1992). See also, in addition to Connell, Calvin Thomas, *Male Matters: Masculinity, Anxiety, and the Male Body on the Line* (Urbana: University of Illinois Press, 1996), and the following collections of essays: *Constructing Masculinity,* ed. Maurice Berger, Brian Wallis, and Simon Watson (New York: Routledge, 1995); *Fictions of Masculinity: Crossing Cultures, Crossing Sexualities,* ed. Peter F. Murphy (New York: New York University Press, 1995); and *Men's Bodies, Men's Gods: Male Identities in a (Post-)Christian Culture,* ed. Björn Krondorfer (New York: New York University Press, 1996). Specifically on medieval masculinity, see *Becoming Male in the Middle Ages,* ed. Jeffrey Jerome Cohen and Bonnie Wheeler (New York: Garland, 1997).
15. See *The Riverside Chaucer,* p. xxix.
16. See Ernst Robert Curtius, *European Literature and the Latin Middle Ages,* trans. Willard R. Trask (Princeton: Princeton University Press, 1953), p. 414, and John A. Alford, "The Grammatical Metaphor: A Survey of Its Use in the Middle Ages," *Speculum* 57 (1982), pp. 731–33 and 750–54, as well as Ziolkowski's book, cited below (n. 18).
17. Alan of Lille, *De planctu naturae,* 1.15–22, ed. Nikolaus M. Häring, *Studi Medievali,* serie terza 19.2 (1978), p. 806; *Plaint of Nature,* trans. James J.

Sheridan (Toronto: Pontifical Institute of Mediaeval Studies, 1980), pp. 67–68.

18. Jan Ziolkowski, *Alan of Lille's Grammar of Sex* (Cambridge, MA: Medieval Academy, 1985), p. 15.

19. Alan of Lille, *De planctu Naturae,* 8.83–87, ed. Häring, p. 835; *Plaint,* trans. Sheridan, p. 136.

20. Ziolkowski, *Grammar of Sex,* p. 20.

21. Monique Wittig, "The Mark of Gender," in her *The Straight Mind and Other Essays* (Boston: Beacon Press, 1992), p. 76. cf. Luce Irigaray on "the unconscious translation of gender into discourse" in "The Three Genders," in her *Sexes and Genealogies,* trans. Gillian C. Gill (New York: Columbia University Press, 1993), pp. 172–76.

22. Dinshaw, "Chaucer's Queer Touches," p. 80.

23. Luce Irigaray, *This Sex Which Is Not One,* trans. Catherine Porter with Carolyn Burke (Ithaca, NY: Cornell University Press, 1985), p. 122.

24. Irigaray, *This Sex,* p. 28.

25. Elaine Tuttle Hansen shows that the "feminization" of men is problematic throughout Chaucer's works, though she does not consider the case of the Pardoner. See her *Chaucer and the Fictions of Gender* (Berkeley: University of California Press, 1992), pp. 10–25.

26. Caroline Walker Bynum, "Women Mystics and Eucharistic Devotion in the Thirteenth Century," in her *Fragmentation and Redemption: Essays on Gender and the Human Body in Medieval Religion* (New York: Urzone, 1992), pp. 146–47.

27. While historical and critical studies on pederasty in premodern cultures are numerous, though less so for the Middle Ages than for the ancient world, no critic to my knowledge has linked the Pardoner with this practice. For some general remarks on medieval pederasty, see John Boswell, *Christianity, Social Tolerance, and Homosexuality: Gay People in Western Europe from the Beginning of the Christian Era to the Fourteenth Century* (Chicago: University of Chicago Press, 1980), pp. 143–44 and 251–52. (Boswell assimilates medieval pederasty to the modern category of "child abuse" without demonstrating that it was regarded this way in the Middle Ages.) Mathew S. Kuefler asserts a connection between castration and the preservation of attractive prepubescent qualities: see "Castration and Eunuchism in the Middle Ages," in *Handbook of Medieval Sexuality,* ed. Vern L. Bullough and James A. Brundage (New York: Garland, 1996), pp. 286–87. On religious and secular sanctions against pederasty, see Michael Goodich, *The Unmentionable Vice: Homosexuality in the Later Medieval Period* (Santa Barbara [?], Dorset Press, 1979), pp. 27 and 83. The eroticized gender ambiguity of boys has been theorized by Marjorie Garber, *Vested Interests: Cross-Dressing and Cultural Anxiety* (1992; repr. HarperCollins: New York, 1993), pp. 165–85.

28. Evanthius, "De Fabula," 1.2, in Aelius Donatus, *Commentum Terenti,* ed. Paul Wessner, 2 vols. (Leipzig: Teubner, 1902–1905), 1:13; "On Drama," trans. O. B. Hardison, Jr., in *Medieval Literary Criticism: Translations and In-*

terpretations, ed. O. B. Hardison, Jr., et al. (New York: Frederick Ungar, 1974), p. 42.

29. Aelius Donatus, "De Comoedia," 5.7, in *Commentum Terenti,* 1:24; "On Comedy," trans. Hardison, in *Medieval Literary Criticism,* p. 46.

30. On this entire tradition, I am indebted to A. Philip McMahon, "Seven Questions on Aristotelian Definitions of Tragedy and Comedy," *Harvard Studies in Classical Philology* 40 (1929): 97–198, which traces the influence of definitions of tragedy from the Greeks to the Renaissance. For the period from Evanthius to Chaucer, see especially pp. 126–50.

31. Extracts from Trevet's "Commentary on Seneca's Tragedies" are translated in *Medieval Literary Theory and Criticism c. 1100-c.1375: The Commentary Tradition,* ed. A. J. Minnis and A. B. Scott with David Wallace, rev. ed. (Oxford: Clarendon Press, 1991), p. 344; Dante Alighieri, *Epistole,* XIII, ed. Arsenio Frugoni and Giorgio Brugnoli, in his *Opere minori,* 2 vols. (Milan: Riccardo Ricciardi, 1979), 2:616; trans. "Epistle to Can Grande della Scala: Extract," in *Medieval Literary Theory and Criticism,* ed. Minnis and Scott, p. 461. See also the "Prologue" to Guido da Pisa's *Commentary on Dante's Comedy,* trans. in *Medieval Literary Theory and Criticism,* trans. Minnis and Scott, p. 474.

32. Evanthius, "De Fabula," 1.2, ed. Wessner, 1:13; trans. Hardison, *Medieval Literary Criticism,* p. 41.

33. Aelius Donatus, "De Comoedia," 5.8, ed. Wessner, 1:24; trans. Hardison, *Medieval Literary Criticism,* p. 46. Donatus also mentions the altar to Bacchus present on the ancient stage: see 6.2, ed. Wessner, 1:26; trans. Hardison, *Medieval Literary Criticism,* p. 48.

34. Isidore of Seville, for example, makes the connection between drama and Dionysus (or "Liber") at least twice in the *Etymologiae,* 18.16.3 and 18.51: *Etimologías,* ed. José Oroz Reta and Manuel-A. Marcos Casquero, 2 vols. (Madrid: Biblioteca de Autores Cristianos, 1982), 2:404, 2:420.

35. Many critics have noted the Pardoner's fondness for drink; John Bowers, for one, links him to "alcoholism." See Bowers, "'Dronkenesse Is Ful of Stryvyng': Alcoholism and Ritual Violence in Chaucer's *Pardoner's Tale,*" *ELH* 57 (1990): 757–84. Chaucer relates Bacchus to drunkenness in the *Manciple's Prologue* (IX, 99–101). The ancient myths of Bacchus reveal further suggestive parallels with the Pardoner: Bacchus is a stranger, a god who always comes from elsewhere (compare the Pardoner who comes both from "Rouncivale" and "the court of Rome" (I, 670–71); Bacchus has consistent difficulties being accepted as a god, as the Pardoner finds it difficult to gain acceptance as a religious authority among the pilgrims (as we saw in the introduction); and Bacchus is regularly, like the Pardoner, associated with dismemberment (see chapter 6). For these aspects of the god, see Marcel Detienne, *Dionysos at Large,* trans. Arthur Goldhammer (Cambridge: Harvard University Press, 1989), pp. 3–26.

36. Ovid [P. Ovidii Nasonis], *Metamorphoseon libri XV,* 3.323, ed. B. A. van Proosdij (Leiden: E. J. Brill, 1982), p. 78; *Metamorphoses,* trans. Mary M. Innes (Harmondsworth: Penguin, 1955), p. 82.

37. Ovid, *Metamorphoseon libri XV,* 3.532–37, 553–56, pp. 86–87; *Metamorphoses,* trans. Innes, p. 88.
38. Ovid, *Metamorphoseon libri XV,* 3.605–09, p. 88; *Metamorphoses,* trans. Innes, p. 90. Medieval authors thought of Dionysus/Bacchus/Liber as effeminate, too: see Isidore's *Etymologiae,* 8.11.43 and 10.160, ed. Reta and Casquero, 1:726 and 1:830.
39. Ovid, *Metamorphoseon libri XV,* 4.18–20, p. 95; *Metamorphoses,* trans. Innes, p. 94.
40. Susan Crane, *Gender and Romance in Chaucer's* Canterbury Tales (Princeton, NJ: Princeton University Press, 1994), p. 5.
41. It should be added that another of Chaucer's favorite authors points out a similar ambiguity: for Boccaccio in the *Genealogy of the Gentile Gods,* there were two poets named Orpheus, and the younger "hic Bachi orgia adinvenit et Menadum nocturnos cetus" [invented the rites of Bacchus, and the nocturnal gatherings of the Maenads] and was therefore "a posteris primus creditus est Orpheus" [regarded as the great Orpheus by posterity]—even though the "great Orpheus" was also a victim of these same Maenads. Giovanni Boccaccio, *Genealogie deorum gentilium libri,* 14.7, ed. Vincenzo Romano, 2 vols. (Bari: Laterza, 1951), 2:704; *Boccaccio on Poetry: Being the Preface and the Fourteenth and Fifteenth Books of Boccaccio's* Genealogia Deorum Gentilium, trans. Charles G. Osgood (1930; repr. Library of Liberal Arts, New York: Bobbs-Merrill, 1956), p. 45.

Chapter 2: The Pardoner's (Over-)Sexed Body

1. Glenn Burger, "Kissing the Pardoner," *PMLA* 107 (1992), p. 1145. Burger is responding specifically to the following: Eugene Vance, "Chaucer's Pardoner: Relics, Discourse, and Frames of Propriety," *New Literary History* 20 (1988–89): 723–45; H. Marshall Leicester, Jr., *The Disenchanted Self: Representing the Subject in the* Canterbury Tales (Berkeley: University of California Press, 1990), especially pp. 161–94; and Carolyn Dinshaw, *Chaucer's Sexual Poetics* (Madison: University of Wisconsin Press, 1989), pp. 156–86.
2. Burger, "Kissing," p. 1147.
3. Jonathan Dollimore, *Sexual Dissidence: Augustine to Wilde, Freud to Foucault* (Oxford: Clarendon Press, 1991), p. 87.
4. Walter Clyde Curry, *Chaucer and the Mediaeval Sciences,* 2nd ed. (New York: Barnes and Noble, 1960), pp. 54–70. The *Oxford English Dictionary* defines "gelding" as "a gelded person or eunuch" and "a gelded or castrated animal, esp. a horse," illustrating it with a quotation from Wyclif contemporary with Chaucer (s.v. "gelding"). The *Middle English Dictionary* is somewhat more equivocal, defining "gelding" as both "a castrated man, a eunuch" and as "a naturally impotent man" (s.v. "gelding"); "gelded" itself is invariably defined as "castrated."
5. Curry, *Chaucer and the Mediaeval Sciences,* pp. 61–64.

6. Curry, *Chaucer and the Mediaeval Sciences*, pp. 57–58, citing *Secreta Secretorum*, ed. R. Steele, EETS e.s. 74, pp. 223, 231.

7. Curry, *Chaucer and the Mediaeval Sciences*, pp. 60–61, citing *Bartholomeus de Proprietatibus Rerum*, trans. Trevisa (1495), 5.66, 5.23, 5.29, 5.25, 5.15, respectively.

8. See, for instance, David F. Greenberg, *The Construction of Homosexuality* (Chicago: University Of Chicago Press, 1988), p. 293:

   > Only incidentally do these clerical passages deplore homosexuality; their deepest preoccupation is with men dressing and acting like women. Sexual stratification in the feudal aristocracy had been sharp. . . . The new styles of clothing and bodily appearance cultivated by the men of the post-Conquest Norman aristocracy were incompatible with their traditional pastimes (hunting, fighting); gender conservatives interpreted them as involving the imitation of women, who had been traditionally been subordinate to men. The clergy found this voluntary adoption of the life-style of a subordinate sex repugnant, perhaps incompatible with the expectations of a ruling class.

   See also pp. 292–98 generally. On the association of effeminacy with male-male desire, see also John Boswell, *Christianity, Social Tolerance, and Homosexuality: Gay People in Western Europe from the Beginning of the Christian Era to the Fourteenth Century* (Chicago: University of Chicago Press, 1980), pp. 229–35. On the Pardoner's "normality," see Richard Firth Green, "The Sexual Normality of Chaucer's Pardoner," *Mediaevalia* 8 (1982): 351–58, discussed below.

9. "Si vero plus de muliebri spermate in dextra parte collocetur, femina virago generatur. Si plus in sinistram quam in dextram, et si plus sit de virili semine quam muliebri, vir effeminatus nascitur." [If more of the womanly sperm is set in the right part {of the womb}, a manly woman {*femina virago*} will be generated. If more in the left than the right, and there is more of the manly seed than the womanly, an effeminate man {*vir effeminatus*} will be born.] *The Prose Salernitan Questions Edited from a Bodleian Manuscript (Auct. F.3.10),* ed. Brian Lawn, Auctores Britannici Medii Aevi 5 (London: British Academy at Oxford University Press, 1979), B.193, p. 103, quoted in Joan Cadden, *Meanings of Sex Difference in the Middle Ages: Medicine, Science, and Culture* (Cambridge, Eng.: Cambridge University Press, 1993), p. 201, n. 116; trans. Cadden, p. 201. Cadden's entire chapter on "Feminine and Masculine Types," pp. 169–227, is useful in this context.

10. The *OED,* s.v. "gelded," defines the term unequivocally as "castrated," and illustrates it with another example from Trevisa; cf. the *MED,* s.v. "gelden," "to castrate."'

11. Mathew Kuefler cites satyriasis, elephantiasis, hernias, leprosy, gout, and epilepsy, among others, as diseases treatable by castration: see his "Castration and Eunuchism in the Middle Ages," in *Handbook of Medieval Sexuality,* ed. Vern L. Bullough and James A. Brundage (New York: Garland,

1996), pp. 279–306; the references to castration as cure and as legal punishment occur at p. 289 and pp. 288–89. See also Boswell, *Christianity, Social Tolerance, and Homosexuality*, p. 288, and James A. Brundage, *Law, Sex, and Christian Society in Medieval Europe* (Chicago: University of Chicago Press, 1987), pp. 472–74.

12. That is, those who, according to the *Glossa ordinaria*, "deceptively put on the guise of religion, but in reality are not chaste: the wolves in sheeps' clothing. 'Inter hos computantur etiam hic qui specie religionis simulant castitastem.'" [Among those are also reckoned those who simulate chastity under the guise of religion.] Robert P. Miller, "Chaucer's Pardoner, the Scriptural Eunuch, and the Pardoner's Tale," in *Chaucer Criticism: The Canterbury Tales*, ed. Richard Schoeck and Jerome Taylor (Notre Dame: University of Notre Dame Press, 1960), p. 226, quoting the *Glossa ordinaria* to Matthew 19:12 (*PL* 94, col. 148); trans. Miller, p. 242, n. 6. And cf. G. G. Sedgewick, "The Progress of Chaucer's Pardoner, 1880–1940," *Modern Language Quarterly* 1 (1940): 431–58, repr. in *Chaucer: Modern Essays in Criticism*, ed. Edward Wagenknecht (New York: Oxford University Press, 1959), pp. 126–58. Miller's essay is a revision of an earlier (1955) version, but despite its age Miller's article remains influential among recent critics concerned with medieval gender theory, for instance Carolyn Dinshaw, who cites Miller approvingly in her chapter on the Pardoner in her *Chaucer's Sexual Poetics*, pp. 159 and 164. For another example, see Gregory W. Gross, "Trade Secrets: Chaucer, the Pardoner, the Critics," *Modern Language Studies* 25.4 (1995), pp. 11–13. Gross usefully surveys Curry's influence on readings of the Pardoner, pp. 9–15.

13. Cadden, *Meanings of Sex Difference*, p. 198.

14. Monica McAlpine, "The Pardoner's Homosexuality and How It Matters," *PMLA* 95 (1980), pp. 10–11; and see the *MED* and *OED*, both s.v. "mare."

15. Beryl Rowland, "Animal Imagery and the Pardoner's Abnormality," *Neophilologus* 48 (1964), p. 58.

16. Carolyn Dinshaw, "Chaucer's Queer Touches / A Queer Touches Chaucer," *Exemplaria* 7 (1995), p. 80.

17. Rowland, "Animal Imagery," p. 60 n. 19.

18. See Rowland, "Chaucer's Idea of the Pardoner," *Chaucer Review* 14 (1979), pp. 149–50:

> According to late medieval writers the hermaphrodite's dual nature represented a duplicity, a doubleness of character. The word is used in the fourteenth and fifteenth centuries to convey the idea of *biplicitas, duplicitas,* deceitfulness, lack of sincerity, unreliability, complexity, and it is this sense which the hermaphrodite epitomizes. To the bestiarist of the thirteenth century the hare, because it is a hermaphrodite, exemplifies the double-minded man. Wycliffe, when discussing temporal and spiritual interests, observes that no man can serve two masters: "us thinkith that hermafrodita or ambidexter where a god name to sich maner of men of duble astate." . . . When the Pardoner, with his confession and sermon behind him, tries once more to play

his shamanistic role, to serve God and Mammon simultaneously, his conduct is wholly credible because Chaucer has carefully prepared for it by presenting a disastrous physical ambivalence as both counterpart and cause.

19. Rowland, "Animal Imagery," p. 57.

20. Rowland, "Animal Imagery," pp. 56–57.

21. Rowland, "Chaucer's Idea of the Pardoner," p. 143.

22. Rowland, "Chaucer's Idea of the Pardoner," pp. 143–44.

23. C. David Benson, "Chaucer's Pardoner: His Sexuality and Modern Critics," *Mediaevalia* 8 (1982), p. 344.

24. Benson, "Chaucer's Pardoner," p. 345. Benson uses the alternative scheme for labeling the fragments of *The Canterbury Tales* by letter rather than number; his C is what I refer to as Fragment VI, D is III.

25. Benson, "Chaucer's Pardoner," p. 345.

26. Richard Firth Green, "The Sexual Normality of Chaucer's Pardoner," *Mediaevalia* 8 (1982): 351–58; on the "Canterbury Interlude," see p. 353.

27. Green, "Sexual Normality," pp. 354–56, quoting *Three Prose Versions of the Secreta Secretorum,* ed. R. Steele, EETS e.s. 74 (London, 1898), p. 14.

28. Green, "Sexual Normality," p. 355, quoting John Gower, *Confessio Amantis,* ed. G. C. Macaulay, 2 vols., EETS 81–82 (London, 1900–01), 2:356 (Book VII, ll. 4318–27).

29. Monique Wittig, "The Straight Mind," in her *The Straight Mind and Other Essays* (Boston: Beacon Press, 1992), p. 29.

30. See the discussion of Alan of Lille in chapter 1 and the critical works cited in that chapter's note 16. See also Alexandre Leupin, "The Hermaphrodite: Alan of Lille's *De planctu Naturae,"* in his *Barbarolexis: Medieval Writing and Sexuality,* trans. Kate M. Cooper (Cambridge, MA: Harvard University Press, 1989), pp. 59–78. Rita Copeland more generally surveys the classical and medieval association of the dangers of undisciplined rhetoric with bodily perversions, and reads the Pardoner's ambiguous body as a figure for the dangerous "disciplinary autonomy of rhetoric," in "The Pardoner's Body and the Disciplining of Rhetoric," in *Framing Medieval Bodies,* ed. Sarah Kay and Miri Rubin (Manchester: Manchester University Press, 1994), p. 149.

31. Monique Wittig, "The Mark of Gender," in her *The Straight Mind and Other Essays,* p. 78.

32. See, for instance, Luce Irigaray, *Je, tu, nous: Toward a Culture of Difference,* trans. Alison Martin (New York: Routledge, 1993): "In any case, our need first and foremost is for a right to human dignity for everyone. That means we need laws that valorize difference. . . . That's particularly true for the sexes," p. 22. And cf. her *Thinking the Difference: For a Peaceful Revolution,* trans. Karin Montin (New York: Routledge, 1994). For an instructive consideration, and partial deconstruction, of these differences between Irigaray and Wittig, see Diana J. Fuss, *Essentially Speaking: Feminism, Nature and Difference* (New York: Routledge, 1989), pp. 39–72.

NOTES   183

33. Michel Foucault, "The Ethic of Care for the Self as a Practice of Freedom,"
    in *The Final Foucault,* ed. James Bernauer and David Rasmussen (Cam-
    bridge, MA: MIT Press, 1988), p. 12, quoted in John Champagne, *The
    Ethics of Marginality: A New Approach to Gay Studies* (Minneapolis: Univer-
    sity Of Minnesota Press), 1995, p. 5. See also Foucault's discussion of power
    and bodies in "Body/Power," in his *Power/Knowledge: Selected Interviews and
    Other Writings, 1972–1977,* ed. Colin Gordon (New York: Pantheon,
    1980): once power produces a disciplinary effect on the body, "there in-
    evitably emerge the responding claims and affirmations, those of one's own
    body against power. . . . Power, after investing itself in the body, finds itself
    exposed to a counterattack in that same body," p. 56.
34. Rowland, "Chaucer's Idea of the Pardoner," pp. 145–46. She also cites St.
    Augustine, Isidore of Seville, Bartholomaeus Anglicus, Lanfranc, Guy de
    Chauliac, and Trevisa.
35. Michel Foucault, "Introduction" to *Herculine Barbin: Being the Recently Dis-
    covered Memoirs of a Nineteenth-Century French Hermaphrodite,* trans. Richard
    McDougall (New York: Pantheon, 1980), pp. vii-viii. And cf. John W. Bald-
    win, *The Language of Sex: Five Voices from Northern France Around 1200*
    (Chicago: University of Chicago Press, 1994), pp. 44–45.
36. Judith Butler, *Gender Trouble: Feminism and the Subversion of Identity* (New
    York: Routledge, 1990), p. 96.
37. Another influential historian of sexuality who argues that the typical man-
    ner of differentiating anatomically between the sexes before the eighteenth
    century was radically different from ours is Thomas Laqueur, whose "one-
    sex" model (the view that in earlier periods female genitals were imagined
    as the same as male ones except for their positioning inside the body) has
    gained considerable currency: see his *Making Sex: Body and Gender from the
    Greeks to Freud* (Cambridge, MA: Harvard University Press, 1990). Laqueur
    has little to say about the Middle Ages, however, and, as in Foucault's case,
    the facts appear to be considerably more complex than can be accounted
    for by his theory. As Cadden, in *Meanings of Sex Difference,* mildly puts it,
    "medieval views on the status of the uterus and the opinions of medieval
    physiognomers about male and female traits suggest evidence of other
    models not reducible to Laqueur's," p. 3. Cadden's work provides the care-
    fully researched specifics lacking in such grand theories as Laqueur's and
    Foucault's.
38. Cadden, *Meanings of Sex Difference,* p. 203. Incisive recent studies that im-
    plicitly critique Foucault's understanding of the premodern categories of
    sex include, for Chaucer's own culture, Ruth Mazo Karras and David
    Lorenzo Boyd, "'*Ut cum muliere*': A Male Transvestite Prostitute in Four-
    teenth-Century London," in *Premodern Sexualities,* ed. Louise Fradenburg
    and Carla Freccero (New York: Routledge: 1996), pp. 101–116: gender
    transgression, rather than sodomy or prostitution, is at issue in the legal
    proceedings against the man in question, one John Rykener, who, despite
    his male anatomy, had to be categorized as a woman in order to allay the

anxieties about the sex/gender system that his unique case raised. See also, in the same volume, Lorraine Daston and Katharine Park, "The Hermaphrodite and the Orders of Nature: Sexual Ambiguity in Early Modern France," pp. 117–36. For more explicit critiques, see the "Introduction" to *Constructing Medieval Sexuality,* ed. Karma Lochrie, Peggy McCracken, and James A. Schultz, Medieval Cultures 11 (Minneapolis: University of Minnesota Press, 1997), pp. ix–xviii; and Allen J. Frantzen, *Before the Closet: Same-Sex Love from* Beowulf *to* Angels in America (Chicago: University of Chicago Press, 1998), pp. 7–13.

39. Albertus Magnus, *De animalibus,* 18.11.3.66, quoted and trans. in Cadden, *Meanings of Sex Difference,* p. 212, n. 151 and p. 212.

40. Cadden, *Meanings of Sex Difference,* p. 212. For a brief survey of "medieval challenges to bodily 'order,'" see Miri Rubin, "The Person in the Form: Medieval Challenges to Bodily 'Order,'" in *Framing Medieval Bodies,* pp. 100–122.

41. Judith Butler, *Bodies That Matter: On the Discursive Limits of "Sex"* (New York: Routledge, 1993), p. 4.

42. Caroline Walker Bynum, "Women Mystics and Eucharistic Devotion in the Thirteenth Century," in her *Fragmentation and Redemption: Essays on Gender and the Human Body in Medieval Religion* (New York: Urzone, 1992), pp. 146–47.

43. Donna J. Haraway, "In the Beginning was the Word: The Genesis of Biological Theory," in her *Simians, Cyborgs, and Women: The Reinvention of Nature* (New York: Routledge, 1991), p. 77. On biology as politics, see also Haraway's "FemaleMan©_Meets_OncoMouse™: Mice into Wormholes: A Technoscience Fugue in Two Parts" in her *Modest_Witness@Second_Millenium.FemaleMan©_Meets_OncoMouse™* (New York: Routledge, 1997), pp. 49–118.

44. Jacqueline Urla and Jennifer Terry, "Introduction: Mapping Embodied Deviance," in *Deviant Bodies: Critical Perspectives on Difference in Science and Popular Culture,* ed. Jacqueline Urla and Jennifer Terry (Bloomington: Indiana University Press, 1995), p. 16.

Chapter 3: The Pardoner's Different Erotic Practices

1. George Lyman Kittredge, *Chaucer and His Poetry* (Cambridge: Harvard University Press, 1915; repr. 1927), p. 211.

2. Kittredge, *Chaucer and His Poetry,* p. 180.

3. Walter Clyde Curry, *Chaucer and the Mediaeval Sciences,* 2nd ed. (New York: Barnes and Noble, 1960), pp. 54–70. See chapter 2.

4. Melvin Storm, "The Pardoner's Invitation: Quaestor's Bag or Becket's Shrine?" (abstract), *PMLA* 97 (1982), p. 797.

5. See Storm's essay, "The Pardoner's Invitation: Quaestor's Bag or Becket's Shrine?," *PMLA* 97 (1982), p. 813, and the articles he cites there.

6. Muriel Bowden, *A Commentary on the General Prologue to the Canterbury Tales* (New York: Macmillan, 1948), pp. 274–76.

7. Cited above, chapter 1, n. 9.

8. Monica McAlpine, "The Pardoner's Homosexuality and How It Matters," *PMLA* 95 (1980), p. 14.

9. Steven F. Kruger, "Claiming the Pardoner: Toward a Gay Reading of Chaucer's Pardoner's Tale," *Exemplaria* 6 (1994), p. 138. A progressive and very useful critique of the essentialist assumptions of a number of earlier critics on the subject of the Pardoner's erotic practices may be found in Gregory W. Gross, "Trade Secrets: Chaucer, the Pardoner, the Critics," *Modern Language Studies* 25.4 (1995): 1–33, especially pp. 2–15.

10. McAlpine, "The Pardoner's Homosexuality," pp. 10–13.

11. C. David Benson, "Chaucer's Pardoner: His Sexuality and Modern Critics," *Mediaevalia* 8 (1982): 337–49.

12. Richard Firth Green, "The Sexual Normality of Chaucer's Pardoner," *Mediaevalia* 8 (1982): 351–58.

13. Storm, "Invitation," p. 812.

14. Storm, "Invitation," p. 813.

15. Donald R. Howard, *The Idea of the Canterbury Tales* (Berkeley: University of California Press, 1976), pp. 344–45.

16. Michel Foucault, *The History of Sexuality, Volume I: An Introduction,* trans. Robert Hurley (1978; repr. Vintage: New York, 1980), p. 101.

17. Joan Cadden, *Meanings of Sex Difference in the Middle Ages: Medicine, Science, and Culture* (Cambridge, Eng.: Cambridge University Press, 1993), pp. 214–18.

18. Peter of Abano, *Expositio problematum Aristotelis* (ed. 1475), 4.26, trans. in Cadden, *Meanings of Sex Difference,* p. 214, quoted p. 214 n. 161.

19. Cadden, *Meanings of Sex Difference,* p. 214.

20. See Cadden, *Meanings of Sex Difference,* p. 215.

21. Peter of Abano, *Expositio,* 4.26, trans. in Cadden, *Meanings of Sex Difference,* p. 214, quoted p. 214, n. 161.

22. Cadden, *Meanings of Sex Difference,* pp. 215–16, translating Peter of Abano, *Expositio* 4.26; quoted p. 216, n. 167·" . . . propter pravam consuetundinem obscenam advenit, quales sunt sodomite."

23. Cadden, *Meanings of Sex Difference,* p. 215. See also Cadden, "Sciences/Silences: The Natures and Languages of 'Sodomy' in Peter of Abano's *Problemata* Commentary," in *Constructing Medieval Sexuality,* Medieval Cultures 11, eds. Karma Lochrie, Peggy McCracken, and James A. Schultz (Minneapolis: University of Minnesota Press, 1997), pp. 40–57.

24. Mark D. Jordan, *The Invention of Sodomy in Christian Theology* (Chicago: University of Chicago Press, 1997), p. 133.

25. Peter Damian, "Letter 31" (*Liber Gomorrhianus*) in *Die Briefe des Petrus Damiani,* ed. Kurt Reindel, 4 vols. (Munich: Monumenta Germaniae Historica, 1983), 1:287; "Letter 31" (*The Book of Gommorah*), trans. Owen J. Blum, O.F.M., in *Peter Damian: Letters 31–60,* The Fathers of the Church: Mediaeval Continuation 2 (Washington, D.C.: Catholic University of America Press, 1990), pp. 6–7.

26. Damian, *Liber Gomorrhianus,* 1:302; *Book of Gommorah,* trans. Blum, p. 23. See Jordan's discussion of these issues in *Invention of Sodomy,* pp. 51–58. A variety of specific penances for male same-sex eroticism in the medieval

penitentials can be found in *Medieval Handbooks of Penance: A Translation of the Principal* Libri Poenitentiales, trans. John T. McNeill and Helena M. Gamer, Records of Western Civilization (New York: Columbia University Press, 1938, repr. 1990), indexed under "homosexuality" and "sodomy." These texts are usefully discussed in Pierre J. Payer, *Sex and the Penitentials: The Development of a Sexual Code, 550–1150* (Toronto: University of Toronto Press, 1984), pp. 40–44 and 135–39. Payer seems to agree that the penitentials' view of sodomy is contradictory: "The attitude betrayed by their treatment of homosexuality can be argued endlessly," p. 135.

27. Jordan, *Invention of Sodomy*, pp. 65–66.

28. James A. Brundage, *Law, Sex, and Christian Society in Medieval Europe* (Chicago: University of Chicago Press, 1987), p. 533. And cf. John W. Baldwin, *The Language of Sex: Five Voices From Northern France Around 1200* (Chicago: University of Chicago Press, 1994), pp. 43–47, on the wide variety of erotic practices condemned as sodomitical.

29. Elizabeth B. Keiser, *Courtly Desire and Medieval Homophobia: The Legitimation of Sexual Pleasure in* Cleanness *and Its Contexts* (New Haven: Yale University Press, 1997), p. 95. See also Jordan's discussion of Aquinas on pleasure, *Invention of Sodomy*, pp. 155–56, and his essay, "Homosexuality, *Luxuria,* and Textual Abuse" in *Constructing Medieval Sexuality*, pp. 24–39.

30. The poet's "extraordinary intellectual and imaginative" breakthrough is discussed throughout Keiser's book, but see especially pp. 65–70. And cf. Carolyn Dinshaw, "A Kiss Is Just a Kiss: Heterosexuality and its Consolations in *Sir Gawain and the Green Knight,*" in *Critical Crossings,* ed. Judith Butler and Biddy Martin, special issue of *Diacritics* 24.2–3 (Summer-Fall, 1994), especially pp. 216–20.

31. John Boswell, *Christianity, Social Tolerance, and Homosexuality: Gay People in Western Europe from the Beginning of the Christian Era to the Fourteenth Century* (Chicago: University of Chicago Press, 1980), p. 330.

32. Keiser, *Courtly Desire,* p. 112.

33. Michael Goodich, *The Unmentionable Vice: Homosexuality in the Later Medieval Period* (Santa Barbara [?]: Dorset Press, 1979).

34. Jordan, *Invention of Sodomy*, pp. 106 and 111–12.

35. Jordan, *Invention of Sodomy*, p. 98, paraphrasing Paul of Hungary's *Summa de poenitentia* (ed. 1880), 208a.

36. Jordan, *Invention of Sodomy*, p. 113.

37. P. L. Heyworth, "Jocelin of Brakelond, Abbot Samson, and the Case of William the Sacrist," in *Middle English Studies Presented to Norman Davis in Honour of his Seventieth Birthday*, ed. Douglas Gray and E. G. Stanley (Oxford: Clarendon Press, 1983), p. 186. Heyworth's entire discussion of these issues, pp. 184–93, is relevant and useful.

38. Keiser, *Courtly Desire,* p. 236 n. 19. Cf. Heyworth, "Jocelin of Brakelond," p. 186, and see also Goodich, *Unmentionable Vice,* p. 38, on the association of the Ephesians passage with the story of Sodom, as well as Jordan's discussion of the Ephesians passage, *Invention of Sodomy*, pp. 150–51.

39. Jordan, *Invention of Sodomy*, p. 90. See also Heyworth, "Jocelin of Brakelond," p. 185.

40. Alan of Lille, *De planctu naturae*, 8.92–95, ed. Nikolaus M. Häring, *Studi Medievali*, serie terza 19.2 (1978), p. 839; *Plaint of Nature*, trans. James J. Sheridan (Toronto: Pontifical Institute of Mediaeval Studies, 1980), p. 144.

41. Alan of Lille, *De planctu naturae*, 10.50–57, ed. Häring, p. 846; *Plaint of Nature*, trans. Sheridan, p. 157.

42. *Plaint of Nature*, trans. Sheridan, p. 157, n.11.

43. It should be noted at this point that Jan Ziolkowski, by decoding Alan's metaphors, has emphatically not made it possible to discuss same-sex erotic practices in medieval literature unambiguously; in a curious disclaimer, he states at the outset that his book is not really concerned with "homosexuality," but only with linguistic metaphors: "the first chapter is not intended as a contribution to the study of medieval views on homosexuality. Rather, it is meant to set the stage for an exploration of the attitudes toward grammar which prompted Alan to choose grammatical metaphors as a vehicle of expression for his thoughts on many issues." Like such heterosexist Chaucerians as Storm, Ziolkowski's language erases same-sex desrie even when it is crucial to his own argument. See Jan Ziolkowski, *Alan of Lille's Grammar of Sex* (Cambridge, MA: Medieval Academy, 1985), p. 4. Despite Ziolkowski's reservation, at least one recent critic has attempted a "queer" reading of Alan's text itself: see Elizabeth Pittenger, "Explicit Ink," in *Premodern Sexualities*, ed. Louise Fradenburg and Carla Freccero (New York: Routledge, 1996), pp. 223–42. See also Alexandre Leupin's deconstruction of Alan's use of the sodomite and hermaphrodite: "The Hermaphrodite: Alan of Lille's *De planctu Naturae*," in his *Barbarolexis: Medieval Writing and Sexuality*, trans. Kate M. Cooper (Cambridge, MA: Harvard University Press, 1989), pp. 59–78. And cf. Keiser, *Courtly Desire*, pp. 74–86. Gross explores another manner in which Chaucer translates Alan's rhetorical strategies in order to associate the Pardoner with sodomy: Alan's term for rhetorical defects, *uicium*, is also used metaphorically to designate the practices of the sodomites, and in English becomes Chaucer's "vice," as in the Pardoner's admission that he is "a ful vicious man" (Gross, "Trade Secrets," pp. 23–31).

44. Keiser, *Courtly Desire*, p. 57.

45. Eve Kosofsky Sedgwick, *Epistemology of the Closet* (Berkeley: University of California Press, 1990), p. 74, apparently referring to Ephesians 5:3–12; see n. 38, above.

46. Luce Irigaray, *This Sex Which Is Not One*, trans. Catherine Porter with Carolyn Burke (New York: Columbia University Press, 1985), p. 26.

47. Irigaray, *This Sex*, p. 193.

48. Judith Butler, *Gender Trouble: Feminism and the Subversion of Identity* (New York: Routledge, 1990), p. 17.

49. Monique Wittig, "The Straight Mind," in her *The Straight Mind and Other Essays* (Boston: Beacon Press, 1992), p. 32.

50. Butler, *Gender Trouble*, p. 127. The possibility that Wittig and Butler seem to be approaching, that of an anatomical male claiming a lesbian identity, has been explored by Jacquelyn N. Zita, "Male Lesbians and the Postmodernist Body," *Hypatia* 7.4 (Fall, 1992): 106–127; because it represents a postmodern failure to value the "historical gravity" of the body, Zita finally rejects this possibility, but only "tentatively," p. 126.

Chapter 4: The Pardoner Unveiled

1. David F. Greenberg, *The Construction of Homosexuality* (Chicago: University of Chicago Press, 1988).

2. Marjorie Garber, *Vested Interests: Cross-Dressing and Cultural Anxiety* (1992; repr. HarperCollins: New York, 1993), pp. 304–52.

3. C. David Benson, "Chaucer's Pardoner: His Sexuality and Modern Critics," *Mediaevalia* 8 (1982), p. 339, and Carolyn Dinshaw, *Chaucer's Sexual Poetics* (Madison: University of Wisconsin Press, 1989), pp. 256–57, n. 1; Ralph W. V. Elliott, *Chaucer's English* (London: André Deutsch, 1974), pp. 87–88; Ewald Standop, "Chaucers Pardoner: das Charakterproblem und die Kritiker," in *Geschichtlichkeit und Neuanfang im sprachlichen Kunstwerk: Studien zur englischen Philologie zu Ehren von Fritz W. Schulze*, ed. Peter Erlebach, Wolfgang G. Müller, and Klaus Reuter (Tübingen: Gunter Narr, 1981), pp. 63–64; Walter Clyde Curry, *Chaucer and the Mediaeval Sciences,* p. 59; J. Swart, "Chaucer's Pardoner," *Neophilologus* 36 (1952), p. 45. (And I realize that I myself am taking the pronoun "I" for granted along with the subjectivity it implies, as lying outside the scope of this book.)

4. On medieval masculinity more generally in this context, see also Jeffrey Jerome Cohen and Bonnie Wheeler, "Becoming and Unbecoming," the introduction to *Becoming Male in the Middle Ages*, ed. Jeffrey Jerome Cohen and Bonnie Wheeler (New York: Garland, 1997), pp. vii–xx, and the essays collected therein.

5. Homi K. Bhabha, "Are You a Man or a Mouse?" in *Constructing Masculinity*, ed. Maurice Berger, Brian Wallis, and Simon Watson (New York: Routledge, 1995), p. 57.

6. *Jacobi a Voragine Legenda aurea vulgo historica lombardica dicta*, ed. Th. Graesse, 2nd ed. (Leipzig: Arnold, 1850), p. 233.

7. See James F. Rhodes, "The Pardoner's Vernycle and His Vera Icon," *Modern Language Studies* 13 (1983), pp. 35–36.

8. The complex history of the Veronica legend is carefully described by Rhodes, "The Pardoner's Vernycle," pp. 34–37.

9. E. Kölbing and Mabel Day, eds., *The Siege of Jerusalem,* EETS o.s. 188 (1932; repr. Kraus Reprint Co.: New York, 1971), p. xxix.

10. *The Siege of Jerusalem,* ll. 161–64; emphasis added. See also ll. 231, 249, 259.

11. 2 Corinthians 3:13–16 (Douay-Rheims translation).

12. St. Augustine, *Confessions,* 6.4, ed. W. H. D. Rouse, trans. William Watts, 2 vols., Loeb Classical Library 26–27 (Cambridge, MA: Harvard University Press, 1912), 1:278–79.

13. I am indebted to D. W. Robertson, Jr., *A Preface to Chaucer: Studies in Medieval Perspectives* (Princeton, NJ: Princeton University Press, 1962), pp. 291, 294, and 319–20 for all of these examples of the veil as a figure for Scriptural allegory.

14. O. B. Hardison et al, eds., *Medieval Literary Criticism: Translations and Interpretations* (New York: Ungar, 1974), p. 20; Robertson, *Preface,* p. 280.

15. Giovanni Boccaccio, *Genealogie deorum gentilium libri,* 14.10, ed. Vincenzo Romano, 2 vols. (Bari: Laterza, 1951), 2:710; *Boccaccio on Poetry: Being the Preface and the Fourteenth and Fifteenth Books of Boccaccio's* Genealogia Deorum Gentilium, trans. Charles G. Osgood (1930; repr. Bobbs-Merrill: New York, 1956), p. 53.

16. J. S. McQuade, "Robert Grosseteste's Commentary on the 'Celestial Hierarchy' of Pseudo-Dionysius the Areopagite: An Edition Translation, and Introduction to his Text and Commentary, chapters 10–15," diss. Queen's University of Belfast, 1961, p. 50, qtd. in A. J. Minnis and A. B. Scott, eds., *Medieval Literary Theory and Criticism, c. 1100–c. 1375: The Commentary Tradition,* rev. ed. (Oxford: Clarendon Press, 1991), p. 172, n. 40.

17. Boccaccio, *Genealogia,* 14.9, ed. Romano, 2:706; *On Poetry,* trans. Osgood, p.48.

18. The reference to Veronica's veil in *The Siege of Jerusalem,* cited above, is unusual in its description of the image of Christ's face as a painting; more typically, it is miraculously imprinted on the veil, transferred directly by contact with Christ's body. See, for instance, Veronica's narrative in *Legenda aurea,* p. 233. Even the *Siege,* however, traces the image directly back to Christ ("for loue he left hit hir"), thus linking the vernicle once again to the originary transcendental signified.

19. Rhodes, "The Pardoner's Vernycle," pp. 36–37.

20. Marie-José Baudinet, "The Face of Christ, the Form of the Church," in *Fragments for a History of the Human Body, Part One,* ed. Michael Feher with Ramona Naddaff and Nadia Tazi, *Zone* 3 (New York: Urzone, 1989), p. 153. The text of Nicephorus on which Baudinet is commenting in this passage appears as an appendix, pp. 157–59.

21. Rhodes, "The Pardoner's Vernycle," p. 34.

22. Bhabha, "Are You a Man or a Mouse?," p. 59, quoting Johann G. Fichte's 1807–1808 *Address to the German Nation* (Chicago: Open Court Publishing, 1968), p. 173.

23. Jacques Derrida, *Spurs: Nietzsche's Styles / Eperons: Les Styles de Nietzsche,* trans. Barbara Harlow (Chicago: University of Chicago Press, 1979), pp. 94–101.

24. Carolyn Burke, "Irigaray Through the Looking Glass," in *Engaging with Irigaray: Feminist Theory and Modern European Thought,* ed. Carolyn Burke, Naomi Schor, and Margaret Whitford (New York: Columbia University Press, 1994), p. 42. Burke's entire discussion of this term's history (pp. 41–43) is useful and relevant. Jean-Joseph Goux helpfully discusses the mythic origins of the association between phallus and logos in "The Phallus: Masculine Identity and the 'Exchange of Women,'" *differences* 4.1

(1992): 40–58; see especially pp. 48–49: "As the male organ of generation, the phallus is therefore essentially logos or source of the logos: rational power, or intelligible reason," p. 49.

25. Beryl Rowland, *Blind Beasts: Chaucer's Animal World* (Kent, OH: Kent State University Press, 1971), p. 100; John Boswell, *Christianity, Social Tolerance, and Homosexuality: Gay People in Western Europe from the Beginning of the Christian Era to the Fourteenth Century* (Chicago: University of Chicago Press, 1980), pp. 137–38, 306.

26. Critical opinion is divided as to whether or not the "walet" and the "male" are in fact the same bag. The Ellesmere miniature depicts only one, suggesting that they are identical, although, departing from the verbal description, it depicts the bag neither in the Pardoner's lap nor in a fold, but hanging from his horse's neck.

27. Chaucer uses the term unambiguously in this modern sense later in *The Canterbury Tales:* In *The Monk's Tale,* Ugolino's children lie "in his lappe adoun" to die (VII, 2454). The text's unambiguous uses of the term in its other sense (in *The Second Nun's Prologue* and *The Clerk's Tale*) do not include the possessive pronoun, but refer to "a lappe" or "the lappe" (VIII, 12; IV, 585). Another occurrence of "lappe" with the possessive pronoun, in *The Squire's Tale* (V, 635), could also be read either way, but again the modern sense seems more likely.

28. See, for example, Dinshaw, *Chaucer's Sexual Poetics,* p. 164.

29. Slavoj Žižek's Lacanian analysis of the insult mocking an adversary's phallic power suggests an interesting reading of the Pardoner's silence: "'Yours is so big and powerful, but in spite of that, you are impotent. You cannot hurt me with it.' . . . In this way the adversary is caught in a forced choice which . . . defines the experience of castration: if he cannot, he cannot; but even if he can, any attesting to his power is doomed to function as denial— that is, as a masking of his fundamental impotence, as a mere showing-off which just confirms, in a negative way, that he cannot do anything." *The Sublime Object of Ideology* (London: Verso, 1989), p. 157.

30. Jacques Lacan, "The Signification of the Phallus," in his *Ecrits: A Selection,* trans. Alan Sheridan (New York: Norton, 1977), p. 285. The slippage between "phallus" and "penis" in Lacan's own usage, however, has been noted by several critics as itself an instance of the phallogocentrism Derrida exposes in psychoanalytic discourse; see Jane Gallop, *Reading Lacan* (Ithaca, NY: Cornell University Press, 1985), pp. 133–36. Goux, "The Phallus," argues that such slippage is inevitable: "If the phallus is a simulacrum and not an organ, this phallus undeniably derives a part of its signifying attributes from what the real penis can evoke," p. 60.

31. Goux, "The Phallus," p. 43. The Osiris myth was well known in the Western Middle Ages; Martianus Capella, for instance, refers to it in *The Marriage of Philology and Mercury,* a text with which Chaucer claims familiarity in *The Merchant's Tale* (IV, 1732–1735). See Martianus Capella, *De Nuptiis Philologiae et Mercurii,* 1.4, in *Martianus Capella Accedunt Scholia in Caesaris*

Germanici Aratea, ed. Francis Eyssenhardt (Leipzig:Teubner, 1866), p. 3. For medieval commentaries on Martianus Capella's references to Osiris, see Remigius of Auxerre, *Remigii Autissiodorensis Commentum in Martianum Capellam,* 1.6.2, ed. Cora E. Lutz, 2 vols. (Leiden: E. J. Brill, 1962–1965), 1:73, and Bernardus Silvestris, *The Commentary on Martianus Capella's De Nuptiis Philologiae et Mercurii Attributed to Bernardus Silvestris,* 5.874–95, ed. Haijo Jan Westra (Toronto: Pontifical Institute of Mediaeval Studies, 1986), p. 123. Dionysos, whose connection with the Pardoner was examined in chapter 1, is a similarly phallic god, one whom Detienne associates with Osiris: see Marcel Detienne, *Dionysos at Large,* trans. Arthur Goldhammer (Cambridge, MA: Harvard University Press, 1989), pp. 1 and 32.

32. Luce Irigaray offers a critique of this aspect of the veiled phallus from the perspective of the female body in her suggestively titled essay "Veiled Lips":

    Nature can be loved only if she is concealed: as if in a dream. No sooner do they sense nature than the men of yesterday and today climb high onto the roofs and towers of fantasy. They are born to climb—to rise up. . . . Their dream: to cover the natural with veils. To climb ever higher, get farther and farther off, turn away from nature toward certainties that they can no longer even see, as an escape onto dangerous heights—their plains, their plans. As a way to rid their thoughts of the disgusting things to which nature subjects every woman (?).

    Marine Lover of Friedrich Nietzsche, trans. Gillian C. Gill (New York: Columbia University Press, 1991), p. 108. In this fascinating passage, the veiling of the phallus is simply one aspect of the veiling of the natural, which is here assimilated to "woman"—though Irigaray's concluding question mark seems to warn against the very essentialism her writings so often appear to promote.

33. Lacan, "Signification," p. 288. Catherine S. Cox proposes that the veiled phallus can also be read as a sign specifically of gender inequality, thus making explicit what remains implicit in Lacan: "It is a commonplace of medieval theology that an awareness of sexual difference is a consequence of the fall; as noted, the first gesture of shame exhibited by humans is the covering up of the genitals, a veiling of sexual difference and the troubling issues it seems to promote. Appropriately, too, the veil comprises animal hides, a trophy of human conquest. What seems inextricable from the awareness of sexual difference and gender distinction is inequality, the subordination of the feminine." *Gender and Language in Chaucer* (Gainesville: University Press of Florida, 1997), p. 84.

34. Jean Baudrillard, "The Precession of Simulacra," in his *Simulation and Simulacra,* trans. Sheila Faria Glaser (Ann Arbor: University of Michigan Press, 1994), p. 3.

35. Baudrillard, "Precession," p. 6.

36. Garber, *Vested Interests,* p. 343.

37. Lacan, "Signification," p. 289.
38. Goux, "The Phallus," p. 53.
39. Bhabha, "Are You a Man or a Mouse?," p. 58.
40. Dinshaw, *Chaucer's Sexual Poetics,* pp. 160–68 and 176–77.
41. Lacan, "Signification," p. 290. Goux, "The Phallus," also relates such "sacred objects" (p. 62) to the phallus and, interestingly for the Pardoner's case, to the concept of *agalma,* or "ornament, costume, glory, honor, offering, gift object, beautiful image, sign," p. 73, n. 7.
42. Bice Benvenuto and Roger Kennedy, *The Works of Jacques Lacan: An Introduction* (New York: St. Martin's Press, 1986), pp. 132–33.
43. Goux, "The Phallus," p. 69.
44. Bhabha, "Are You a Man or a Mouse?," p. 60.
45. Bhabha, "Are You a Man or a Mouse?," p. 58.
46. Lacan, "Signification," p. 288.
47. Calvin Thomas, *Male Matters: Masculinity, Anxiety, and the Male Body on the Line* (Urbana: University of Illinois Press, 1996), p. 115. Thomas follows Leo Bersani's celebrated essay, "Is the Rectum a Grave?" (1987), repr. in *Reclaiming Sodom,* ed. Jonathan Goldberg (New York: Routledge, 1994), pp. 249–64, though Bersani's understanding of the rectal potential for deconstructing an idealized phallic subjectivity is more positive: " . . . if the rectum is the grave in which the masculine ideal (an ideal shared—differently—by men *and* women) of proud subjectivity is buried, then it should be celebrated for its very potential for death. . . . It may, finally, be in the gay man's rectum that he demolishes his own perhaps otherwise uncontrollable identification with a murderous judgment against him," p. 262.
48. Goux, "The Phallus," p. 41.
49. Goux, "The Phallus," p. 70.
50. Goux, "The Phallus," p. 73.
51. Baudrillard, "Precession," p. 25.
52. Baudrillard, "Precession," p. 20.
53. Baudrillard, "Precession," p. 12.
54. Baudrillard, "Precession," pp. 19–27 and 32–40.
55. Baudrillard, "Precession," p. 33.
56. See Baudinet, "Face of Christ."
57. Dinshaw, *Chaucer's Sexual Poetics,* pp. 182–83. Dinshaw's positive understanding of this supposed refusal of difference would, perhaps, be challenged by Irigaray, who sees the "annihilation of difference" as a typical patriarchal move in the erasure of woman: "Once the phallic show—what he has kept in reserve—is over, the question must be taken up and reconsidered. See if the process of taking over would still be master even to this point over 'the unceasing war between the sexes,' 'the mortal hate between the sexes'. . . . For the affirmation or annihilation of difference, perhaps?" "Veiled Lips," p. 111; ellipsis in text.
58. See, e.g., Dinshaw, *Chaucer's Sexual Poetics,* pp. 157.

59. Garber, *Vested Interests,* pp. 339–45.

60. I do not wish to claim that this constellation of details appeared in the medieval versions of Salome's story or that her story influenced Chaucer in any way: neither the Bible nor any medieval source mentions the veils or the kiss, which appear to be nineteenth-century additions. My interest lies only in comparing how these two entirely independent stories function.

61. Garber, *Vested Interests,* p. 342.

62. Judith Butler, *Gender Trouble: Feminism and the Subversion of Identity* (New York: Routledge, 1990), p. 136.

63. Joan Rivière, "Womanliness as a Masquerade" (1929), repr. in *Formations of Fantasy,* ed. Victor Burgin, James Donald, and Cora Kaplan (London: Methuen, 1986), pp. 35–44. See also Butler's discussion of Rivière, *Gender Trouble,* pp. 50–54.

64. Butler, *Bodies That Matter: On the Discursive Limits of "Sex"* (New York: Routledge, 1993), p. 230.

65. Benvenuto and Kennedy, *The Works of Jacques Lacan,* p. 133.

66. Baudrillard, "Precession," pp. 4–5.

67. Goux, "The Phallus," p. 55.

Chapter 5: A Speaking and Singing Subject

1. On the Summoner's erotics, see Catherine S. Cox, *Gender and Language in Chaucer* (Gainesville: University Press of Florida, 1997), pp. 113–32. She discusses his relationship with the Pardoner specifically on pp. 115–18. Laurel Braswell-Means, "A New Look at an Old Patient: Chaucer's Summoner and Medieval Physiognomia," *Chaucer Review* 25.3 (1991): 266–75, discusses, among other things, the sexual implications of the Summoner's physiognomy, though she draws an unsupported connection between impotence and "his implied homosexual preferences," p. 272.

2. Julia Kristeva, "From One Identity to Another," in her *Desire in Language: A Semiotic Approach to Literature and Art,* ed. Leon S. Roudiez, trans. Thomas Gora, Alice Jardine, and Leon S. Roudiez (New York: Columbia University Press, 1980), p. 133.

3. Kristeva, "From One Identity," p. 133.

4. Kristeva, "From One Identity," p. 140.

5. Kristeva, "From One Identity," p. 136. On the relationship of the feminine to song, see also Hélène Cixous, "The Laugh of the Medusa" (1975), repr. in *Feminisms: An Anthology of Literary Theory and Criticism,* ed. Robyn Warhol and Diane Price Herndl (New Brunswick, NJ: Rutgers University Press, 1991), pp. 334–49, especially p. 339.

6. Julia Kristeva, "Stabat Mater," in her *Tales of Love,* trans. Leon S. Roudiez (New York: Columbia University Press, 1987), p. 235.

7. Kristeva, "From One Identity," p. 132.

8. Carolyn Dinshaw, *Chaucer's Sexual Poetics* (Madison: University of Wisconsin Press, 1989), p. 158; H. Marshall Leicester, *The Disenchanted Self: Representing*

the Subject in the Canterbury Tales (Berkeley: University of California Press, 1990), pp. 181–94.

9. See chapter 4, "The Pardoner Unveiled."

10. Martin Irvine, *The Making of Textual Culture: 'Grammatica' and Literary Theory 350–1100* (Cambridge: Cambridge University Press, 1994), p. 91.

11. Donatus, *De voce,* in *Grammatici Latini,* ed. Heinrich Keil and H. Hagen, 7 vols. (Leipzig: Teubner, 1857–1880), 4:367, quoted and trans. in Irvine, *Making of Textual Culture,* p. 92.

12. Diomedes, *De voce,* in *Grammatici Latini,* 1:420, quoted and trans. in Irvine, *Making of Textual Culture,* pp. 92–93.

13. Priscian, *De voce,* in *Grammatici Latini,* 2:5, quoted and trans. in Irvine, *Making of Textual Culture,* pp. 93–94.

14. Irvine, *Making of Textual Culture,* p. 91.

15. Stephen G. Nichols, "Voice and Writing in Augustine and in the Troubadour Lyrics," in *Vox Intexta: Orality and Literacy in the Middle Ages,* ed. A. N. Doane and Carol Braun Pasternack (Madison: University of Wisconsin Press, 1991), p. 146.

16. Paul Zumthor, *La Lettre et la voix: De la "littérature" médiévale* (Paris: Seuil, 1987), p. 270.

17. Augustine, *Confessions,* 11.27, ed. P. Knöll, trans. William Watts, rev. W. H. D. Rouse, 2 vols., Loeb Classical Library 26–27 (Cambridge, MA: Harvard University Press, 1912), 2:274, 275.

18. Augustine, *Confessions,* 12.16, ed. Knöll, 2:322, 323.

19. Nichols, "Voice and Writing," p. 147.

20. Nichols, "Voice and Writing," p. 149.

21. Thomas Walsingham, *Historia Anglicana,* ed. Henry Thomas Riley, 2 vols. (Rolls Series, 1863–64), 1:460; trans. R. B. Dobson, *The Peasants' Revolt of 1381,* ed. R. B. Dobson, 2nd. ed. (London: Macmillan, 1983), p. 173. This passage was drawn to my attention by Jesse M. Gellrich, *Discourse and Dominion in the Fourteenth Century: Oral Contexts of Writing in Philosophy, Politics, and Poetry* (Princeton, NJ: Princeton University Press, 1995), p. 163.

22. Gellrich, *Discourse and Dominion,* p. 163; and see the discussion of the political ideology of Walsingham's use of voice in Steven Justice, *Writing and Rebellion: England in 1381* (Berkeley: University of California Press, 1994), pp. 205–08. The anonymous "Canterbury Interlude" added to *The Canterbury Tales* in the 1420s gives the Pardoner a song with similarly disruptive qualities: see John M. Bowers, ed., The Canterbury Tales: *Fifteenth-Century Continuations and Additions,* TEAMS Middle English Texts Series (Kalamazoo, MI: Medieval Institute Publications, 1992), pp. 60–79, especially ll. 407–21, p. 71.

23. Gellrich, *Discourse and Dominion,* p. 163.

24. Dobson, ed., *Peasants' Revolt,* p. 172. The Latin text is "ribaldi perditissimi, ganeones dæmoniaci," Walsingham, *Historia Anglicana,* 1:459.

25. Nichols, "Voice and Writing," p. 146.

26. Bernardus Silvestris, *The Commentary on the First Six Books of the* Aeneid *of Vergil Commonly Attributed to Bernardus Silvestris,* book 4, ed. Julian Ward Jones and Elizabeth Frances Jones (Lincoln: University of Nebraska Press, 1977), p. 25; *Commentary on the First Six Books of Virgil's* Aeneid, trans. Earl G. Schreiber and Thomas E. Maresca (Lincoln: University of Nebraska Press, 1979), p. 27; both qtd. inaccurately in Nichols, "Voice and Writing," p. 150.

27. Nichols, "Voice and Writing," p. 150.

28. R. Howard Bloch, *Medieval Misogyny and the Invention of Western Romantic Love* (Chicago: University of Chicago Press, 1991), pp. 54, 18; on the connection of the feminine to the body, senses, and materiality, see pp. 13–63 generally. And recall Caroline Walker Bynum's similar points, cited above, chapter 1, n. 26, and chapter 2, n. 42. See also the essays collected in *Feminist Approaches to the Body in Medieval Literature,* ed. Linda Lomperis and Sarah Stanbury (Philadelphia: University of Pennsylvania Press, 1993).

29. E. Jane Burns, *Bodytalk: When Women Speak in Old French Literature* (Philadelphia: University of Pennsylvania Press, 1993), pp. 48–70.

30. Gellrich, *Discourse and Dominion,* p. 166.

31. This is demonstrated, for example, by the need for English translations of widely available Latin texts such as the pseudo-Augustinian *Soliloquies:* see Robert S. Sturges, "Anti-Wycliffite Commentary in Richardson MS 22," *Harvard Library Bulletin* 34 (1986), p. 381.

32. Kristeva, "From One Identity," p. 133.

33. Cf. Judith Ferster, "'Your Praise is Performed by Men and Children': Language and Gender in the *Prioress's Prologue and Tale,*" in *Reconceiving Chaucer: Literary Theory and Historical Interpretation,* ed. Thomas Hahn, special issue of *Exemplaria* 2.1 (Spring, 1990), p. 151, nn. 14–15.

34. Corey J. Marvin, "'I Will Thee Not Forsake':The Kristevan Maternal Space in Chaucer's *Prioress's Tale* and John of Garland's *Stella maris,*" *Exemplaria* 8 (1996), pp. 38–39.

35. See Marvin, "'I Will Thee Not Forsake,'" p. 41, n. 9. This description corresponds to the actual acquisition of Latin literacy as described, for example, by Suzanne Reynolds: "It is significant that the young student can come to the point of reciting parts of the sacred page of the Bible without fully understanding them, for the most elementary Latin grammar, the *Ars minor* of Donatus, comes after these rudiments." *Medieval Reading: Grammar, Rhetoric, and the Classical Text,* Cambridge Studies in Medieval Literature 27 (Cambridge, Eng.: Cambridge University Press, 1996), p. 10. Reynolds also notes the typical gendering of a pupil's vernacular and Latin instruction:" . . . while the teaching of a vernacular to children is entrusted to an upper-class woman, the grammatical exposition of a Latin text is in the hands of the male *magistri*" (*Medieval Reading,* p. 66). On Latin as the father tongue, see also the essays collected in *The Tongue of the Fathers: Gender and Ideology in Twelfth-Century Latin,* ed. David Townsend and Andrew Taylor (Philadelphia: University of Pennsylvania Press, 1998).

36. Marvin, "'I Will Thee Not Forsake,'" p. 45.

37. Marvin, "'I Will Thee Not Forsake,'" p. 52.

38. See Robert S. Sturges, "*The Canterbury Tales'* Women Narrators: Three Traditions of Female Authority," *Modern Language Studies* 12 (1983): 41–51.

39. Marvin, "'I Will Thee Not Forsake,'" p. 46.

40. Ferster, "'Your Praise Is Performed,'" p. 156.

41. A recent scholarly controversy has played out the question of how late medieval religious texts (verbal and visual) gendered Christ. Caroline Walker Bynum's response to Leo Steinberg's observations about "the sexuality of Christ"—that is, his masculinity—in late medieval and Renaissance representations emphasizes instead the association of the physical aspect of Christ with the feminine (Bynum, "The Body of Christ in the Later Middle Ages: A Reply to Leo Steinberg," in *Fragmentation and Redemption,* pp. 79–117). Steinberg's second edition of his book takes issue with some of Bynum's claims (Leo Steinberg, *The Sexuality of Christ in Renaissance Art and in Modern Oblivion,* 2nd ed. [Chicago: University of Chicago Press, 1996], pp. 364–89). It seems clear that both historians' arguments reveal valid findings about different traditions, and that they represent two complementary (or competing?) medieval and Renaissance views of gender in relation to the body of Christ. The Prioress' association of Christ with the masculine grammatical tradition suggests that her *Tale* belongs to the tradition discerned by Steinberg, at least in its representation of Christ. The fact that two major scholars each insists that her/his perspective is the "correct" one is a good example of modern attempts to reduce medieval discourses to univocity, an attempt I am arguing against throughout this book.

42. Marvin, "'I Will Thee Not Forsake,'" p. 49.

43. Ferster, "'Your Praise Is Performed,'" p. 159.

44. St. Augustine, *De civitate dei libri XXII,* 22.24, ed. Bernard Dombart and Alphonse Kalb, 2 vols., 1928–1929, repr. Corpus Christianorum, Series Latina 17–18 (Turnhout: Brepols, 1955), 2:849–50; *City of God,* trans. Henry Bettenson (Harmondsworth: Penguin, 1972), p. 1073. My discussion of this passage is indebted to Nichols, "Voice and Writing," p. 148.

45. Nichols, "Voice and Writing," p. 148. The Wife of Bath, it should be remembered, asserts her final sovereignty over her husband's discourse by taking control specifically of his tongue and hands: "To han the governance of hous and lond, / And of his tonge, and of his hond also" (III, 814–815).

46. Derek Pearsall, "Chaucer's Pardoner: The Death of a Salesman," *Chaucer Review* 17 (1983), pp. 361 and 362. See also Pearsall's book *The Canterbury Tales* (London: George Allen and Unwin, 1985), pp. 98–101.

47. Dinshaw, *Chaucer's Sexual Poetics,* p. 179, and see, among many others, the critics she cites, pp. 274–75, nn. 72–73. A particularly fruitful association of the Pardoner with the Old Man is Derek Pearsall's, in *The Canterbury Tales,* pp. 101–4. For a survey of "The Old Body in Medieval Culture," see Shulamith Shahar's essay of that title in *Framing Medieval Bodies,* ed. Sarah Kay and Miri Rubin (Manchester: Manchester University Press, 1994), pp. 160–86.

48. Kristeva, "From One Identity," pp. 136 and 139.
49. Quoted and trans. in R. A. Shoaf, *Dante, Chaucer, and the Currency of the Word: Money, Images, and Reference in Late Medieval Poetry* (Norman, OK: Pilgrim, 1983), pp. 10–11. For a further discussion of the opposition between money and materiality that can be applied to gender theory, see Andrew Cowell, "The Fall of the Oral Economy: Writing Economics on the Dead Body," *Exemplaria* 8 (1996): "['Du denier et de la brebis'] nostalgically equates oral knowledge and economy to a pre-lapsarian plenitude between the body and the world," p. 167.
50. Shoaf, *Dante, Chaucer, and the Currency of the Word,* p. 11.
51. "[T]he three young men and the old man express conflicting sides of the Pardoner's personality." Alfred David, *The Strumpet Muse: Art and Morals in Chaucer's Poetry* (Bloomington: Indiana University Press, 1976), p. 201.
52. Kristeva, "From One Identity," p. 143.
53. Kristeva, "Word, Dialogue, and Novel," in *Desire in Language,* pp. 78–79.
54. Noted by David, *Strumpet Muse,* p. 200.
55. Shoaf, *Dante, Chaucer, and the Currency of the Word,* p. 9. What Catherine Cox says of the Wife of Bath seems true of the Pardoner as well: " . . . in her quest to fill the empty spaces, she is depicted as consuming far more than needed but remains necessarily unfulfilled by the vicariousness of her excessive supplementation." *Gender and Language in Chaucer,* p. 24.
56. Anne Laskaya, *Chaucer's Approach to Gender in the* Canterbury Tales, Chaucer Studies 25 (Cambridge, Eng.: D. S. Brewer, 1995), p. 192.
57. Lee Patterson, to whom Laskaya also refers, provides support for this more nuanced view, though he regards the Pardoner through the lens of confessional subjectivity rather than gender: " . . . the Pardoner at once enacts masculinism's deepest fears and challenges a theological orthodoxy that is itself sustained by profoundly masculinist assumptions." Lee Patterson, *Chaucer and the Subject of History* (Madison: University of Wisconsin Press, 1991), p. 397.

Chapter 6: The Dismemberment of the Pardoner

1. Ovid [P. Ovidii Nasonis], *Metamorphoseon libri XV,* ed. B. A. van Proosdij, 7th ed. (Leiden: E. J. Brill, 1982), 10.26–29, 37–39, p. 301; *Metamorphoses,* trans. Mary M. Innes (Harmondsworth: Penguin, 1955), pp. 225–26.
2. Ovid, *Metamorphoseon,* 5.524–26, p. 144; *Metamorphoses,* trans. Innes, p. 130.
3. Ovid, *Metamorphoseon,* 10.46–49, p. 302; *Metamorphoses,* trans. Innes, p. 226.
4. Ovid, *Metamorphoseon,* 10.60–63, p. 302; *Metamorphoses,* trans. Innes, p. 226.
5. Ovid, *Metamorphoseon,* 11.64–66, p. 335; *Metamorphoses,* trans. Innes, p. 247. Catherine S. Cox offers a comparable reading of Chaucer's reworking of another Ovidian story in *The Manciple's Tale:* "once dead . . . the wife is reclaimed by Phebus as his prize property, restored to her former status as his 'gemme.' In the Manciple's reworking of the Ovidian myth, the wife is of greater value to Phebus dead than alive, for Phebus can then rewrite her history to suit his own desires without fear of having his reconfiguration

exposed or betrayed." *Gender and Language in Chaucer* (Gainesville: University Press of Florida, 1997), p. 102.

6. Ovid, *Metamorphoseon*, 10.79–85, pp. 303–04; *Metamorphoses*, trans. Innes, p. 227.

7. Ovid, *Metamorphoseon*, 10.152–54, p. 307; *Metamorphoses*, trans. Innes, p. 229.

8. Ovid, *Metamorphoseon*, 10.159–61, p. 307; *Metamorphoses*, trans. Innes, p. 229.

9. Ovid, *Metamorphoseon*, 10.199–203, 204–05, p. 309; *Metamorphoses*, trans. Innes, p. 230.

10. Ovid, *Metamorphoseon*, 11.1–7, 15–19, pp. 333–34; *Metamorphoses*, trans. Innes, p. 246.

11. Ovid, *Metamorphoseon*, 11.39–43, 50–53, p. 335; *Metamorphoses*, trans. Innes, p. 247.

12. Ovid, *Metamorphoseon*, 11.86, p. 336; *Metamorphoses*, trans. Innes, p. 248.

13. Emmet Robbins, "Famous Orpheus," in *Orpheus: The Metamorphoses of a Myth*, ed. John Warden (Toronto: University of Toronto Press, 1982), p. 13.

14. Quoted and trans. by W. S. Anderson, "The Orpheus of Virgil and Ovid: *flebile nescio quid,"* in *Orpheus*, ed. Warden, p. 30.

15. Quoted and trans. in Anderson, "The Orpheus of Virgil and Ovid," p. 33.

16. Anderson, "The Orpheus of Virgil and Ovid," p. 46.

17. Anderson, "The Orpheus of Virgil and Ovid," p. 39.

18. *The "Vulgate" Commentary on Ovid's* Metamorphoses: *The Creation Myth and the Story of Orpheus*, 10.10, 10.13, 10.17, etc., ed. Frank T. Coulson (Toronto: Pontifical Institute of Mediaeval Studies for the Center for Medieval Studies, 1991), pp. 119, 121, 123, etc.

19. For a survey of interpretations of the Orpheus myth in medieval Boethius commentaries, see John Block Friedman, *Orpheus in the Middle Ages* (Cambridge, MA: Harvard University Press, 1970), pp. 98–117. Patricia Vicari, "*Sparagmos:* Orpheus Among the Christians," in *Orpheus*, ed. Warden, pp. 63–83, is heavily dependent on Friedman. John M. Fyler, *Chaucer and Ovid,* (New Haven, CT: Yale University Press, 1979) makes no mention of the Orpheus story.

20. See Bernardus Silvestris, *The Commentary on the First Six Books of the* Aeneid *of Vergil Commonly Attributed to Bernardus Silvestris,* book 6, ed. Julian Ward Jones and Elizabeth Frances Jones (Lincoln: University of Nebraska Press, 1977), p. 30; and Bernardus Silvestris, *Commentary on the First Six Books of Virgil's* Aeneid, trans. Earl G. Schreiber and Thomas E. Maresca (Lincoln: University of Nebraska Press, 1979), p. 32:

> Est autem alius virtutis qui fit dum sapiens aliquis ad mundana per considerationem descendit, non ut in eis intentionem ponat, sed ut eorum cognita fragilitate, eis abiectis, ad invisibilia penitus se convertat et per creaturarum cognitionem creatorem evidentius cognoscat. Sed hoc modo Orpheus et Hercules qui sapientes habiti sunt descenderunt. Est vero tercius vitii, qui vulgaris est, quo ad temporalia pervenitur atque in eis tota intentio ponitur eisque tota

mente servitur nec ab eis amplius dimovetur. Taliter Euridicem legimus descendisse. Hic autem irrevocabilis est.

[The second descent is through virtue, and it occurs when any wise person descends to mundane things through meditation, not so that he may put his desire in them, but so that, having recognized their frailty, he may thoroughly turn from the rejected things to the invisible things and acknowledge more clearly in thought the Creator of creatures. In this manner, Orpheus and Hercules, who are considered wise men, descended. The third is the descent of vice, which is common and by which one falls to temporal things, places his whole desire in them, serves them with his whole mind, and does not turn away from them at all. We read that Eurydice descended in this way. Her descent, however, is irreversible.]

21. Bernardus Silvestris, *Commentary,* book 6, ed. Jones and Jones, pp. 54–55; trans. Schreiber and Maresca, pp. 54–55.

22. Fausto Ghisalberti, ed., "Arnolfo d'Orléans, un Cultore di Ovidio nel secolo XII," *Memorie del Reale Istituto Lombardo di Scienze e Lettere* 24 (1932), p. 222, quoted and trans. in Friedman, *Orpheus in the Middle Ages,* pp. 120–121. Friedman's survey of medieval commentaries on Ovid's version of the Orpheus story, pp. 118–136, is the basis for my account.

23. John of Garland, *Integumenta Ovidii, poemetto inedito del secolo XIII,* ed. Fausto Ghisalberti (Milan: 1933), 10.67, quoted in Friedman, *Orpheus in the Middle Ages,* p. 121.

24. Pierre Bersuire [Petrus Berchorius], *Reductorium morale, Liber XV, cap. ii-xv: "Ovidius moralizatus,"* book 5, ed. J. Engels and D. van Nes (Utrecht: Instituut voor Laat Latijn der Rijksuniversiteit Utrecht, 1962), p. 147. Trans. Friedman, *Orpheus in the Middle Ages,* p. 127.

25. Remigius of Auxerre, *Remigii Autissiodorensis Commentum in Martianum Capellam,* 9.480.19, ed. Cora E. Lutz, 2 vols. (Leiden: E. J. Brill, 1962–1965), 2:310; trans. Friedman, *Orpheus in the Middle Ages,* p. 101.

26. Friedman, *Orpheus in the Middle Ages,* pp. 89–90.

27. Martianus Capella, *De Nuptiis Philologiae et Mercurii,* in *Martianus Capella Accedunt Scholia in Caesaris Germanici Aratea,* 9.906, ed. Francis Eyssenhardt (Leipzig: Teubner, 1866), pp. 338–39; Martianus Capella, *Martianus Capella and the Seven Liberal Arts, Volume II: The Marriage of Philology and Mercury,* trans. William Harris Stahl and Richard Johnson with E. H. Burge (New York: Columbia University Press, 1977), p. 351.

28. See Martianus Capella, *De Nuptiis,* 1.4, p. 2; *The Marriage,* trans. Stahl and Johnson, p. 5.

29. As proposed by Jane Chance, *The Mythographic Chaucer: The Fabulation of Sexual Politics* (Minneapolis: University of Minnesota Press, 1995), in her discussion of *The House of Fame,* pp. 75–76; Chance follows B. G. Koonce, *Chaucer and the Tradition of Fame: Symbolism in* The House of Fame (Princeton, NJ: Princeton University Press, 1966), pp. 199–200. My remaining observations on this text and *The Merchant's Tale* should make it clear why I find these references more ambiguous. Chance's preference

for the alternative tradition is also evident in her discussion of *The Merchant's Tale*, p. 237.

30. Compare Chance's observations on Orpheus in *The Book of the Duchess* and in *Troilus and Criseyde, Mythographic Chaucer,* pp. 28 and 148.

31. Guillaume de Lorris and Jean de Meun, *Le Roman de la rose,* ll. 19645–56, ed. Daniel Poirion (Paris: Garnier-Flammarion, 1974), pp. 520–21; *The Romance of the Rose,* trans. Charles Dahlberg (Princeton, NJ: Princeton University Press, 1971, repr. University Press of New England: Hanover, NH, 1983), p. 324.

32. Alan of Lille, *De planctu naturae,* 8.54–55, ed. Nikolaus Häring, *Studi Medievali,* serie terza, 19.2 (1978), p. 834; Alan of Lille, *Plaint of Nature,* trans. James J. Sheridan, Mediaeval Sources in Translation 26 (Toronto: Pontifical Institute of Mediaeval Studies, 1980), p. 133; *The Romance of the Rose,* trans. Dahlberg, p. 418n. Michael A. Calabrese, "'Make a Mark That Shows': Orphean Song, Orphean Sexuality, and the Exile of Chaucer's Pardoner," *Viator* 24 (1993): 269–86, examines the links between the Pardoner and Jean de Meun's use of the Orpheus story, suggesting that the latter serves as a metaphor for the spiritual exile of the former.

33. Guillaume de Lorris and Jean de Meun, *Le Roman de la Rose,* ll. 19663–80, ed. Poirion, p. 521; *The Romance of the Rose,* trans. Dahlberg, p. 324.

34. Chance, *Mythographic Chaucer,* p. 148, and see p. 342, n. 12.

35. See *The Riverside Chaucer's* explanatory note on line 651, p. 909. For a striking visual example of the *arma Christi,* including both instruments of torture and an unanchored wound, see Michael Camille, *Gothic Art: Glorious Visions* (New York: Harry N. Abrams, 1996), p. 118, fig. 82.

36. For example, Carolyn Dinshaw, *Chaucer's Sexual Poetics* (Madison: University of Wisconsin Press, 1989), p. 179. See also the works cited above, chapter 5, n. 47.

37. Jacques Lacan, "The Mirror Stage as Formative of the Function of the I as Revealed in Psychoanalytic Experience," in his *Ecrits: A Selection,* trans. Alan Sheridan (New York: Norton, 1977), p. 4. My reading of Lacan on the *corps morcelé* is indebted throughout to Bice Benvenuto and Roger Kennedy, *The Works of Jacques Lacan: An Introduction* (New York: St. Martin's Press, 1986), especially pp. 47–62.

38. Lacan, "The Mirror Stage," pp. 4–5.

39. Jacques Lacan, "Aggressivity in Psychoanalysis," in his *Ecrits: A Selection,* pp. 11–12.

40. Lacan, "Aggressivity," p. 12. This imagery is also, of course, part and parcel of late medieval culture as a whole; for visual examples and analysis of such phenomena as the "transi" tomb, see Camille, *Gothic Art,* pp. 153–61.

41. Lacan, "Aggressivity," p. 10.

42. Lacan, "The Mirror Stage," p. 4.

43. Benvenuto and Kennedy, *The Works of Jacques Lacan,* p. 172.

44. Benvenuto and Kennedy, *The Works of Jacques Lacan,* p. 177.

45. Benvenuto and Kennedy, *The Works of Jacques Lacan,* p. 176.

46. Jacques Lacan, "The Subversion of the Subject and the Dialectic of Desire in the Freudian Unconscious," in his *Ecrits: A Selection*, pp. 314–15.
47. Jacqueline Rose, "Introduction II" in Jacques Lacan and the *école freudienne, Feminine Sexuality,* ed. Juliet Mitchell and Jacqueline Rose, trans. Jacqueline Rose (New York: Norton, 1982), pp. 38–39.
48. For example, Jane Gallop, *Reading Lacan* (Ithaca, NY: Cornell University Press, 1985), pp. 143–49 (and see my discussion of this passage in chapter 4, "The Pardoner Unveiled").
49. Gallop, *Reading Lacan,* p. 80, her emphasis. She cites Jean Laplanche and Jean-Baptiste Pontalis, *Vocabulaire de la psychanalyse* (Paris: PUF, 1967), p. 453.
50. This assumption is spelled out in, for example, Jean-Michel Palmier, *Lacan* (Paris: PUF, 1972), p. 23, quoted in Gallop, *Reading Lacan,* p. 79.
51. Gallop, *Reading Lacan,* p. 86.
52. Jane Flax, *Thinking Fragments: Psychoanalysis, Feminism, and Postmodernism in the Contemporary West* (Berkeley: University of California Press, 1990), p. 106.
53. Flax, *Thinking Fragments,* p. 146.
54. Flax, *Thinking Fragments,* pp. 172–73, emphasis added, quoting Hélène Cixous and Catherine Clément, *The Newly Born Woman* (Minneapolis: University of Minnesota Press, 1986), p. 67. cf. Flax's "Postmodernism and Gender Relations in Feminist Theory": "Feminist theories, like other forms of postmodernism, should encourage us to tolerate and interpret ambivalence, ambiguity, and multiplicity as well as to expose the roots of our needs for imposing order and structure no matter how arbitrary and oppressive these needs may be." In *Feminism/Postmodernism,* ed. Linda J. Nicholson (New York: Routledge, 1990), p. 56. Diana J. Fuss even suggests that "woman" is present in Lacan's own notoriously "difficult and equivocal style." (*Essentially Speaking: Feminism, Nature and Difference* [New York: Routledge, 1989], p. 12.)
55. Caroline Walker Bynum, "Material Continuity, Personal Survival and the Resurrection of the Body: A Scholastic Discussion in Its Medieval and Modern Contexts," in her *Fragmentation and Redemption: Essays on Gender and the Human Body in Medieval Religion* (New York: Urzone, 1992), p. 296. See also Miri Rubin, "The Person in the Form: Medieval Challenges to Bodily 'Order,'" in *Framing Medieval Bodies,* pp. 100–122, especially pp. 113–116.
56. Bynum, "Material Continuity," p. 287.
57. Bynum, *The Resurrection of the Body in Western Christianity, 200–1336,* Lectures on the History of Religions Sponsored by the American Council of Learned Societies, New Series 15 (New York: Columbia University Press), pp. 205–09.
58. Bynum, *Resurrection,* pp. 323–27. Like the feminized, nonscriptible voice examined in chapter 5, the feminized, fragmented body may also have political implications of disorder, as in the common high and late medieval image of the body politic. In Marie de France's twelfth-century "Fable of a Man, His Belly, and His Limbs," the dissolution of a body into its com-

ponent parts is likened to the rebellion of subjects against a lord (*Medieval Political Theory, a Reader: The Quest for the Body Politic, 1100–1400,* ed. Cary J. Nederman and Kate Langdon Forhan [NewYork: Routledge, 1993], pp. 24–25). Fifteenth-century thinkers such as Christine de Pizan were still developing the implications of this image, as in her *Book of the Body Politic* (see *Medieval Political Theory,* ed. Nederman and Forhan, pp. 230–47).

59. Bynum, *Resurrection,* pp. 322–23.

60. Bynum, *Resurrection,* p. 203.

61. Bynum, *Resurrection,* p. 213. Bynum, in fact, has also found that in some cases the part was considered to be the equivalent of the whole, thus denying—for those of proper moral status—the reality of fragmentation altogether: "Claims that holy bodies do not decay, and especially that parts of holy bodies are incorrupt or intact, represent a widespread concern to cross or deny the part/whole boundary by asserting the part to *be* the whole" ("Material Continuity," p. 285). See also, for a slightly later period, David Hillman and Carla Mazzo: "The body in parts, which occupies such a privileged place in the public and private fantasies of early modern Europe, perhaps does so because it ultimately never takes place." In "Introduction: Individual Parts," in *The Body in Parts: Fantasies of Corporeality in Early Modern Europe,* ed. Hillman and Mazzo (New York: Routledge, 1997), p. xxiv.

62. Bynum, "Material Continuity," p. 259.

63. Bynum, "Material Continuity," p. 260. Bynum, p. 405 n. 66, quotes Durandus, *In Sententias theologicas Petri Lombardi commentariorum libri quatuor* (Lyon: Apud Gasparem, 1556), 44.1.

64. Bynum, "Material Continuity," p. 294.

65. Once again, Dinshaw's concluding vision of the Pardoner's "poetics" as founded on the Incarnate Word or Body of Christ "in whom there is no lack, no division, no separation" (*Chaucer's Sexual Poetics,* p. 183) seems from this perspective sentimental and over optimistic. On the female as imperfect male, see Joan Cadden, *Meanings of Sex Difference in the Middle Ages: Medicine, Science, and Culture* (Cambridge, Eng.: Cambridge University Press, 1993), pp. 177–83; and compare the notion of man as unity and woman as division, explored by R. Howard Bloch, *Medieval Misogyny and the Invention of Western Romantic Love* (Chicago: University of Chicago Press, 1991), pp. 22–29.

66. See the remarkable visual evidence marshaled by Bynum in *Resurrection,* especially plate 3 (from Herrad's twelfth-century *Hortus deliciarum*), plate 6 (the eleventh-century Last Judgment mosaic in the Torcello cathedral), plate 26 (a fourteenth-century wall painting from the Strozzi chapel in Florence), and plate 31 (a late-thirteenth-century mosaic from the Baptistry at Florence), each depicting a different period's vision of "bodily partition in the lowest levels of hell" (commentary accompanying plate 3).

67. The Wandering Jew has been regarded as an analogue for the Old Man since 1893, according to Frederick Tupper in his chapter on *The Pardoner's Tale* in W. F. Bryan and Germaine Dempster, eds., *Sources and Analogues of*

Chaucer's Canterbury Tales (1941; repr. Humanities Press: Atlantic Highlands, NJ, 1958), p. 436 n. 2. The similarities between the two stories have been suggestive for several later critics; a full discussion of them can be found in N. S. Bushnell, "The Wandering Jew and *The Pardoner's Tale,*" *Studies in Philology* 28 (1931), pp. 450–60. And cf. the Pardoner's repeated association of his false relics with a "holy Jew" (VI, 351, 364).

68. Alan of Lille, *De planctu naturae,* 8.54–58, ed. Häring, p. 834; *Plaint of Nature,* pp. 133–34.

69. Peter Damian, "Letter 31" (*Liber Gomorrhianus*), in *Die Briefe des Petrus Damiani,* ed. Kurt Reindel, 4 vols. (Munich: Monumenta Germaniae Historica, 1983), 1:294; "Letter 31" (*Book of Gommorah*), in *Peter Damian: Letters 31–60,* trans. Owen J. Blum, O.F.M., The Fathers of the Church, Medieval Continuation 2 (Washington, D.C.: Catholic University of America Press, 1990), p. 15. c.f. his later comment on the "vir evirate . . . homo effeminate," *Liber Gomorrhianus,* ed. Reindel, 1:313; "you unmanly and effeminate man," *Book of Gommorah,* trans. Blum, p. 35.

70. Monica McAlpine, "The Pardoner's Homosexuality and How It Matters," *PMLA* 95 (1980): 8–22, documents aspects of this ambiguous conflation of sex, gender, and erotic practice in Guillaume de Lorris, Gautier de Leu, Dante, and Chaucer's contemporary, the *Pearl*-poet, specifically in *Cleanness.* Keiser, in *Courtly Desire and Medieval Homophobia: The Legitimation of Sexual Pleasure in* Cleanness *and Its Contexts* (New Haven, CT: Yale University Press, 1997), taking up the subject of *Cleanness,* demonstrates the continued influence of Alan of Lille in the fourteenth century, pp. 71–92.

71. Carolyn Dinshaw argues for a similar relationship between images of dismemberment and the fragmentation of straight masculine identity (a fragmentation that, in the logic of the text, must be repressed) in *Sir Gawain and the Green Knight:* see her "A Kiss Is Just a Kiss: Heterosexuality and its Consolations in *Sir Gawain and the Green Knight,*" in *Critical Crossings,* ed. Judith Butler and Biddy Martin, special issue of *Diacritics* 24.2–3 (Summer-Fall, 1994), especially pp. 213–16 and 220–22.

72. Chance, *Mythographic Chaucer,* p. 71; for her discussion of Ganymede, see pp. 59–71.

Conclusions: The Pardoner In and Out of *The Canterbury Tales*

1. Brief discussions of the various possible orders for the individual tales, including the "Bradshaw shift," with relevant bibliographies, can be found in most editions of *The Canterbury Tales,* including the following: Walter W. Skeat's "Introduction" to his edition of *The Complete Works of Geoffrey Chaucer,* 4: *The Canterbury Tales: Text* (Oxford: Clarendon Press, 1894), p. xxiii; the introduction and textual notes to *The Canterbury Tales* in *The Riverside Chaucer,* pp. 5, 1120–21; and Robert A. Pratt's "Introduction" to his edition of Geoffrey Chaucer, *The Tales of Canterbury*

(Boston: Houghton Mifflin, 1974), pp. xxv–xxvii. See also Derek Pearsall's book *The Canterbury Tales* (London: George Allen and Unwin, 1985), pp. 14–23. A thoroughgoing discussion of the classification of the manuscripts of *The Canterbury Tales* can be found in the second volume (*Classification of the Manuscripts*) of *The Text of The Canterbury Tales,* ed. John M. Manly and Edith Rickert, 8 vols. (Chicago: University of Chicago Press, 1940); see especially pp. 475–94 and the tables following p. 494 on the order of the tales.

2. See Alfred David, *The Strumpet Muse: Art and Morals in Chaucer's Poetry* (Bloomington: Indiana University Press, 1976), p. 6; Carolyn Dinshaw, *Chaucer's Sexual Poetics* (Madison: University of Wisconsin Press, 1989), p. 160, etc. Anne Laskaya argues less convincingly that Chaucer simply distances himself from the Pardoner by making the latter unsympathetic: see *Chaucer's Approach to Gender in the* Canterbury Tales (Cambridge, Eng.: D. S. Brewer, 1995), pp. 191–92.

3. For a review of these critical positions, see Jerome Mandel, *Geoffrey Chaucer: Building the Fragments of the* Canterbury Tales (London: Associated University Presses, 1992), pp. 13–17.

4. See the textual note on this link in *The Riverside Chaucer,* p. 1126.

5. A. J. Minnis, "Ordering Chaucer," review of Helen Cooper, *The Structure of the* Canterbury Tales, *Essays in Criticism* 35 (1985), p. 267. As Minnis points out, the same scribe produced two manuscripts with the tales in different orders, Hengwrt and Ellesmere, p. 266.

6. Mandel, *Geoffrey Chaucer,* p. 17. Much of Mandel's work on the unity of the individual fragment has been anticipated by previous scholars, especially by Helen Cooper, *The Structure of the* Canterbury Tales (Athens, GA: University of Georgia Press, 1984), pp. 108–207.

7. For example, Mandel's chapter on fragment VI (that which contains the *Pardoner's Prologue* and *Tale*) emphasizes the structural, and to a lesser degree the thematic, similarities between the *Pardoner's Tale* and the one other tale contained in this fragment (and preceding the Pardoner's), the *Physician's Tale.* He finds numerous correspondences between the two: the themes of fraud and of governance, for example. See Mandel, pp. 50–70, as well as his comment on these two tales in his introduction: "[t]hey are structurally identical" (p. 18), a comparison—of one of Chaucer's worst tales with one of his best—that, if correct (and Mandel makes a reasonably good case for his assertion) serves only to demonstrate that structural similarity is less meaningful than Mandel believes.

8. Ihab Hassan, *The Dismemberment of Orpheus: Toward a Postmodern Literature,* 2nd ed. (Madison: University of Wisconsin Press, 1982), pp. 267–68.

9. Luce Irigaray, *This Sex Which Is Not One,* trans. Catherine Porter with Carolyn Burke (Ithaca, NY: Cornell University Press, 1985).

10. David Greetham, "(En)gendering the Text/Texting Gender" (paper presented at the 33rd International Congress on Medieval Studies, Western Michigan University, May 9, 1998), pp. 19–20, citing Irigaray, *This Sex,*

p. 26. This paper was presented in a session, sponsored by *Exemplaria* and organized by R. Allen Shoaf, entitled "Theories of Editing and Editing Theory." R. Allen Shoaf presided; the present author was the respondent. The paper presented at the conference differed somewhat from the hard copy I am quoting, but Greetham preserved all the passages I quote in his presentation. For a more elaborate development of his ideas on gender and textual theory, see Greetham's chapter on "Gender in the Text" in his *Theories of the Text* (Oxford: Oxford University Press, 1999), pp. 433–86.

11. Greetham discusses "the modern" as a historical "interruption to book history," p. 21; see also Robert S. Sturges, "Textual Scholarship: Ideologies of Literary Production" in *Reflections in the Frame: New Perspectives on the Study of Medieval Literature,* ed. Peter Allen and Jeff Rider, special issue of *Exemplaria* 3.1 (March, 1991), pp. 109–31. Greetham's views, no doubt, could also be extended to later forms of textuality, but print tends to disguise a textual fluidity that manuscripts make manifest. See Bernard Cerquiglini, *Eloge de la variante: Histoire critique de la philologie* (Paris: Seuil, 1989), specifically on medieval textuality:

> Non encore serrée au carcan des formes instituées de l'écrit (auteur comme origine tutélaire, stabilité textuelle, etc.), dont nous avons vu combien elles étaient tardives, cette littérature donne à voir, de façon exemplaire, l'appropriation euphonique par la langue maternelle du geste qui la transcende.
>
> Cette appropriation se traduit par une variance essentielle, dans laquelle la philologie, pensée moderne du texte, n'a vu que maladie infantile, désinvolture coupable ou déficience première de la culture scribale, ce qui est seulement un excès joyeux (p. 42).
>
> [Not yet locked into the pillory of institutionalized forms of writing (author as guardian origin, textual stability, etc.), the degree of whose recency we have observed, this literature demonstrates in ex emplary fashion the mother tongue's euphonic appropriation of the gesture that transcends it.
>
> This appropriation betrays itself in an essential variance, in which philology, the modern idea of the text, saw only an infantile sickness, a guilty frivolity, or a primary deficiency of scribal culture, but which is merely a pleasurable excess.]

12. Greetham, p. 20, citing Hélène Cixous, "Coming to Writing," in her *"Coming to Writing" and Other Essays,* ed. Deborah Jenson, trans. Sarah Cornell, Deborah Jenson, Ann Liddle, and Susan Sellers, p. 31.

13. Irigaray, "This Sex Which Is Not One," in *This Sex,* p. 30.

14. See, for example, Ann Rosalind Jones, "Writing the Body: Toward an Understanding of *l'écriture féminine*" (1981), repr. in *Feminisms: An Anthology of Literary Theory and Criticism,* ed. Robyn R. Warhol and Diane Price Herndl (New Brunswick, NJ: Rutgers University Press, 1991), pp. 357–70. See also *Engaging with Irigaray: Feminist Theory and Modern European Thought,* ed.

Carolyn Burke, Naomi Schor, and Margaret Whitford (New York: Columbia University Press, 1992); and Diana J. Fuss' defense of Irigaray in "Essentially Speaking: Luce Irigaray's Language of Essence" (1989), repr. in *Revaluing French Feminism: Critical Essays on Difference, Agency, and Culture,* ed. Nancy Fraser and Sandra Lee Bartky (Bloomington: Indiana University Press, 1992), pp. 94–112. The fluidity and fragmentariness of *écriture féminine* has remained a useful tool for contemporary feminist analysis, especially of the body: see, for example, two essays in the recent volume *Sexy Bodies: The Strange Carnalities of Feminism,* ed. Elizabeth Grosz and Elspeth Probyn (New York: Routledge, 1995): Nicole Brossard, "Green Night of Labyrinth Park," trans. Lou Nelson, pp. 128–36; and Sue Golding, "Pariah Bodies," pp. 172–80.

15. Irigaray, *This Sex,* p. 30. Judith Butler in *Gender Trouble: Feminism and the Subversion of Identity* (New York: Routledge, 1990) analyzes the views of Monique Wittig, too, both in her fiction and in her theoretical essays, in terms of both a negative fragmentation (imposed on Being by the cultural category of "sex," pp. 114–115) and a positive one (producing "the body itself as an incoherent center of attributes, gestures, and desires," p. 125). Wittig herself, however, rejects the notion of *écriture féminine:* see her essay "The Point of View: Universal or Particular?" in *The Straight Mind and Other Essays* (Boston: Beacon Press, 1992), pp. 59–67.

16. Irigaray, *This Sex,* p. 28.

17. Irigaray, *This Sex,* p. 25.

18. Irigaray, *This Sex,* p. 29.

19. Hélène Cixous, "The Laugh of the Medusa" (1976), repr. in *Feminisms,* ed. Warhol and Price Herndl, pp. 345, 344–45.

20. Cixous, "The School of Roots," in her *Three Steps on the Ladder of Writing,* trans. Sarah Cornell and Susan Sellers (New York: Columbia University Press, 1993), p. 135; Verena Andermatt Conley, *Hélène Cixous: Writing the Feminine,* expanded edition (Lincoln: University of Nebraska Press, 1991), p. 80.

21. Derek Pearsall, "Editing Medieval Texts: Some Developments and Some Problems," in James J. McGann, ed., *Textual Criticism and Literary Interpretation* (Chicago: University of Chicago Press, 1985), p. 97; see also p. 105. Pearsall goes on to state that a state of unfinished fluidity is typical of much medieval textuality. David Greetham usefully discusses Pearsall's essay at several points in his *Textual Transgressions: Essays Toward the Construction of a Biobibliography* (New York: Garland, 1998), especially in "The Place of Fredson Bowers in Medieval Editing," pp. 231, 235–36.

22. Cixous cites both Joyce and Genet as possible models: see "Laugh," pp. 341, 342, 349, n. 3. This attribution of *écriture féminine* to anatomical males should be taken into consideration by those who accuse Cixous, like Irigaray, of biological essentialism. See also her response to this accusation in "The School of Roots," pp. 128–29.

23. Cixous, "Laugh," p. 342.

24. Cixous, "Laugh," p. 343.
25. On Fragment VI as the "floating fragment," see Donald R. Howard, *The Idea of the* Canterbury Tales (Berkeley: University of California Press, 1976); Howard also relates the ambiguous Pardoner to the unanchored position of this fragment: "The Pardoner . . . is a pariah among the pilgrims, and his tale seems to be in a similar position among the other tales—the fragment it belongs to is sometimes called the 'floating' fragment," p. 338. See also Dolores Warwick Frese, *An Ars Legendi for Chaucer's* Canterbury Tales: *Re-constructive Reading* (Gainesville: University of Florida Press, 1991), p. 178.
26. All these points about the possible ordering of the fragments are thoroughly discussed in the Riverside edition: see the general introduction to *The Canterbury Tales* and the explanatory notes to each fragment. And cf. Howard, *Idea,* pp. 333–39.
27. Susan Bordo, "Reading the Male Body," in *The Male Body: Features, Destinies, Exposures,* ed. Laurence Goldstein (Ann Arbor: University of Michigan Press, 1994), p. 266, emphases in text. See also Bordo's elaboration of these ideas in her *The Male Body: A New Look at Men in Public and in Private* (New York: Farrar, Straus, and Giroux, 1999), pp. 36–104.
28. Greetham, "(En)gendering the Text," pp. 18–19, citing Wittig, "The Straight Mind," in *The Straight Mind and Other Essays,* p. 28, and Jonathan Goldberg, ed., *Queering the Renaissance* (Durham, NC: Duke University Press, 1994).
29. See Wittig, "The Straight Mind," p. 29: "This ontological characteristic of the difference between the sexes affects all the concepts which are part of the same conglomerate"—presumably including even the textual concepts of good and bad readings.
30. I take the variant readings from the fifth volume (*Corpus of Variants, Part I*) of *The Text of* The Canterbury Tales, ed. Manly and Rickert, p. 62. Definitions of "ioly" and "feere" come from *The Riverside Chaucer's* Glossary, s.v. "joly" and "fere." The fourteenth-century definitions of "grom," from the *Oxford English Dictionary,* s.v. "groom," include "a man, male person"; the *Middle English Dictionary,* s.v. "grom," gives simply "a man" as a possible meaning beginning in 1375. This entire section speculating about a "queer edition" of Chaucer has been inspired not only by Greetham, but also by Jonathan Goldberg, "Under the Covers with Caliban," in *The Margins of the Text,* ed. D. C. Greetham (Ann Arbor: University of Michigan Press, 1997), pp. 105–28.
31. See Wittig, "The Straight Mind," p. 30. On the specifically medieval book as embodiment, see Michael Camille, "Glossing the Flesh: Scopophilia and the Margins of the Medieval Book" in *The Margins of the Text,* pp. 245–67, as well as the essays collected in *The Book and the Body,* ed. Dolores Warwick Frese and Katherine O'Brien O'Keeffe (Notre Dame, IN: University of Notre Dame Press, 1997).
32. On Urry's edition, see Derek Brewer, ed., *Chaucer: The Critical Heritage,* 2 vols. (London: Routledge and Kegan Paul, 1978), 1:36.

33. Pasolini's 1972 film is available on videotape: see Pier Paolo Pasolini, dir., *The Canterbury Tales* (Water Bearer Films Videocassette WBF8003). Dyson's *Canterbury Pilgrims* (1940) has been recorded by the London Symphony Chorus and Orchestra, cond. Richard Hickox: see George Dyson, *The Canterbury Pilgrims* (Chandos Compact Disks CHAN9531[2], 1997). Despite its title, John Wain's distinguished novel *The Pardoner's Tale* (1978; repr. Viking Press: New York, 1979) is also unconcerned with the Pardoner.

34. "Spurious Links, Series 1: BL Lansdowne 851," in John M. Bowers, ed., *The Canterbury Tales: Fifteenth-Century Continuations and Additions*, TEAMS Middle English Texts Series (Kalamazoo, MI: Medieval Institute Publications, 1992), pp. 44–45.

35. Bowers, *Continuations and Additions*, p. 42. These links appear in "Spurious Links, Series 2: BL Royal 18.C.ii," in Bowers, pp. 48–50.

36. "Spurious Links, Series 2," in Bowers, *Continuations and Additions*, pp. 49–50, ll. 10–18.

37. As Bowers points out, *Continuations and Additions*, p. 53, note to ll. 12–13.

38. "John Lydgate's Prologue to the *Siege of Thebes*," in Bowers, *Continuations and Additions*, pp. 3–22, ll. 32–35.

39. Bowers, *Continuations and Additions*, p. 19, note to ll. 32–36.

40. See Bowers, *Continuations and Additions*, p. 57.

41. "The Canterbury Interlude and Merchant's Tale of Beryn," in Bowers, *Continuations and Additions*, pp. 60–196, l. 301.

42. "Canterbury Interlude," l. 22.

43. "Canterbury Interlude," ll. 438–46.

44. "Canterbury Interlude," ll. 450–58.

45. "Canterbury Interlude," ll. 523–30.

46. "Canterbury Interlude," ll. 569–75.

47. "Canterbury Interlude," ll. 640–44.

48. "Canterbury Interlude," l. 612.

49. "Canterbury Interlude," l. 514.

50. For Pearsall in *The Canterbury Tales*, the "Canterbury Interlude" includes "some recognition . . . of the hints of effeminacy in Chaucer's portrait" of the Pardoner, p. 301.

51. A palmer, of course, is a pilgrim, in particular one who had visited the Holy Land, betokened by a palm frond. A pothecary is a pharmacist or apothecary.

52. According to Malcolm Andrew, Todd in 1810 compared Heywood's use of the Pardoner's relics to that of Chaucer; and in 1894 Skeat regarded Heywood's adaptation as "a shameless plagiarism" of the *Pardoner's Prologue*. See Andrew's explanatory notes to *The Canterbury Tales: The General Prologue Part One B*, vol. 2 of *A Variorum Edition of the Works of Geoffrey Chaucer* (Norman, OK: University of Oklahoma Press, 1993), pp. 528–29. Heywood also uses a Chaucerian Pardoner in his play *The Pardoner and the Friar;* the connection is discussed by David Boocker, "Heywood's Indulgent Pardoner," *English Language Notes* 29.2 (1991): 21–30.

53. John Heywood, *The Four P.P.,* in John S. Farmer, ed., *John Heywood: The Dramatic Writings* (1905), rpt. New York: Georg Olms, 1977, pp. 29–64; p. 43.
54. Heywood, *The Four P.P.,* p. 44.
55. Heywood, *The Four P.P.,* p. 44.
56. Heywood, *The Four P.P.,* p. 44.
57. Heywood, *The Four P.P.,* p. 43.
58. Heywood, *The Four P.P.,* p. 44.
59. Heywood, *The Four P.P.,* p. 44. The Pothecary also opines of the slipper that "[o]ne of the Seven Sleepers trod in a turd," p. 44.
60. Heywood, *The Four P.P.,* p. 45.
61. Heywood, *The Four P.P.,* pp. 50–51.
62. Heywood, *The Four P.P.,* pp. 55–56.
63. Heywood, *The Four P.P.,* p. 57.
64. Heywood, *The Four P.P.,* p. 56.
65. Heywood, *The Four P.P.,* p. 57.
66. Heywood, *The Four P.P.,* p. 56.
67. Heywood, *The Four P.P.,* pp. 50–51.
68. Heywood, *The Four P.P.,* p. 50.
69. M. M. Bakhtin's theories of the carnivalesque are familiar from his *Rabelais and His World,* trans. Hélène Iswolsky (Bloomington: Indiana University Press, 1984). The most sophisticated critique of Bakhtin (and of his critics) can be found in Peter Stallybrass and Allon White, *The Politics and Poetics of Transgression* (Ithaca, NY: Cornell University Press, 1986). For Bakhtinian readings of medieval culture, including the present author's, see *Bakhtin and Medieval Voices,* ed. Thomas J. Farrell (Gainesville: University of Florida Press, 1995). A specifically feminist reading of the carnivalesque is Dale Bauer, "Gender in Bakhtin's Carnival," in her *Feminist Dialogics* (1988), repr. in *Feminisms,* ed. Warhol and Price Herndl, pp. 671–84.
70. Heywood, *The Four P.P.,* p. 57.
71. Heywood, *The Four P.P.,* pp. 57–58.
72. Heywood, *The Four P.P.,* p. 61.
73. Heywood, *The Four P.P.,* p. 64.
74. Sir Walter Scott, *The Abbot,* 2 vols. (1820; repr. Thos. Y. Crowell and Co.: New York, n.d.), 2:89. In one-volume editions, these passages occur in chapter 27.
75. Scott, *The Abbot,* 2:89.
76. Scott, *The Abbot,* 2:90.
77. Cixous, "Laugh," p. 336.
78. Scott, *The Abbot,* 2:90.
79. Scott, *The Abbot,* 2:92.
80. Scott, *The Abbot,* 2:97–98.
81. Scott, *The Abbot,* 2:98.
82. Scott, *The Abbot,* 2:98.
83. Scott, *The Abbot,* 2:99.

84. Bauer, "Gender," p. 680.
85. Bauer, "Gender," p. 679.
86. Robert Glück, *Margery Kempe* (London and New York: HIGH RISK Books / Serpent's Tail, 1994), pp. 81–82.
87. On the importance of the midpoint in medieval and early modern literary texts, see, among many others, John D. Niles, "Ring Composition in *La Chanson de Roland* and *La Chançun de Willame*," *Olifant* 1.2 (1973): 4–12, and Michael Baybak, Paul Delany, and A. Kent Hieatt, "Placement 'in the middest' in *The Faerie Queene*," in Alastair Fowler, ed., *Silent Poetry: Essays in Numerological Analysis* (London: Routledge and Kegan Paul, 1970), pp. 141–52.
88. Glück, *Margery Kempe,* p. 136.
89. Glück, *Margery Kempe,* p. 154 (emphases in text).
90. Glück, *Margery Kempe,* p. 157 (emphases in text).
91. Glück, *Margery Kempe,* pp. 161–62 (emphases in text).

WORKS CITED

Primary Sources

Aelius Donatus. "De Comoedia." In his *Commentum Terenti*. Ed. Paul Wessner. 2 vols. Leipzig: Teubner, 1902–1905. Vol. 1: 22–31.

Alan of Lille. *Anticlaudianus*. Ed. R. Bossuat. Paris: Vrin, 1955.

———. *Anticlaudianus or the Good and Perfect Man*. Trans. James J. Sheridan. Toronto: Pontifical Institute of Mediaeval Studies, 1973.

———. *De planctu naturae*. Ed. Nikolaus M. Häring. *Studi Medievali,* serie terza 19.2 (1978): 797–879.

———. *Plaint of Nature*. Trans. James J. Sheridan. Toronto: Pontifical Institute of Mediaeval Studies, 1980.

Augustine, St. *City of God*. Trans. Henry Bettenson. Harmondsworth: Penguin, 1972.

———. *De civitate dei libri XXII*. Ed. Bernard Dombart and Alphonse Kalb. 2 vols. 1928. Repr. Corpus Christianorum, Series Latina 17–18. Turnhout: Brepols, 1955.

———. *Confessions*. Ed. W. H. D. Rouse. Trans. William Watts. 2 vols. Loeb Classical Library 26–27. Cambridge, MA: Harvard University Press, 1912.

Bernardus Silvestris. *The Commentary on Martianus Capella's* De Nuptiis Philologiae et Mercurii *Attributed to Bernardus Silvestris*. Ed. Haijo Jan Westra. Toronto: Pontifical Institute of Mediaeval Studies, 1986.

———. *The Commentary on the First Six Books of the* Aeneid *of Vergil Commonly Attributed to Bernardus Silvestris*. Ed. Julian Ward Jones and Elizabeth Frances Jones. Lincoln: University of Nebraska Press, 1977.

———. *Commentary on the First Six Books of Virgil's* Aeneid. Trans. Earl G. Schreiber and Thomas E. Maresca. Lincoln: University of Nebraska Press, 1979.

Bersuire, Pierre [Petrus Berchorius]. *Reductium morale, Liber XV, cap. ii-xv: "Ovidius moralizatus."* Ed. J. Engels and D. van Nes. Utrecht: Instituut voor Laat Latijn der Rijksuniversiteit Utrecht, 1962.

Boccaccio, Giovanni. *Boccacio on Poetry: Being the Preface and the Fourteenth and Fifteenth Books of Boccaccio's* Genealogia Deorum Gentilium. Trans. Charles G. Osgood. 1930. Repr. Bobbs-Merrill: Library of Liberal Arts. New York, 1956.

———. *Genealogie deorum gentilium libri*. Ed. Vincenzo Romano. 2 vols. Bari: Laterza, 1951.

Bowers, John M., ed. The Canterbury Tales: *Fifteenth-Century Continuations and Additions*. TEAMS Middle English Texts Series. Kalamazoo, MI: Medieval Institute Publications, 1992.

Coulson, Frank T., ed. *The "Vulgate" Commentary on Ovid's* Metamorphoses: *The Creation Myth and the Story of Orpheus.* Toronto Medieval Latin Texts. Toronto: Pontifical Institute of Mediaeval Studies for the Center for Medieval Studies, 1991.

Damian, St. Peter. "Letter 31." *(Liber Gomorrhianus).* In *Die Briefe des Petrus Damiani.* Ed. Kurt Reindel. 4 vols. Munich: Monumenta Germaniae Historica, 1983. Vol. 1: 284–330.

————. "Letter 31" *(Book of Gommorah).* In *Peter Damian: Letters 31–60.* Trans. Owen J. Blum, O.F.M. The Fathers of the Church: Mediaeval Continuation 2. Washington, D.C: Catholic University of America Press, 1990. 3–53.

Dante Alighieri. *Epistole,* XIII. Ed. Arsenio Frugoni and Giorgio Brugnoli. In his *Opere minori.* 2 vols. Milan: Riccardo Ricciardi, 1979. Vol. 2: 598–643.

Dobson, R. B., ed. *The Peasants' Revolt of 1381.* 2nd ed. London: Macmillan, 1983.

Dyson, George. *The Canterbury Pilgrims.* 1940. Soloists, London Symphony Chorus, London Symphony Orchestra. Richard Hickox. 1997. Chandos Compact Disks CHAN9531(2).

Eulogium Historiarum sive Temporis. Ed. F. S. Haydon. 3 vols. Rolls Series. 1858–63.

Evanthius. "De Fabula." In Aelius Donatus, *Commentum Terenti.* Ed. Paul Wessner. 2 vols. Leipzig: Teubner, 1902–1905. Vol. 1: 13–22.

Froissart, Jean. *Les Chroniques de Sire Jean Froissart.* Ed. J. A. C. Buchon. 3 vols. Paris: A. Desrez, 1835.

Galbraith, V. H., ed. *The Anonimalle Chronicle, 1333–1381.* Historical Series 45. Manchester: Manchester University Press, 1927.

Glück, Robert. *Margery Kempe.* London and New York: HIGH RISK Books /Serpent's Tail. 1994.

Graesse, Th., ed. *Jacobi a Voragine Legenda aurea vulgo historia lombardica dicta.* 2nd ed. Leipzig: Arnold, 1850.

Guillaume de Lorris and Jean de Meun. *Le Roman de la rose.* Ed. Daniel Poirion. Paris: Garnier-Flammarion, 1974.

————. *The Romance of the Rose.* Trans. Charles Dahlberg. 1971. Repr. University Press of New England: Hanover, NH, 1983.

Hardison, O. B., Jr., et al, eds. *Medieval Literary Criticism: Translations and Interpretations.* New York: Frederick Ungar, 1974.

Heywood, John. *The Four P.P.* In *John Heywood: The Dramatic Writings.* Ed. John S. Farmer. 1905. Repr. Georg Olms: New York, 1977. 26–64.

Isidore of Seville. *Etimologías.* Ed. José Oroz Reta and Manuel-A. Marcos Casquero. 2 vols. Madrid: Biblioteca de Autores Cristianos, 1982.

John of Salisbury. *Policraticus.* Ed. and trans. Cary J. Nederman. Cambridge: Cambridge University Press, 1990.

Knighton, Henry. *Knighton's Chronicle 1337–1396.* Ed. and trans. G. H. Martin. Oxford Medieval Texts. Oxford: Clarendon Press, 1996.

Kölbing, E., and Mabel Day, eds. *The Siege of Jerusalem.* EETS o.s. 188. 1932. Repr. New York: Kraus Reprint Co.: New York, 1971.

Manly, John M., and Edith Rickert, eds. *The Text of The Canterbury Tales.* 8 vols. Chicago: University of Chicago Press, 1940.

Martianus Capella. *Martianus Capella and the Seven Liberal Arts, volume II: The Marriage of Philology and Mercury*. Trans. William Harris Stahl and Richard Johnson with E. L. Burge. Records of Western Civilization 84. New York: Columbia University Press, 1977.

———. *De Nuptiis Philologiae et Mercurii*. In *Martianus Capella Accedunt Scholia in Caesaris Germanici Aratea*. Ed. Francis Eyssenhardt. Leipzig: Teubner, 1866. 1–375.

McNeill, John T., and Helena M. Gamer, trans. *Medieval Handbooks of Penance: A Translation of the Principal Libri Poenitentiales*. Records of Western Civilization. New York: Columbia University Press, 1938. Repr. 1990.

Minnis, A. J., and A. B. Scott, with David Wallace, eds. *Medieval Literary Theory and Criticism c. 1100-c. 1375: The Commentary Tradition*. Rev. ed. Oxford: Clarendon Press, 1991.

Nederman, Cary J., and Kate Langdon Forhan, eds. *Medieval Political Theory, A Reader: The Quest for the Body Politic, 1100–1400*. New York: Routledge, 1993.

Ovid [P. Ovidii Nasonis]. *Metamorphoseon libri XV.* Ed. B. A. van Proosdij. Leiden: E. J. Brill, 1982.

———. *Metamorphoses*. Trans. Mary M. Innes. Harmondsworth: Penguin, 1955.

Ovide moralisé: poème du commencement du quatorzième siècle. Ed. C. de Boer et al. 5 vols. 1915–1938. Repr. Martin Sändig: Wiesbaden, 1966–68.

Pasolini, Pier Paolo, dir. *The Canterbury Tales*. 1972. Water Bearer Films Videocassette WBF8003.

Pratt, Robert A., ed. *Geoffrey Chaucer, The Tales of Canterbury*. Boston: Houghton Mifflin, 1974.

Remigius of Auxerre. *Remigii Autissiodorensis Commentum in Martianum Capellam, Libri I-II*. Ed. Cora E. Lutz. Leiden: E. J. Brill, 1962.

Scott, Sir Walter. *The Abbot*. 1820. Repr. 2 vols. Thomas Y. Crowell Co: New York, n.d.

Skeat, Walter W., ed. *Geoffrey Chaucer, The Canterbury Tales: Text*. Vol. 4 of *The Complete Works of Geoffrey Chaucer.* Oxford: Clarendon Press, 1894.

Wain, John. *The Pardoner's Tale*. 1978. Repr. Viking Press: New York, 1979.

Walsingham, Thomas. *Historia Anglicana*. Ed. Henry Thomas Riley. 2 vols. Rolls Series. 1863–1864.

Secondary Sources

Abramson, Paul, and Steven D. Pinkerton, eds. *Sexual Nature, Sexual Culture*. Chicago: University of Chicago Press, 1995.

Alford, John A. "The Grammatical Metaphor: A Survey of Its Use in the Middle Ages." *Speculum* 57 (1982): 728–60.

Anderson, W. S. "The Orpheus of Virgil and Ovid: *flebile nescio quid.*" In Warden. 25–50.

Andrew, Malcolm. "Explanatory Notes." *The Canterbury Tales: The General Prologue Part One B*. Vol. 2 of *A Variorum Edition of the Works of Geoffrey Chaucer*. Norman, OK: University of Oklahoma Press, 1993.

Bakhtin, Mikhail. *Rabelais and His World*. Trans. Hélène Iswolsky. Bloomington: Indiana University Press, 1986.

Baldwin, John W. *The Language of Sex: Five Voices from Northern France Around 1200*. Chicago: University of Chicago Press, 1994.

Baudinet, Marie-José. "The Face of Christ, the Form of the Church." In *Fragments for a History of the Human Body, Part One*. Ed. Michael Feher with Ramona Naddaff and Nadia Tazi. *Zone* 3. New York: Urzone, 1989. 149–59.

Baudrillard, Jean. "The Precession of Simulacra." In his *Simulacra and Simulation*. Trans. Sheila Faria Glaser. Ann Arbor: University of Michigan Press, 1994. 1–42.

Bauer, Dale. "Gender in Bakhtin's Carnival." In her *Feminist Dialogics*. 1988. Repr. in Warhol and Price Herndl. 671–84.

Baybak, Michael, Paul Delany, and A. Kent Hieatt. "Placement 'in the middest' in *The Faerie Queene*." In *Silent Poetry: Essays in Numerological Analysis*. Ed. Alastair Fowler. London: Routledge and Kegan Paul, 1970. 141–52.

Benson, C. David. "Chaucer's Pardoner: His Sexuality and Modern Critics." *Mediaevalia* 8 (1982): 337–49.

Benvenuto, Bice, and Roger Kennedy. *The Works of Jacques Lacan: An Introduction*. New York: St. Martin's Press, 1986.

Berger, Maurice, Brian Wallis, and Simon Watson, eds. *Constructing Masculinity*. New York: Routledge, 1995.

Bersani, Leo. "Is the Rectum a Grave?" 1987. Repr. in *Reclaiming Sodom*. Ed. Jonathan Goldberg. New York: Routledge, 1994. 249–64.

Bhabha, Homi K. "Are You a Man or a Mouse?" In Berger, Wallace, and Watson. 57–65.

Bloch, R. Howard. "Critical Communities and the Shape of the Medievalist's Desire: A Response to Judith Ferster and Louise Fradenburg." In *Reconceiving Chaucer: Literary Theory and Historical Interpretation*. Ed. Thomas Hahn. Special issue of *Exemplaria* 2.1 (Spring, 1990): 203–20.

———. *Medieval Misogyny and the Invention of Western Romantic Love*. Chicago: University of Chicago Press, 1991.

Boocker, David. "Heywood's Indulgent Pardoner." *English Language Notes* 29.2 (1991): 21–30.

Bordo, Susan. *The Male Body: A New Look at Men in Public and in Private*. New York: Farrar, Straus, and Giroux, 1999.

———. "Reading the Male Body." In *The Male Body: Features, Destinies, Exposures*. Ed. Laurence Goldstein. Ann Arbor: University of Michigan Press, 1994. 265–306.

Boswell, John. "Categories, Experience, and Sexuality." In *Forms of Desire: Sexual Orientation and the Social Constructionist Controversy*. Ed. Edward Stein. 1990. Repr. Routledge: New York, 1992. 133–73.

———. *Christianity, Social Tolerance, and Homosexuality: Gay People in Western Europe from the Beginning of the Christian Era to the Fourteenth Century*. Chicago: University of Chicago Press, 1980.

———. "Revolutions, Universals, and Sexual Categories." In Duberman, Vicinus, and Chauncey. 17–36.

Bowden, Muriel. *A Commentary on the General Prologue to the Canterbury Tales*. New York: Macmillan, 1948.

Bowers, John M. "'Dronkenesse Is Ful of Stryvyng': Alcoholism and Ritual Violence in Chaucer's *Pardoner's Tale.*" *ELH* 57 (1990): 757-84.

Braswell-Means, Laurel. "A New Look at an Old Patient: Chaucer's Summoner and Medieval Physiognomia." *Chaucer Review* 25.3 (1991): 266–75.

Bravmann, Scott. *Queer Fictions of the Past: History, Culture, and Difference.* Cambridge, Eng.: Cambridge University Press, 1997.

Brewer, Derek, ed. *Chaucer: The Critical Heritage.* 2 vols. Critical Heritage Series. London: Routledge and Kegan Paul, 1978.

Brossard, Nicole. "Green Night of Labyrinth Park." Trans. Lou Nelson. In Grosz and Probyn. 128–36.

Brundage, James A. *Law, Sex, and Christian Society in Medieval Europe.* Chicago: University of Chicago Press, 1987.

Burger, Glen. "Kissing the Pardoner." *PMLA* 107 (1992): 1143–56.

Burke, Carolyn. "Irigaray Through the Looking Glass." In Burke, Schor, and Whitford. 39–56.

Burke, Carolyn, Naomi Schor, and Margaret Whitford, eds. *Engaging with Irigaray: Feminist Theory and Modern European Thought.* New York: Columbia University Press, 1994.

Burns, E. Jane. *Bodytalk: When Women Speak in Old French Literature.* Philadelphia: University of Pennsylvania Press, 1993.

Bushnell, N. S. "The Wandering Jew and *The Pardoner's Tale.*" *Studies in Philology* 28 (1931): 450–60.

Butler, Judith. *Bodies That Matter: On the Discursive Limits of "Sex."* New York: Routledge, 1993.

———. *Gender Trouble: Feminism and the Subversion of Identity.* New York: Routledge, 1990.

———. *The Psychic Life of Power: Theories in Subjection.* Stanford, CA: Stanford University Press, 1997.

Bynum, Caroline Walker. "The Body of Christ in the Later Middle Ages: A Reply to Leo Steinberg." In her *Fragmentation and Redemption.* 79-117.

———. *Fragmentation and Redemption: Essays on Gender and the Human Body in Medieval Religion.* New York: Urzone, 1992.

———. "Material Continuity, Personal Survival, and the Resurrection of the Body: A Scholastic Discussion in its Medieval and Modern Contexts." In her *Fragmentation and Redemption.* 239–97.

———. *The Resurrection of the Body in Western Christianity, 200–1336.* Lectures on the History of Religions Sponsored by the American Council of Learned Societies, New Series 15. New York: Columbia University Press, 1995.

———. "Women Mystics and Eucharistic Devotion in the Thirteenth Century." In her *Fragmentation and Redemption.* 119–150.

Cadden, Joan. *Meanings of Sex Difference in the Middle Ages: Medicine, Science, and Culture.* Cambridge, Eng.: Cambridge University Press, 1993.

———. "Sciences/Silences: The Natures and Languages of 'Sodomy' in Peter of Abano's *Problemata* Commentary." In Lochrie, McCracken, and Schultz. 40–57.

Cain, James D. "Re: Facts, Texts, and Theories." Electronic communication posted to medgay-l@ksu.edu. June 9, 1999.

Calabrese, Michael A. "'Make a Mark That Shows': Orphean Song, Orphean Sexuality, and the Exile of Chaucer's Pardoner." *Viator* 24 (1993): 269–86.

Camille, Michael. "Glossing the Flesh: Scopophilia and the Margins of the Medieval Book." In Greetham, *Margins.* 245–67.

———. *Gothic Art: Glorious Visions.* New York: Harry N. Abrams, 1996.

Cerquiglini, Bernard. *Eloge de la variante: Histoire critique de la philologie.* Paris: Seuil, 1989.

Champagne, John. *The Ethics of Marginality: A New Approach to Gay Studies.* Minneapolis: University Of Minnesota Press, 1995.

Chance, Jane. *The Mythographic Chaucer: The Fabulation of Sexual Politics.* Minneapolis: University of Minnesota Press, 1995.

Chay, Deborah G. "Reconstructing Essentialism." *Diacritics* 21.2–3 (1991): 135–47.

Cixous, Hélène. "Coming to Writing." In her *"Coming to Writing" and Other Essays.* Ed. Deborah Jenson. Trans. Sarah Cornell, Deborah Jenson, Ann Liddle, and Susan Sellers. Cambridge, MA: Harvard University Press, 1991. 2–58.

———. "The Laugh of the Medusa." 1975. Repr. in Warhol and Price Herndl. 334–49.

———. "The School of Roots." In her *Three Steps on the Ladder of Writing.* Trans. Sarah Cornell and Susan Sellers. New York: Columbia University Press, 1993. 109–56.

Cohen, Jeffrey Jerome, and Bonnie Wheeler, eds. *Becoming Male in the Middle Ages.* New York: Garland, 1997.

Cohen, Jeffrey Jerome, and Bonnie Wheeler. "Introduction." In Cohen and Wheeler. vii–xx.

Conley, Verena Andermatt. *Hélène Cixous: Writing the Feminine.* Expanded edition. Lincoln: University of Nebraska Press, 1991.

Connell, R. W. *Masculinities.* Berkeley: University of California Press, 1995.

Cooper, Helen. *The Structure of the* Canterbury Tales. Athens, GA: University of Georgia Press, 1984.

Copeland, Rita. "The Pardoner's Body and the Disciplining of Rhetoric." In Kay and Rubin. 138–59.

Cowell, Andrew. "The Fall of the Oral Economy: Writing Economics on the Dead Body." *Exemplaria* 8 (1996): 145–67.

Cox, Catherine S. *Gender and Language in Chaucer.* Gainesville: University Press of Florida, 1997.

Crane, Susan. *Gender and Romance in Chaucer's* Canterbury Tales. Princeton, NJ: Princeton University Press, 1994.

———. "The Writing Lesson of 1381." In *Chaucer's England: Literature in Historical Context.* Ed. Barbara Hanawalt. Medieval Studies at Minnesota 4. Minneapolis: University of Minnesota Press, 1992. 201–21.

Curry, Walter Clyde. *Chaucer and the Mediaeval Sciences.* 2nd ed. New York: Barnes and Noble, 1960.

Curtius, Ernst Robert. *European Literature and the Latin Middle Ages.* Trans. Willard R. Trask. Princeton, NJ: Princeton University Press, 1953.

Daston, Lorraine, and Katharine Park. "The Hermaphrodite and the Orders of Nature: Sexual Ambiguity in Early Modern France." In Fradenburg and Freccero. 117–36.

David, Alfred. *The Strumpet Muse: Art and Morals in Chaucer's Poetry.* Bloomington: Indiana University Press, 1976.

Delany, Samuel R. "Appendix: Closures and Openings." In his *Return to Nevèrÿon.* 1987. Repr. University Press of New England/Wesleyan University Press: Hanover, NH, 1994. 269–91.

Derrida, Jacques. *Spurs: Nietzsche's Styles / Eperons: Les Styles de Nietzsche.* Trans. Barbara Harlow. Chicago: University of Chicago Press, 1979.

Detienne, Marcel. *Dionysos at Large.* Trans. Arthur Goldhammer. Revealing Antiquity 1. Cambridge, MA: Harvard University Press, 1989.

Dinshaw, Carolyn. "Chaucer's Queer Touches / A Queer Touches Chaucer." *Exemplaria* 7 (1995): 75–92.

———. *Chaucer's Sexual Poetics.* Madison: University of Wisconsin Press, 1989.

———. "A Kiss Is Just a Kiss: Heterosexuality and its Consolations in *Sir Gawain and the Green Knight.*" In *Critical Crossings.* Ed. Judith Butler and Biddy Martin. Special issue of *Diacritics* 24.2–3 (Summer-Fall, 1994): 205–26.

Dollimore, Jonathan. *Sexual Dissidence: Augustine to Wilde, Freud to Foucault.* Oxford: Clarendon Press, 1991.

Duberman, Martin Bauml, Martha Vicinus, and George Chauncey, eds. *Hidden From History: Reclaiming the Gay and Lesbian Past.* New York: New American Library, 1989.

Elliott, Ralph W. V. *Chaucer's English.* Language Library. London: André Deutsch, 1974.

Farrell, Thomas J., ed. *Bakhtin and Medieval Voices.* Gainesville: University of Florida Press, 1995.

Ferster, Judith. "'Your Praise is Performed by Men and Children': Language and Gender in the *Prioress's Prologue and Tale.*" In *Reconceiving Chaucer: Literary Theory and Historical Interpretation.* Ed. Thomas Hahn. Special issue of *Exemplaria* 2.1 (Spring, 1990): 149–68.

Flax, Jane. "Postmodernism and Gender Relations in Feminist Theory." In *Feminism/Postmodernism.* Ed. Linda J. Nicholson. New York: Routledge, 1990. 39–62.

———. *Thinking Fragments: Psychoanalysis, Feminism, and Postmodernism in the Contemporary West.* Berkeley: University of California Press, 1990.

Foucault, Michel. "Body/Power." In *Power/Knowledge: Selected Interviews and Other Writings, 1972–1977.* Ed. Colin Gordon. New York: Pantheon, 1980. 55–62.

———. *The History of Sexuality, Volume I: An Introduction.* Trans. Robert Hurley. 1978. Repr. Vintage: New York, 1980.

———. "Introduction." *Herculine Barbin: Being the Recently Discovered Memoirs of a Nineteenth-Century French Hermaphrodite.* Trans. Richard McDougall. New York: Pantheon, 1980. vii–xvii.

Fradenburg, Louise, and Carla Freccero, eds. *Premodern Sexualities.* New York: Routledge, 1996.

Frantzen, Allen J. *Before the Closet: Same-Sex Love from* Beowulf *to* Angels in America. Chicago: University of Chicago Press, 1998.

Frese, Dolores Warwick. *An Ars Legendi for Chaucer's* Canterbury Tales: *Re-constructive Reading.* Gainesville: University of Florida Press, 1991.

Frese, Dolores Warwick, and Katherine O'Brien O'Keeffe, eds. *The Book and the Body.* Notre Dame, IN: University of Notre Dame Press, 1997.

Friedman, John Block. *Orpheus in the Middle Ages.* Cambridge, MA: Harvard University Press, 1970.

Fuss, Diana J. *Essentially Speaking: Feminism, Nature, and Difference.* New York: Routledge, 1989.

————. "Essentially Speaking: Luce Irigaray's Language of Essence." 1989. Repr. in *Revaluing French Feminism: Critical Essays on Difference, Agency, and Culture.* Ed. Nancy Fraser and Sandra Lee Bartky. Bloomington: Indiana University Press, 1992. 94–112.

————. "Inside/Out." In *Inside/Out: Lesbian Theories, Gay Theories.* Ed. Diana J. Fuss. New York: Routledge, 1991. 1–10.

Fyler, John M. *Chaucer and Ovid.* New Haven, CT: Yale University Press, 1979.

Gallop, Jane. *Reading Lacan.* Ithaca, NY: Cornell University Press, 1985.

Garber, Marjorie. *Vested Interests: Cross-Dressing and Cultural Anxiety.* 1992. Repr. HarperCollins: New York, 1993.

Gellrich, Jesse M. *Discourse and Dominion in the Fourteenth Century: Oral Contexts of Writing in Philosophy, Politics, and Poetry.* Princeton, NJ: Princeton University Press, 1995.

Goldberg, Jonathan. "Under the Covers with Caliban." In Greetham, *Margins.* 105–28.

Goldberg, Jonathan, ed. *Queering the Renaissance.* Durham, NC: Duke University Press, 1994.

Golding, Sue. "Pariah Bodies." In Grosz and Probyn. 172–80.

Goodich, Michael. *The Unmentionable Vice: Homosexuality in the Later Medieval Period.* Santa Barbara, CA [?]: Dorset Press, 1979.

Goux, Jean-Joseph. "The Phallus: Masculine Identity and the 'Exchange of Women.'" Trans. Maria Amuchastegui, Caroline Benforado, Amy Hendrix, and Eleanor Kaufman. *differences* 4.1 (1992): 40–75.

Green, Richard Firth. "The Sexual Normality of Chaucer's Pardoner." *Mediaevalia* 8 (1982): 351–58.

Greenberg, David F. *The Construction of Homosexuality.* Chicago: University Of Chicago Press, 1988.

Greetham, David. "(En)gendering the Text/Texting Gender." Paper presented at the 33rd International Congress on Medieval Studies. Medieval Institute, Western Michigan University, Kalamazoo, Michigan. May 9, 1998.

————. "The Place of Fredson Bowers in Medieval Editing." In his *Textual Transgressions.* 225–45.

————. *Textual Transgressions: Essays Toward the Construction of a Biobibliography.* New York: Garland, 1998.

————. *Theories of the Text.* Oxford: Oxford University Press, 1999.

Greetham, D. C., ed. *The Margins of the Text.* Ann Arbor: University of Michigan Press, 1997.

Gross, Gregory. "Trade Secrets: Chaucer, the Pardoner, the Critics." *Modern Language Studies* 25.4 (1995): 1–33.

Grosz, Elizabeth, and Elspeth Probyn, eds. *Sexy Bodies: The Strange Carnalities of Feminism.* New York: Routledge, 1995.

Halperin, David. *Saint Foucault: Towards a Gay Hagiography.* Oxford: Oxford University Press, 1995.

———. "Sex Before Sexuality: Pederasty, Politics, and Power in Classical Athens." In Duberman, Vicinus, and Chauncey. 37–53.

Hamer, Dean and Peter Copeland. *The Science of Desire: The Search for the Gay Gene and the Biology of Behavior.* New York: Simon and Schuster, 1994.

Hansen, Elaine Tuttle. *Chaucer and the Fictions of Gender.* Berkeley: University of California Press, 1992.

Haraway, Donna J. "FemaleMan©_Meets_OncoMouse™: Mice into Wormholes: A Technoscience Fugue in Two Parts." In her *Modest_Witness@Second_Millenium.FemaleMan©_Meets_OncoMouse™.* New York: Routledge, 1997. 49–118.

———. "'Gender' for a Marxist Dictionary: The Sexual Politics of a Word." In her *Simians, Cyborgs, and Women.* 127–48.

———. "In the Beginning was the Word: The Genesis of Biological Theory." In her *Simians, Cyborgs, and Women.* 71–80.

———. *Simians, Cyborgs, and Women: The Reinvention of Nature.* New York: Routledge, 1991.

Hassan, Ihab. *The Dismemberment of Orpheus: Toward a Postmodern Literature.* 2nd ed. Madison: University of Wisconsin Press, 1982.

Heyworth, P. L. "Jocelin of Brakelond, Abbot Samson, and the Case of William the Sacrist." In *Middle English Studies Presented to Norman Davis in Honour of his Seventieth Birthday.* Ed. Douglas Gray and E. G. Stanley. Oxford: Clarendon Press, 1983. 175–94.

Hillman, David, and Carla Mazzo. "Introduction: Individual Parts." In *The Body in Parts: Fantasies of Corporeality in Early Modern Europe.* Ed. David Hillman and Carla Mazzo. New York: Routledge, 1997. xi–xxix.

Hoffman, Richard L. *Ovid and the* Canterbury Tales. Philadelphia: University of Pennsylvania Press, 1966.

Howard, Donald R. *The Idea of the* Canterbury Tales. Berkeley: University of California Press, 1976.

"Introduction." In Lochrie, McCracken, and Schultz. ix–xviii.

"Introduction." In Lomperis and Stanbury. vii–xiv.

Irigaray, Luce. *Je, tu, nous: Toward a Culture of Difference.* Trans. Alison Martin. New York: Routledge, 1993.

———. *Marine Lover of Friedrich Nietzsche.* Trans. Gillian C. Gill. New York: Columbia University Press, 1991.

———. *Thinking the Difference: For a Peaceful Revolution.* Trans. Karin Montin. New York: Routledge, 1994.

———. *This Sex Which Is Not One.* Trans. Catherine Porter with Carolyn Burke. Ithaca, NY: Cornell University Press, 1985.

———. "The Three Genders." In her *Sexes and Genealogies.* Trans. Gillian C. Gill. New York: Columbia University Press, 1993. 167–81.

Irvine, Martin. *The Making of Textual Culture: 'Grammatica' and Literary Theory 350–1100.* Cambridge, Eng.: Cambridge University Press, 1994.

Jones, Ann Rosalind. "Writing the Body: Toward an Understanding of *l'écriture féminine.*" 1981. Repr. in Warhol and Price Herndl. 357–70.

Jordan, Mark D. *The Invention of Sodomy in Christian Theology.* Chicago: University of Chicago Press, 1997.

Justice, Steven. *Writing and Rebellion: England in 1381.* Berkeley: University of California Press, 1994.

Karras, Ruth Mazo, and David Lorenzo Boyd. "'*Ut cum muliere*': A Male Transvestite Prostitute in Fourteenth-Century London." In Fradenburg and Freccero. 101–116.

Kay, Sarah, and Miri Rubin, eds. *Framing Medieval Bodies.* Manchester: Manchester University Press, 1994.

Keiser, Elizabeth B. *Courtly Desire and Medieval Homophobia: The Legitimation of Sexual Pleasure in* Cleanness *and Its Contexts.* New Haven, CT: Yale University Press, 1997.

Kittredge, George Lyman. *Chaucer and His Poetry.* Cambridge, MA: Harvard University Press, 1915. Repr. 1927.

Koonce, B. G. *Chaucer and the Tradition of Fame: Symbolism in* The House of Fame. Princeton, NJ: Princeton University Press, 1966.

Kristeva, Julia. *Desire in Language: A Semiotic Approach to Literature and Art.* Ed. Leon S. Roudiez. Trans. Thomas Gora, Alice Jardine, and Leon S. Roudiez. New York: Columbia University Press, 1980.

———. "From One Identity to an Other." In her *Desire in Language.* 124–47.

———. "Stabat Mater." In her *Tales of Love.* Trans. Leon S. Roudiez. New York: Columbia University Press, 1987. 234–63.

———. "Word, Dialogue, and Novel." In her *Desire in Language.* 64–91.

Krondorfer, Björn, ed. *Men's Bodies, Men's Gods: Male Identities in a (Post-)Christian Culture.* New York: New York University Press, 1996.

Kruger, Steven F. "Claiming the Pardoner: Toward a Gay Reading of Chaucer's Pardoner's Tale." *Exemplaria* 6 (1994): 115–39.

Kuefler, Mathew S. "Castration and Eunuchism in the Middle Ages." In *Handbook of Medieval Sexuality.* Ed. Vern L. Bullough and James A. Brundage. New York: Garland, 1996. 279–306.

Lacan, Jacques. "Aggressivity in Psychoanalysis." In his *Ecrits: A Selection.* 8–29.

———. *Ecrits: A Selection.* Trans. Alan Sheridan. New York: Norton, 1977.

———. "The Mirror Stage as Formative of the Function of the I as Revealed in Psychoanalytic Experience." In his *Ecrits: A Selection.* 1–7.

———. "The Signification of the Phallus." In his *Ecrits: A Selection.* 281–91.

———. "The Subversion of the Subject and the Dialectic of Desire in the Freudian Unconscious." In his *Ecrits: A Selection.* 292–325.

Lacan, Jacques, and the *école freudienne. Feminine Sexuality.* Ed. Juliet Mitchell and Jacqueline Rose. Trans. Jacqueline Rose. New York: Norton, 1982.

Laqueur, Thomas. *Making Sex: Body and Gender from the Greeks to Freud.* Cambridge, MA: Harvard University Press, 1990.

Laskaya, Anne. *Chaucer's Approach to Gender in the* Canterbury Tales. Chaucer Studies 25. Cambridge, Eng.: D. S. Brewer, 1995.

Leicester, H. Marshall, Jr. *The Disenchanted Self: Representing the Subject in the* Canterbury Tales. Berkeley: University of California Press, 1990.

Leupin, Alexandre. "The Hermaphrodite: Alan of Lille's *De planctu Naturae.*" In his *Barbarolexis: Medieval Writing and Sexuality.* Trans. Kate M. Cooper. Cambridge, MA: Harvard University Press, 1989. 59–78.

LeVay, Simon. *The Sexual Brain.* Cambridge, MA: MIT Press, 1993.

Lewis, C. S. *The Allegory of Love.* Oxford: Oxford University Press, 1938.

Lochrie, Karma, Peggy McCracken, and James A. Schultz, eds. *Constructing Medieval Sexuality.* Medieval Cultures 11. Minneapolis: University of Minnesota Press, 1997.

Lomperis, Linda, and Sarah Stanbury, eds. *Feminist Approaches to the Body in Medieval Literature.* Philadelphia: University of Pennsylvania Press, 1993.

Lorber, Judith. *Paradoxes of Gender.* New Haven, CT: Yale University Press, 1994.

Mandel, Jerome. *Geoffrey Chaucer: Building the Fragments of the* Canterbury Tales. London: Associated University Presses, 1992.

Marvin, Corey J. "'I Will Thee Not Forsake': The Kristevan Maternal Space in Chaucer's *Prioress's Tale* and John of Garland's *Stella maris.*" *Exemplaria* 8 (1996): 35–58.

McAlpine, Monica. "The Pardoner's Homosexuality and How It Matters." *PMLA* 95 (1980): 8–22.

McMahon, A. Philip. "Seven Questions on Aristotelian Definitions of Tragedy and Comedy." *Harvard Studies in Classical Philology* 40 (1929): 97–198.

Miller, Robert P. "Chaucer's Pardoner, the Scriptural Eunuch, and the Pardoner's Tale." 1955. Repr. in *Chaucer Criticism: The Canterbury Tales.* Ed. Richard Schoeck and Jerome Taylor. Notre Dame, IN: University of Notre Dame Press, 1960. 221–44.

Minnis, A. J. "Ordering Chaucer." Review of Helen Cooper, *The Structure of* The Canterbury Tales. *Essays in Criticism* 35 (1985): 265–69.

Mondimore, Francis Mark. *A Natural History of Homosexuality.* Baltimore: Johns Hopkins University Press, 1996.

Murphy, Peter F., ed. *Fictions of Masculinity: Crossing Cultures, Crossing Sexualities.* New York: New York University Press, 1995.

Nichols, Stephen G. "Voice and Writing in Augustine and in the Troubadour Lyrics." In *Vox Intexta: Orality and Literacy in the Middle Ages.* Ed. A. N. Doane and Carol Braun Pasternack. Madison: University of Wisconsin Press, 1991. 137–61.

Niles, John D. "Ring Composition in *La Chanson de Roland* and *La Chançun de Willame.*" *Olifant* 1.2 (1973): 4–12.

Norton, Rictor. *The Myth of the Modern Homosexual: Queer History and the Search for Cultural Unity.* London: Cassell, 1997.

Padgug, Robert. "Sexual Matters: Rethinking Sexuality in History." In Duberman, Vicinus, and Chauncey. 54–64.

Patterson, Lee. *Chaucer and the Subject of History.* Madison: University of Wisconsin Press, 1991.

222 CHAUCER'S PARDONER AND GENDER THEORY

Payer, Pierre J. *Sex and the Penitentials: The Development of a Sexual Code, 550–1150.* Toronto: University of Toronto Press, 1984.

Pearsall, Derek. *The Canterbury Tales.* Unwin Critical Library. London: George Allen and Unwin, 1985.

————. "Chaucer's Pardoner: The Death of a Salesman." *Chaucer Review* 17 (1983): 358–65.

————. "Editing Medieval Texts: Some Developments and Some Problems." In *Textual Criticism and Literary Interpretation.* Ed. Jerome J. McGann. Chicago: University of Chicago Press, 1985. 92–106.

Pittenger, Elizabeth. "Explicit Ink." In Fradenburg and Freccero. 223–42.

Readings, Bill, and Bennett Schaber. "Introduction: The Question Mark in the Midst of Modernity." In *Postmodernism Across the Ages: Essays for a Postmodernity That Wasn't Born Yesterday,* ed. Readings and Schaber. Syracuse, NY: Syracuse University Press, 1993. 1–28.

Reynolds, Suzanne. *Medieval Reading: Grammar, Rhetoric, and the Classical Text.* Cambridge Studies in Medieval Literature 27. Cambridge, Eng.: Cambridge University Press, 1996.

Rhodes, James F. "The Pardoner's Vernycle and his Vera Icon." *Modern Language Studies* 13 (1983): 34–40.

Richards, Jeffrey. *Sex, Dissidence and Damnation: Minority Groups in the Middle Ages.* New York: Routledge, 1991.

Rivière, Joan. "Womanliness as a Masquerade." 1929. Repr. in *Formations of Fantasy.* Ed. Victor Burgin, James Donald, and Cora Kaplan. London: Methuen, 1986. 35–44.

Robbins, Emmet. "Famous Orpheus." In Warden. 3–23.

Robertson, D. W., Jr. *A Preface to Chaucer: Studies in Medieval Perspectives.* Princeton, NJ: Princeton University Press, 1962.

Rowland, Beryl. "Animal Imagery and the Pardoner's Abnormality." *Neophilologus* 48 (1964): 56–60.

————. *Blind Beasts: Chaucer's Animal World.* Kent, OH: Kent State University Press, 1971.

————. "Chaucer's Idea of the Pardoner." *Chaucer Review* 14 (1979): 140–54.

Rubin, Gayle. "The Traffic in Women: Notes on the Political Economy of Sex." In *Toward an Anthropology of Women.* Ed. Rayna R. Reiter. New York: Monthly Review, 1975. 157–210.

Rubin, Miri. "The Person in the Form: Medieval Challenges to Bodily 'Order.'" In Kay and Rubin. 100–122.

Schor, Naomi. "Previous Engagements: The Receptions of Irigaray." In Burke, Schor, and Whitford. 4–14.

Sedgewick, G. G. "The Progress of Chaucer's Pardoner, 1880–1940." 1940. Repr. in *Chaucer: Modern Essays in Criticism.* Ed. Edward Wagenknecht. New York: Oxford University Press, 1959. 126–58.

Sedgwick, Eve Kosofsky. *Epistemology of the Closet.* Berkeley: University of California Press, 1990.

Shahar, Shulamith. "The Old Body in Medieval Culture." In Kay and Rubin. 160–86.

Shoaf, R. A. *Dante, Chaucer, and the Currency of the Word: Money, Images, and Reference in Late Medieval Poetry.* Norman, OK: Pilgrim, 1983.

Silverman, Kaja. *Male Subjectivity at the Margins.* New York: Routledge, 1992.

Stallybrass, Peter, and Allon White. *The Politics and Poetics of Transgression.* Ithaca, NY: Cornell University Press, 1986.

Standop, Ewald. "Chaucers Pardoner: das Charakterproblem und die Kritiker." In *Geschichtlichkeit und Neuanfang im sprachlichen Kunstwerk: Studien zur englischen Philologie zu Ehren von Fritz W. Schulze.* Ed. Peter Erlebach, Wolfgang G. Müller, and Klaus Reuter. Tübingen: Gunter Narr, 1981. 59–69.

"The Status of Evidence: A Roundtable." *PMLA* 111 (1996): 21–31.

Steinberg, Leo. *The Sexuality of Christ in Renaissance Art and in Modern Oblivion.* 2nd ed. Chicago: University of Chicago Press, 1996.

Storm, Melvin. "The Pardoner's Invitation: Quaestor's Bag or Becket's Shrine?" *PMLA* 97 (1982): 810–18.

———. "The Pardoner's Invitation: Quaestor's Bag or Becket's Shrine?" Abstract. *PMLA* 97 (1982): 797.

Strohm, Paul. *Social Chaucer.* Cambridge, MA: Harvard University Press, 1989.

Sturges, Robert S. "Anti-Wycliffite Commentary in Richardson MS 22." *Harvard Library Bulletin* 34 (1986): 380–95.

———. "*The Canterbury Tales'* Women Narrators: Three Traditions of Female Authority." *Modern Language Studies* 12 (1983): 41–51.

———. "La(ca)ncelot." *Arthurian Interpretations* 4.2 (Spring, 1990): 12–23.

———. "Textual Scholarship: Ideologies of Literary Production." In *Reflections in the Frame: New Perspectives on the Study of Medieval Literature.* Ed. Peter Allen and Jeff Rider. Special issue of *Exemplaria* 3.1 (March, 1991): 109–31.

Swart, J. "Chaucer's Pardoner." *Neophilologus* 36 (1952): 45–50.

Thomas, Calvin. *Male Matters: Masculinity, Anxiety, and the Male Body on the Line.* Urbana: University of Illinois Press, 1996.

Townsend, David, and Andrew Taylor, eds. *The Tongue of the Fathers: Gender and Ideology in Twelfth-Century Latin.* Philadelphia: University of Pennsylvania Press, 1998.

Tupper, Frederick. "*The Pardoner's Tale.*" In *Sources and Analogues of Chaucer's Canterbury Tales.* Ed. W. F. Bryan and Germaine Dempster. 1941. Repr. Humanities Press: Atlantic Highlands, NJ, 1958. 415–38.

Urla, Jacqueline, and Jennifer Terry. "Introduction: Mapping Embodied Deviance." In *Deviant Bodies: Critical Perspectives on Difference in Science and Popular Culture.* Ed. Jacqueline Urla and Jennifer Terry. Bloomington: Indiana University Press, 1995. 1–17.

Vance, Eugene. "Chaucer's Pardoner: Relics, Discourse, and Frames of Propriety." *New Literary History* 20 (1988–89): 723–45.

Vicari, Patricia. "*Sparagmos:* Orpheus Among the Christians." In Warden. 63–83.

Warden, John, ed. *Orpheus: The Metamorphoses of a Myth.* Toronto: University of Toronto Press, 1982.

Warhol, Robyn, and Diane Price Herndl, eds. *Feminisms: An Anthology of Literary Theory and Criticism.* New Brunswick, NJ: Rutgers University Press, 1991.

Wittig, Monique. "The Mark of Gender." In her *The Straight Mind.* 76–89.

————. "The Point of View: Universal or Particular?" In her *The Straight Mind*. 59–67.

————. "The Straight Mind." In her *The Straight Mind*. 21–32.

————. *The Straight Mind and Other Essays*. Boston: Beacon Press, 1992.

Woods, Gregory. *A History of Gay Literature: The Male Tradition*. New Haven, CT: Yale University Press, 1998.

Ziolkowski, Jan. *Alan of Lille's Grammar of Sex: The Meaning of Grammar to a Twelfth-Century Intellectual*. Speculum Anniversary Monographs 10. Cambridge, MA: The Medieval Academy of America, 1985.

Zita, Jacquelyn N. "Male Lesbians and the Postmodernist Body." *Hypatia* 7.4 (Spring, 1992): 106–27.

Žižek, Slavoj. *The Sublime Object of Ideology*. New York: Verso, 1989.

Zumthor, Paul. *La Lettre et la voix: De la "littérature" médiévale*. Paris: Seuil, 1987.

INDEX

Book of the Duchess, 119–20
Bordo, Susan 148–49, 151, 207n.
Bosch, Hieronymus, 128, 169n.
Boswell, John, xvii, 52, 169nn., 174n.,
    177n., 180–81nn., 186n., 190n.
Bowden, Muriel, 48, 184n.
Bowers, John, 178n., 208nn.
Boyd, David Lorenzo, 183n.
Bradshaw shift, 147, 203n.
Braswell-Means, Laurel, 193n.
Bravmann, Scott, 160–70n.
Brewer, Derek, 207n.
British Library MS Lansdowne 851, 152
Brossard, Nicole, 206n.
Brundage, James A., 186n.
Burger, Glenn, xx, xxi, 35–36, 171n., 172n.,
    179nn.
Burke, Carolyn, 68, 189n., 205–6n.
Burns, E. Jane, 88, 195n.
Bushnell, N. S., 203n.
Butler, Judith, xix, xxii, 44, 45, 58, 77–79,
    171nn., 175n., 183n., 184n., 187n.,
    188n., 193nn., 206n.
Bynum, Caroline Walker, 11, 28, 45,
    132–35, 174n., 177n., 184n., 195n.,
    196n., 201nn., 202nn.

Cadden, Joan, 37–38, 44, 50, 176n., 180n.,
    181n., 183nn., 184n., 185nn., 202n.
Cain, James D., 171n.
Calabrese, Michael A., 200n.
Cambridge MS Gg.4.27, 150
Camille, Michael, 200n., 207n.
Canon's Yeoman's Tale, 36, 152
"Canterbury Interlude," 40, 152, 153–56,
    194n., 208nn.
Canterbury Tales, 7, 9–10, 11, 15, 25, 30, 35,
    36, 38, 40, 41, 48, 57, 59, 64, 65, 68, 91,
    94, 115, 120, 123, 141, 142, 143, 146,
    147, 151, 152–53; *see also* text of the
    Canterbury Tales
carnivalesque, 103–4, 164–65, 209n.
caro radicalis, 134
castration, 10–11, 36–40, 41, 49, 70, 71, 75,
    77, 79, 124, 134, 155; *see also* genitals;
    testicles
Ceres, 108
Cerquiglini, Bernard, 205n.
Champagne, John, 171n., 183n.
Chance, Jane, 139, 199n., 200nn., 203n.

Chaucer, Geoffrey, xv–xvi, xxi, xxii, 1, 2, 3,
    13, 17, 21, 24, 27, 32, 36, 38, 43, 47, 54,
    56, 59, 64, 77, 89, 94, 96, 118–22, 138,
    141, 142
children, 22, 28, 31–32, 111, 114, 136,
    177n.; *see also Prioress's Prologue; Prioress's
    Tale*
Chrétien de Troyes, 143
Christine de Pizan, 8, 173n., 202n.
Church, 1, 67–68, 92, 101, 103, 139
Cixous, Hélène, 144–47, 162, 193n., 205n.,
    206nn., 207n., 209n.
class, 37, 38, 123
Clerk, 123
Clerk's Tale, 190n.
Cohen, Jeffrey Jerome, 176n., 188n.
Compagnon, Antoine, xxiii, 172n.
"Complaint to His Purse," 15–18
Conley, Verena Andermatt, 206n.
Connell, R. W., 21–22, 23, 24, 28, 33,
    175n., 176nn.
constructionism, xvii–xxi, 48, 50, 63, 64, 71,
    80, 145
Cook, 3, 123
Cooper, Helen, 204n.
Copeland, Peter, 170n.
Copeland, Rita, 182n.
corps morcelé, 127–31, 141
Cowell, Andrew, 197n.
Cox, Catherine S., 191n., 193n., 197n.
Crane, Susan, 3, 7, 12, 32, 173n., 174nn.,
    179n.
cross-dressing, 22, 163–64; *see also* drag
Curry, Walter Clyde, 36–39, 41, 47, 179nn.,
    180n., 184n., 188n.
Curtius, Ernst Robert, 176n.

Dahlberg, Charles, 121
Damian, St. Peter 51, 53, 137, 174n.,
    185nn., 203n.
Dante, 29–30, 178n., 203n.
Daston, Lorraine, 184n.
David, Alfred, 3, 102, 172n., 175n., 197nn.,
    204n.
deconstruction, 43, 75
Delany, Paul, 210n.
Delany, Samuel R., xvii, 169n.
Derrida, Jacques, 68, 189n.
Detienne, Marcel, 178n., 191n.
Dido, 88